Where In The WORLD?
Ancient Empires & More!
2nd Edition

Designed and Authored by Amanda Predmore

Student & Teaching Resource Guide - Book 1

COMPANION STUDENT WORKBOOK SOLD SEPARATELY:
STUDENT MAP WORKBOOK - Book 2 with all map worksheets for TrueReview can be found for purchase at http://bit.ly/WITWgeo

A Classically Based Geography Curriculum On
ANCIENT EMPIRES in EUROPE, ASIA, MESOAMERICA & AFRICA.
Complete present day geography of SOUTH AMERICA,
and present day geography on portions of the MIDDLE EAST,
NORTH ATLANTIC, CANADA, & AFRICA.
Canadian geography for Quebec and Ontario at the time of the
British North America Act of 1867 overlaid with present-day geography.

Part of the **Where in the World** Geography Series
Where the student's learn to memorize through drawing and discussion.
http://bit.ly/WhereInTheWorldGeo

Copyright © 2021 by Amanda Predmore

Where in the World?
Ancient Empires & More - 2nd Edition
Student & Teaching Resource Guide - Book 1

Memorize and Engage Geography Through
Repetition and Discussion

http://bit.ly/WhereInTheWorldGeo

All rights reserved. See restrictions and allowances below.

This book or any portion thereof may not be reproduced and is licensed by purchase
for the use of educational material for one homeschool family, or one student in a
classroom. Copy of maps for personal use in your family is permitted. Beyond this
you may not transmit or distribute without express written permission of the
author/designer except for brief quotations in a book review.

ISBN 978-1-7325085-4-5

Where In The WORLD?

Ancient Empires & More!
2nd Edition

Designed and Authored by Amanda Predmore

Baku Beach on the Caspian Sea in the city of Azerbaijan. Image by Faik Nagiyev from Pixabay

TABLE OF Contents

A Note from Amanda Predmore ix
Learning Levels + Tips on How to Teach 1
Activities, Incentives, and Review Games 3
All the Parts - Get to Know the Curriculum 4
Digging Deeper 6

Discussion Dive 8
Summary Map for Lessons 1-7, 11, 12 10
Summary Map for Lessons 8-10 11
Summary Map for Lessons 13-17 12
Summary Map for Lessons 18, 19, 22, 23 13
Summary Map for Lessons 20-21, 24 14

LESSON DIRECTORY

Lesson 1 15
Lesson 2 19
Lesson 3 27
Lesson 4 33
Lesson 5 39
Lesson 6 46
Lesson 7 55
Lesson 8 65
Lesson 9 71
Lesson 10 79
Lesson 11 86
Lesson 12 93

Lesson 13 99
Lesson 14 104
Lesson 15 110
Lesson 16 117
Lesson 17 123
Lesson 18 131
Lesson 19 137
Lesson 20 142
Lesson 21 148
Lesson 22 154
Lesson 23 162
Lesson 24 170

Each lesson begins with Parts 1 & 2 (See full description of the "Parts on Page 4).

Following the last lesson, there are additional Part 2 "Closer Look" Maps that reflect the TrueReview 6 week schedule. These maps are labeled as "TrueReview 1, 2, 3, 4, 5, 6"

"Closer Look" maps show the geography that needs to be reviewed for the lesson you are currently in plus the last 6 lessons.

Closer Look / TrueReview Pages

Closer Look / TrueReview 1 177
Closer Look / TrueReview 2 178
Closer Look / TrueReview 3 179
Closer Look / TrueReview 4 180
Closer Look / TrueReview 5 181
Closer Look / TrueReview 6 182

Summary and Blank Black Line Maps 183

Dedication

First, thank you Lord for granting this request made to you so long ago. The answer isn't what I thought or expected, it is more than I ever wished. Thank you for knowing me so intimately and loving me so wonderfully!

I dedicate this labor of love to my children, Elijah, Ethan and Isabella.
My whole heart is enraptured with you. I rise to your faces and I watch as you sleep and in between we learn together, grow together and refine each other as is pleasing to our Lord and Savior, Jesus Christ.

I also could not have survived the process of creating this work without my husband, Jacob. His work never ceases by day or night when I am focused with my various endeavors. His loving support without complaint or hesitation gives me the strength to persevere.

You all are my blessing from above and I thank you for your patience and endurance as I toiled away on this curriculum for the greater good.

Lastly and importantly, I wish to thank all of you homeschool parents that have so lovingly reached out to encourage me to continue with geography creation. It started with a desire for my own children and has grown to be a learning tool for all of yours.
For this I am truly and forever grateful.

From my heart to you all, blessings and gratitude!

Amanda

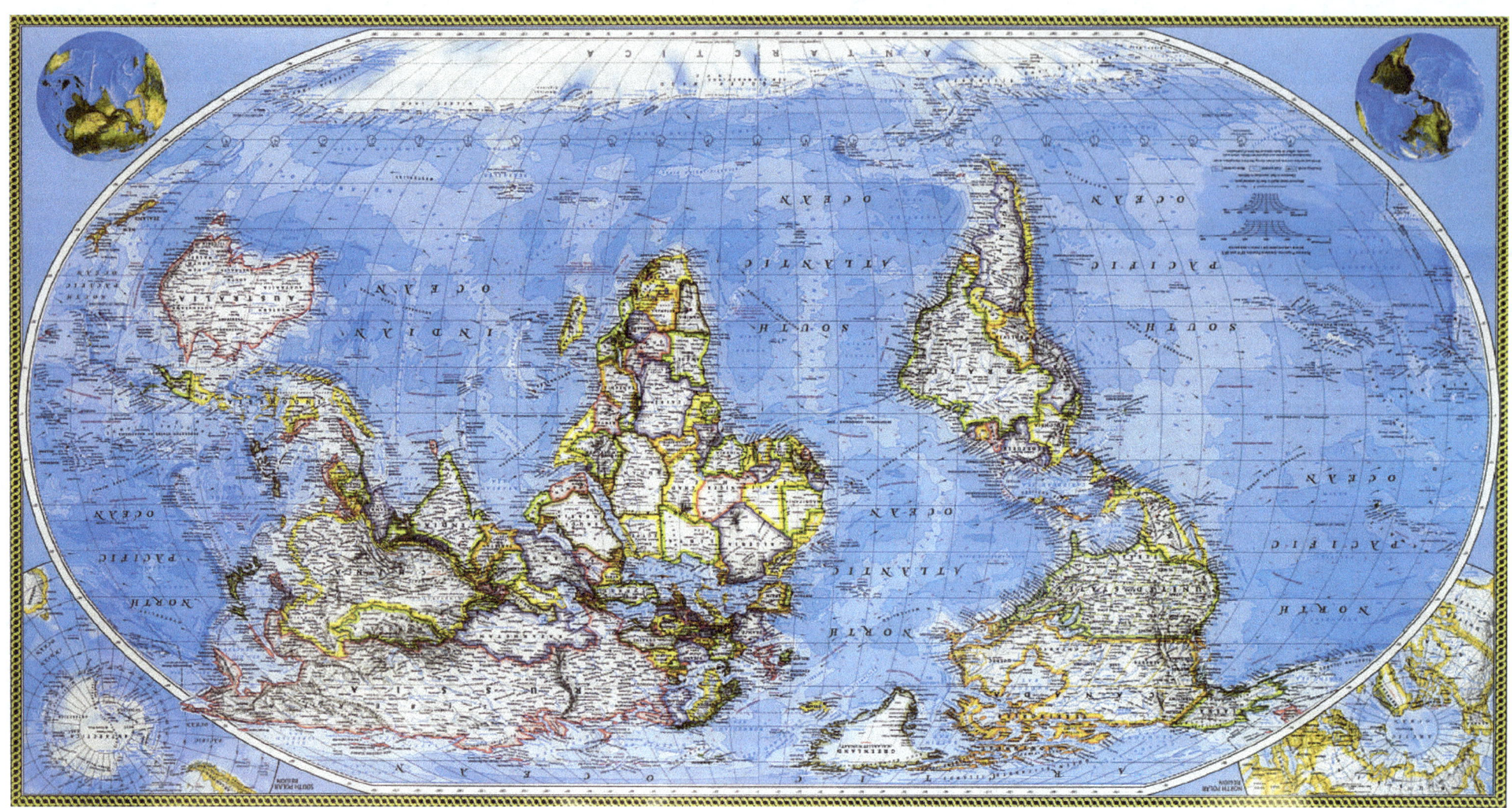

Homeschool Mama of elementary aged triplets and creator of the "Where in the World?" Geography Series

A note from
Amanda Predmore

Creator of the *"Where in the World?"* Geography Curriculum
Where students memorize geography through drawing and discussion!

We are keeping it simple, with endless possibilities for creativity and gentle memorization!

"Ancient Empires and More!" was my first book of a three-cycle series of world geography. Not only my first geography book, the first book I had ever written and designed. So much has changed over these last three years with the development of the additional books—each book went deeper into the historical tid-bits and introduced a better way for students to memorize their geography. And now, "Ancient Empires & More!" has been updated in this 2nd edition, split into two separate books: A Student & Teaching Resource Guide and a Student Geography Worksheet book.

Memorization of geography serves as a launchpad to better understand the world in which we live. In this book, our students learn about the ancient empires of Europe, Asia, Mesoamerica, and Africa. They will also have the opportunity to memorize all modern-day geography of South America and parts of the Middle East and North Atlantic. Along the way, they will learn about the Dominion of Canada through the British North America Act of 1867. The historical tid-bits will entertain and inform while the students utilize the TrueReview platform to memorize the names and locations of the geography. It is fantastic information that, as educators, we have the unique and awesome responsibility to pass along to our students while making it a fun and engaging journey.

The classical method of learning has so much to do with repetition, intensity, and duration. However, this process doesn't have to be daunting or terrible for our students. We can walk through learning together, discovering together, have fun imagining what it would be like to be there, and experience that together!

My heart desires that, within this book, you will find the right tools for your classroom or family to launch into a remarkable discovery of world geography. And hopefully, stepping through this method with a bit of creativity and discussion will make the geography come alive! And in the end, if they have the locations memorized, bonus! But first and foremost, have fun with discovery!

With prayer and blessings,

Amanda Predmore

The great Euphrates River is the longest and historically significant river in Western Asia. Along with the Tigris River, the Euphrates is one of the two defining rivers of Mesopotamia. The source begins in the Armenian Highlands of eastern Turkey, flowing through Syria and Iraq, joining the Tigris in the Shatt al-Arab, that empties into the Persian Gulf.

Photo credit: Eren Demirci from Pixabay

LEARNING LEVELS
with tips on how to teach geography for various ages and learning levels

LEARNING LEVELS WITH TIPS ON HOW TO TEACH GEOGRAPHY

Learning Level 1

Learning geography can be done as early as 4 years of age.

How? The fun way! Make up a song or chant to a rhythm while you and your student place cheerios on the geography being learned. Pick whichever map in each lesson that works best for your student. If they have writing skills learned, even a little, you can have them write the initials of the geography (i.e., "M" for Maine) on the fill-in sheet if it doesn't cause too much angst for the student. Or, use the cut and paste labels. Although, with tiny hands and challenged motor skills, the names are small, and they will need help in this process. You may even need to cut and apply the glue, and the student can stick it in the right place. Be sure not to stick it on; they need to learn where it goes!

Look up 2-3 points from the Tid-Bits section that may interest your student. If it is a good fit, have them draw a picture of one aspect of what is being taught about geography. Take a look at the "Discussion Dive" pages for tips and examples on how you can make geography more engaging. Lightly discussing the geography with your littlest learners will undoubtedly add to their learning experience. Also, be sure to get some photos that will draw visual intrigue of the places they are learning about. With this level and advanced levels of learning, activities are always fun too! Check out some of the suggested geography activities to bring life to learning this material. Depending on your student, doing one geography project per week is enough to give them exposure. You may be surprised what they will learn and retain!

Learning Level 2

As your student gets older

and their motor skills develop, you can begin to utilize the step-by-step process in each lesson. As you learn along with your student, the pages provided in each lesson starts with a complete world picture, then a closer look, and then zooming right in. Just follow the instructions along with your student, helping them in the process. As with Level 1 and Level 3 learners, it is gainful to sing or chant the lesson's geography at the beginning or end of the experience to help pound in the memory pegs. The "Memorization through Repetition" should be done 1-2 times weekly in addition to the "Now Let's Trace, Shade & Label" worksheet, which is used as an introduction to the lesson's geography. Both of these tools will help solidify the whereabouts of these places through tracing, shading, and labeling.

Look up 2-3 points from the Tid-Bits section that may interest your student, allowing for discussion. You can also simply read through this section of the book aloud and have your student tell you what they found most exciting and why. Take a look at the "Discussion Dive" and "Dig Deeper" pages for tips and examples on how you can make geography more engaging. This gives exposure to the dialectic and research skills your students will need. Also, be sure to look up related photos that will draw visual intrigue. Lastly, find kid-friendly videos that talk about these places and their unique history if it is a good fit for your home and educational style.

Learning activities are always fun too! Check out some of the suggested geography activities to bring life to learning this material.

Learning Level 3

For advanced, self-directed students,

as with all learning levels, the goal is to memorize all areas of geography. Through repetition of drawing, your student will create a visual memory. Next, we go to a deeper level of learning.

Engaging in discussion about these places is a great way to make learning connections. Beginning in the Tid-Bits section, your student can learn a little about these places. Then, dig deeper by researching current events. Finally, engage in structured dialogue. See if they understand what they have learned and what they think about what has been studied.

Take a look at the "Discussion Dive" and "Dig Deeper" pages for tips and examples on how you can make geography more engaging. It is good to do a once-to-twice-weekly review utilizing the maps provided in the student workbook for memory retention. You can also play geography games and point-and-name review.

Don't forget that these advanced learners love activities too! Check out some of the suggested geography activities to bring fun into learning this material.

NEW GRAMMAR!
For all levels of learning there are new vocabulary words throughout this book! Be sure to look for learning opportunities!

Why we learn geography!

Geography is a foundational stepping stone in learning culture and social influences, the physical environment, political climate, and the "where" of the events of the world and how they shape and influence our society. To have a mental map of your country and the world as a whole opens the mind to understanding the relationships between nations and the world's interdependence.

Did you know

that drawing improves memory by encouraging a seamless integration of a memory trace's semantic, visual, and motor aspects?
Fun tip for making it stick!

And this curriculum specializes in "making it stick" by utilizing three classical memorization techniques: **repetition, intensity, and duration.**

Activities

These activities need preparations and are offered here as ideas to launch from - on-line searches may be necessary to fuel creativity while trying to stay simple to avoid getting overwhelmed.

- Scavenger hunts (with or without learning to use a compass).
- Learning how to use a compass by placing a geography-related treasure and instructions on how many steps North, East, West and South to find it!
- Mapping out how many miles it is to go from here to geography being learned. How would they get there, and how long would it take?
- Finding out something worth researching in the geography being learned and dig deeper!
- Recreate country shapes with play-doh.
- Create an itinerary for travel to a far-away land and how much would that cost (and why did they choose that place?).
- Map the student's worldwide footprint by checking to see what products they use that are created outside of the United States.
- Pick a country and explore a dish that is traditionally eaten there.
- Learn about time zones. What time is it in Jerusalem, India, or Spain?

Incentives

Many children need incentives and rewards to stay on track with a smile! Here are just a few ideas to make educating a bit easier!

- Lots of encouragement and praise!
- Make a paper airplane out of their geography drawing from the day's lesson and throw towards a globe or map... wherever it lands you can briefly teach them about that area - bonus geography!
- End with a game for accomplishing the goal. It could be a geography game or just any game the student loves best!
- Dominoes/Magformers/Legos/Building Blocks, etc. For every question answered or every goal (big or small) accomplished - the student gets 5 (more or less) pieces to slowly build their own creation.
- Food or Fun Passes - Use an "I got caught being good" jar and place a little something in every time they accomplish the goals that you set for them. At the end of the lesson or school day, they get to reap their reward or accumulate for a bigger reward like a special trip!
- Trinkets Treasure Chest (or rewards basket) Fill a miniature treasure chest with trinkets, stickers, seeds, mystery presents, for the choosing at the end of a successful school day.
- Your child teaching class or being the teacher's assistant.

And the list goes on... check online for homeschool incentives and rewards.

Review Games

Use review games in your homeschool to build relationships, connect with your children, make memories, and pound the memory pegs in a bit further while having fun!

Where in the World! The first step is to number a blank map in order of being taught (for instance: Fertile Crescent (1), Mediterranean Sea (2), Mesopotamia (3). Make geography named labels and place them into a bowl, basket, hat, or bag and pick a geography location for the student to find on the numbered map. If the student gets the number located on the map correctly, they earn a point!

Geo Bingo! Based on the same idea as "Where in the World!" Number your blank maps in order of being taught. Then make the same numbers on little pieces of paper and place them into a bag or basket for drawing from. Call one number (not the geography name) out at a time and have your student(s) find the number on the map and name the geography. If they get it right, they get to color that country or earn a point! Once all geography for that map are colored in, you win! If you have multiple students, they can all win!

We homeschool parents generally like to "DIY" most everything - however if you don't have the time or inclination to prepare these games, I've taken some of the work out of it and made it available for purchase as a download (you just have to cut) combined with a variety of enlarged maps including numbered maps and answer keys!

http://bit.ly/WhereInTheWorldGeo

All the Parts - Get to Know the Curriculum!

TIPS FOR BEING PREPARED!

Having the right tools makes a difference in the quality of drawing and labeling. It is recommended that tracing and coloring be done with colored pencils.

In addition, a fine point sharpie works well over the colored pencil, it is suggested to have a blue for rivers, a black for geography labeling and red for cities.

Pre-grouping the needed colored pencils and pens into a geo-kit will be helpful.

Recommended Product:
Sharpie Pen Stylo Fine Point

There are 2 books that work as a team!
These two books, together, have 6 parts for each lesson. Take a look below to understand each part and where they can be found!

BOOK 1

Book 1 is the Student & Teaching Resource Guide. This guide includes Parts 1, 2, 3, & 4 for each lesson.

BOOK 2

Book 2 is the Student Map Worksheet Book. This book includes Parts 5 & 6 for each lesson.

Parts of each Lesson

1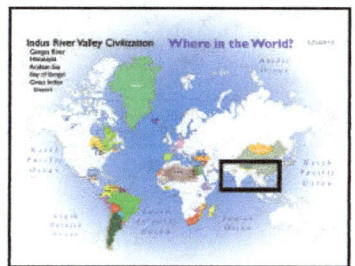

Where in the World? This map is to be presented each week to give context within our great big God created world. Teachers can utilize this as a starting point to show the area that will be taught for the lesson. As an option, the student can pull out a globe to see if they can find the same places! This map is located in the Student & Teaching Resource Guide (Book 1) to be used as an introduction to the lesson's geography.

2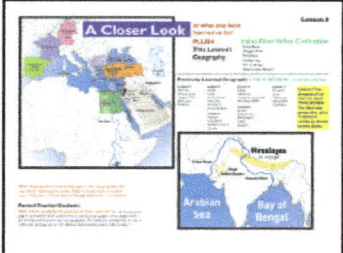

Closer Look! A map showing new geography being learned, alongside geography learned over the last 6 lessons! This map is located in the Student & Teaching Resource Guide (Book 1) to be used as a reference when doing review work.

3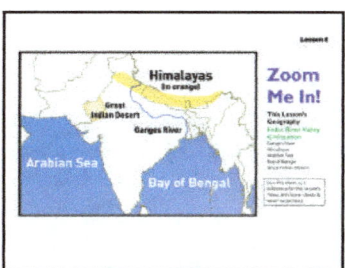

Zoom me in! A map zoomed in to show just the new geography being learned. This map reflects the worksheet called "Now, let's trace, shade, & label!" This map is a great reference when first learning the geography. This map is located in the Student & Teaching Resource Guide (Book 1) to be used as a reference as needed.

4

Tid-Bits! This is the place where you find all of the tid-bits of history, culture, geographical information, science, animals, and more, relating directly to the geography being learned! This section is located in the Student & Teaching Resource Guide (Book 1).

5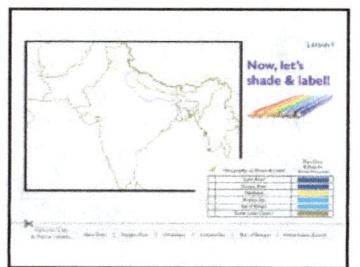

Worksheet - 1 per lesson: "Now, let's trace, shade, & label!" This worksheet is the first introduction to the geography being learned! A gentle way to become familiar with the geography while learning about these places through the tid-bits of information available in the Teaching Resource Guide. This section is located within the Student Worksheet Book (Book 2).

6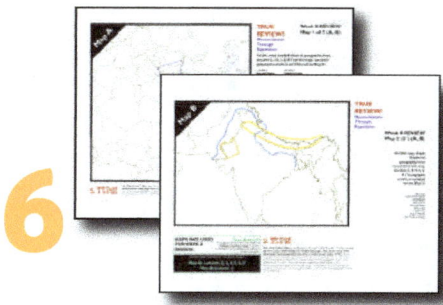

Worksheets - between 2-8 maps per lesson: True Review! "Memorization Through Repetition" It is suggested that each lesson is reviewed 2 times per week for 6 weeks for gentle memorization through repetition. All maps for review are included. All maps are provided for the different portions of the world that fall within new geography and geography that is being reviewed. This section is located within the Student Worksheet Book (Book 2).

DIGGING deeper

to plant the seeds of knowledge for prosperous growth!   Utilized For Learning Level

The Tid-Bits section is just that... tid-bits of information meant to inform you of just a little about a lot of topics to tempt you to dig deeper on the subjects that interest you. In this section you will find example topics relating to the geography that you are teaching for Lessons 1-6. *Happy Digging!*

Lesson 1
- "Epic of Gilgamesh" by the Sumer King
- Reign and fall of Sadaam Hussein
- Tigris River, facts and use
- Euphrates River, facts and use
- Early pottery and other Mesopotamian artifacts - what were they known for?
- Sumer people and their customs
- Ziggurats, what were they like on the inside?
- What equipment did early civilizations in Mesopotamia use for farming?
- What other civilizations followed the Sumer civilization within Mesopotamia.
- What other civilizations lived in the Fertile Crescent in ancient times?

Lesson 2
- Red Sea, what is it famous for?
- Red Sea, facts and use (presently)
- How did people utilize the Red Sea in ancient times?
- Persian Gulf, facts and use
- Caspian Sea, facts and use
- Black Sea, statistics and use
- Babylon, Bible History
- Assyrian Government
- Assyrian Culture
- VOCAB: Deity
- Famous Lamassu Art - how many have been found? What tools did they use to create the art. Are they similar to our tools that we use now?
- What other artifacts have been located from the Assyrian Empire?

Lesson 3
- Hebrew Empire: The people
- Hebrew Empire: The culture
- Hebrew Empire: The rituals
- Hebrew Empire: Their accomplishments
- Judah in ancient times
- Israel, the promised land
- Jordan River, facts... is it salty too?
- The Dead Sea, facts
- Sea of Galilee
- Jordan River, The Dead Sea, Sea of Galilee - from where (the source) does the water flow?
- Hebrew instruments, are they like ours?

Lesson 4
- The city of Hattusa, the people, etymology, culture
- The Hittite Empire: How did it come to be and when?
- Cyprus: How big is the island, who was there first and who is there presently?
- Asia Minor is now called Turkey, how did that happen?
- What animal life exists in the Arabian Desert?
- What is the population in the Arabian Desert.
- What is life like for the people that live in the Arabian Desert.
- What form of government did the Hittites employ?
- What was the Hittite art and culture like?
- What is modern day Turkey like with their government, culture and religion.

Lesson 5
- Nile River, facts
- Upper and Lower Egypt: Why is this an important differentiation?
- Nile River Delta, the river flows into the Mediterranean, what is its' source and what industries utilize the Nile River Delta presently?
- What differentiates these kingdoms in Egypt: Old Kingdom (c. 2575-2130 BC), Middle Kingdom (c. 2040-1600 BC), New Kingdom (c. 1550-1070 BC)
- What is the government structure in present day Egypt and how does that compare to its' past?
- Over time, how have Egypt's people changed in their culture and society?

Lesson 6
- Classical Age - the Greeks ushered this "Age" in, how did it influence European and Western Culture?
- What defines the Classical Age?
- Wars against Persia, what were they fighting for?
- What was Sparta known for?
- Ushering in Democracy, dig deeper with Athens.
- The first Olympic Games
- When were women allowed to compete in the Olympics?
- Greek Mythology
- Greek Theatre

DISCUSSION dive

Utilized For Learning Levels

A few words to help guide you as you dive into discussion with your children.

Diving into discussion allows for your child to better grasp the content that you've read and connect to the geography being taught.

How you ask your questions will determine the breadth of dialogue.

In this curriculum, the "Tid-Bits" section covers a variety of different types of information. Everything from the environment and the people, plants, and animals, to wars and the depths of oceans and lakes, and the largest man-made mineral spa in Iceland. Because of this, the discussions can be quite varied, and your questions, just as much so. As you go through the content, keep in mind what you can make engaging with your child.

There are two types of questions you need to ask, **Review Questions** and **Reflection Questions**. Definition of both, along with examples have been provided from Lesson 1.

Review & Reflection

Review Questions - Step 1

With review questions, you are acting as an investigative reporter asking: **"Who"** are the characters? **"What"** happened? **"Where"** is this place? (pointing back to the geography!) **"When"** did this happen? **"Why"** did this happen? **"How"** did this affect the environment, people, country?

Please note that not all of these will apply to all content that you discuss.

Talking through the material will subtly teach excellent reading skills and think deeply about what is being read. It is the foundation of learning how to read and discuss complex literature and life topics.

Reflection Questions - Step 2

As you may be aware, dialectics is the art or practice of logical discussion. It is the foundation for making a solid argument, which is a powerful tool for your child. Going through this process will allow you to set the foundation of your child's thought process with how they interact with the information they take in through books, the Internet, news, and those around them throughout their lives. This allows them to know why they believe what they do and can logically and powerfully dialogue. The **Reflection Questions** are an exercise in dialectics. You bring forth the deeper elements of the **Review Questions** by building on the answers your students have given. So take notes when they give you answers so that you can bring them back around to those answers and challenge them to dig deeper into what they think about those investigative answers they gave.

Discussion dive

Example Questions from Tid-Bits Section of Lesson 1

Review Questions

1. Who first occupied Mesopotamia?
2. Where and what is the Fertile Crescent?
3. Where is Mesopotamia?
4. When did the first civilization occupy a portion of Mesopotamia within the Fertile Crescent?
5. Where did the Sumerian people live in Mesopotamia?
6. What rivers did the Sumerian people depend on for their water and agriculture needs?
7. Why do you think the Sumer people settled there?
8. What was the Fertile Crescent like before man drained the wetlands?
9. What is the Fertile Crescent like now, and how did it get that way?
10. What did the Sumer people of Mesopotamia live in?
11. Beyond cultivating the land, what else did the Sumer people enjoy?

Reflective Questions

1. If you were there, would you have settled, making a life in Mesopotamia? Why?
2. What do you think it was like to be the first people in a new land?
3. What do you think you would have done as an occupation to provide for yourself and your family?
4. What do you think would be the challenges of living in this new land?
5. What kinds of hobbies do you think you would have enjoyed while living during this time in this place?
6. Do you think you'd like to live back then, or do you think this present time is better for you? Why?
7. Do you think that the people that live there now enjoy their home? Why or why not?

TAKE NOTES of the answers your kiddos give to the Review Questions so that when you get to the Reflective Questions you can have them dive deeper into their initial findings. Plus, note taking is a valuable skill for them to witness!

Open ended questions discourages one word answers!
Closed? What do you think of war?
Open? Is war ever genuinely noble, why or why not?
TIP!

Customize your questions on what your child can answer and have fun with this! If your student doesn't engage, retool and take a break as you want to teach them to love learning not dislike the process!

LOVE IT OR LEAVE IT!

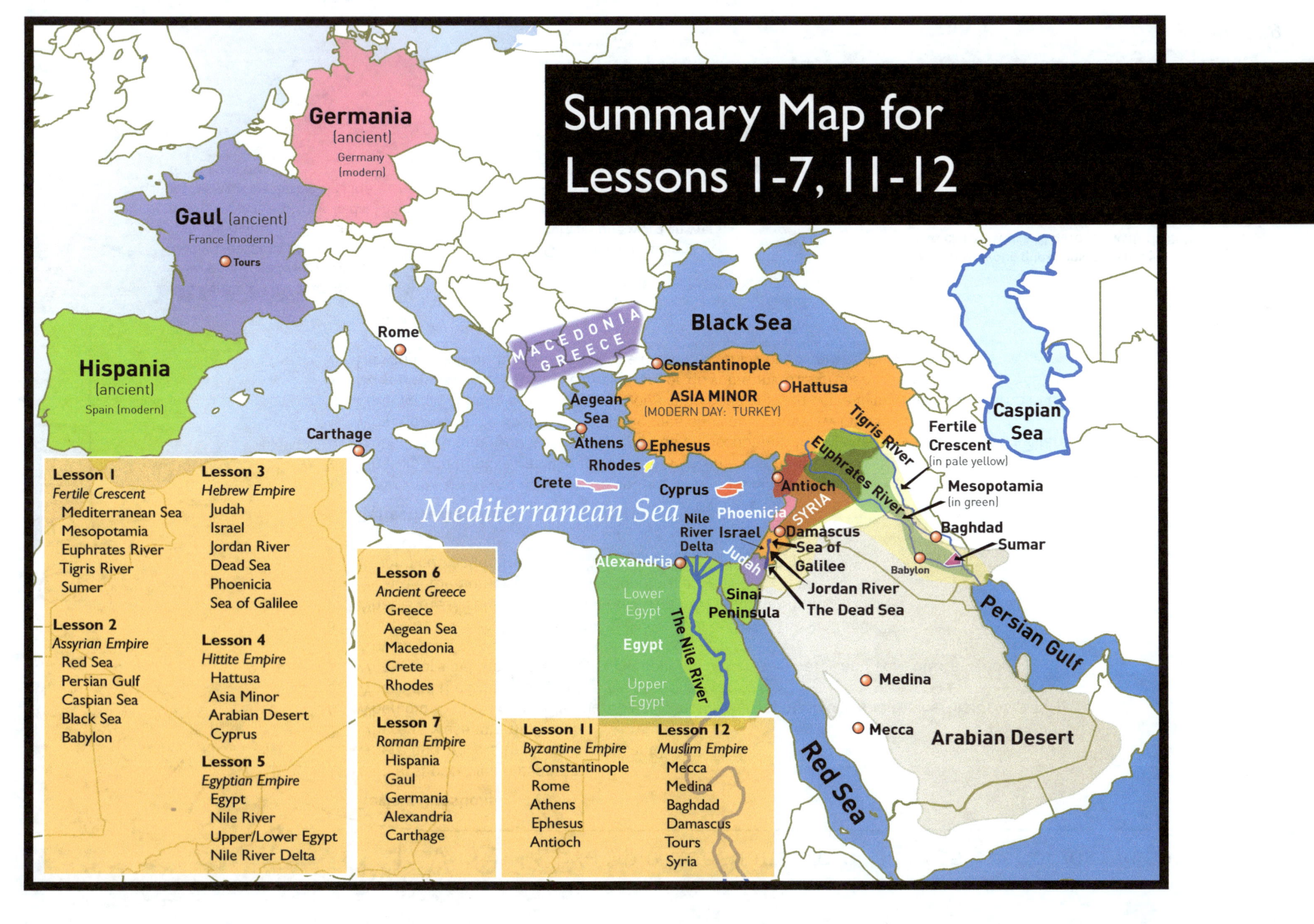

Summary Map for Lessons 1-7, 11-12

Germania (ancient)
Germany (modern)

Gaul (ancient)
France (modern)
• Tours

Hispania (ancient)
Spain (modern)

• Rome

• Carthage

MACEDONIA GREECE

Aegean Sea

Athens

Rhodes

Crete

Black Sea

• Constantinople

• Hattusa

ASIA MINOR (MODERN DAY: TURKEY)

Ephesus

Cyprus

Antioch

Phoenicia

SYRIA

Damascus

Israel

Judah

Sea of Galilee

Jordan River

The Dead Sea

Mediterranean Sea

Nile River Delta

Alexandria

Lower Egypt

Egypt

The Nile River

Upper Egypt

Sinai Peninsula

Tigris River

Euphrates River

Fertile Crescent (in pale yellow)

Mesopotamia (in green)

Baghdad

Sumar

Babylon

Caspian Sea

Persian Gulf

• Medina

• Mecca

Arabian Desert

Red Sea

Lesson 1
Fertile Crescent
Mediterranean Sea
Mesopotamia
Euphrates River
Tigris River
Sumer

Lesson 2
Assyrian Empire
Red Sea
Persian Gulf
Caspian Sea
Black Sea
Babylon

Lesson 3
Hebrew Empire
Judah
Israel
Jordan River
Dead Sea
Phoenicia
Sea of Galilee

Lesson 4
Hittite Empire
Hattusa
Asia Minor
Arabian Desert
Cyprus

Lesson 5
Egyptian Empire
Egypt
Nile River
Upper/Lower Egypt
Nile River Delta

Lesson 6
Ancient Greece
Greece
Aegean Sea
Macedonia
Crete
Rhodes

Lesson 7
Roman Empire
Hispania
Gaul
Germania
Alexandria
Carthage

Lesson 11
Byzantine Empire
Constantinople
Rome
Athens
Ephesus
Antioch

Lesson 12
Muslim Empire
Mecca
Medina
Baghdad
Damascus
Tours
Syria

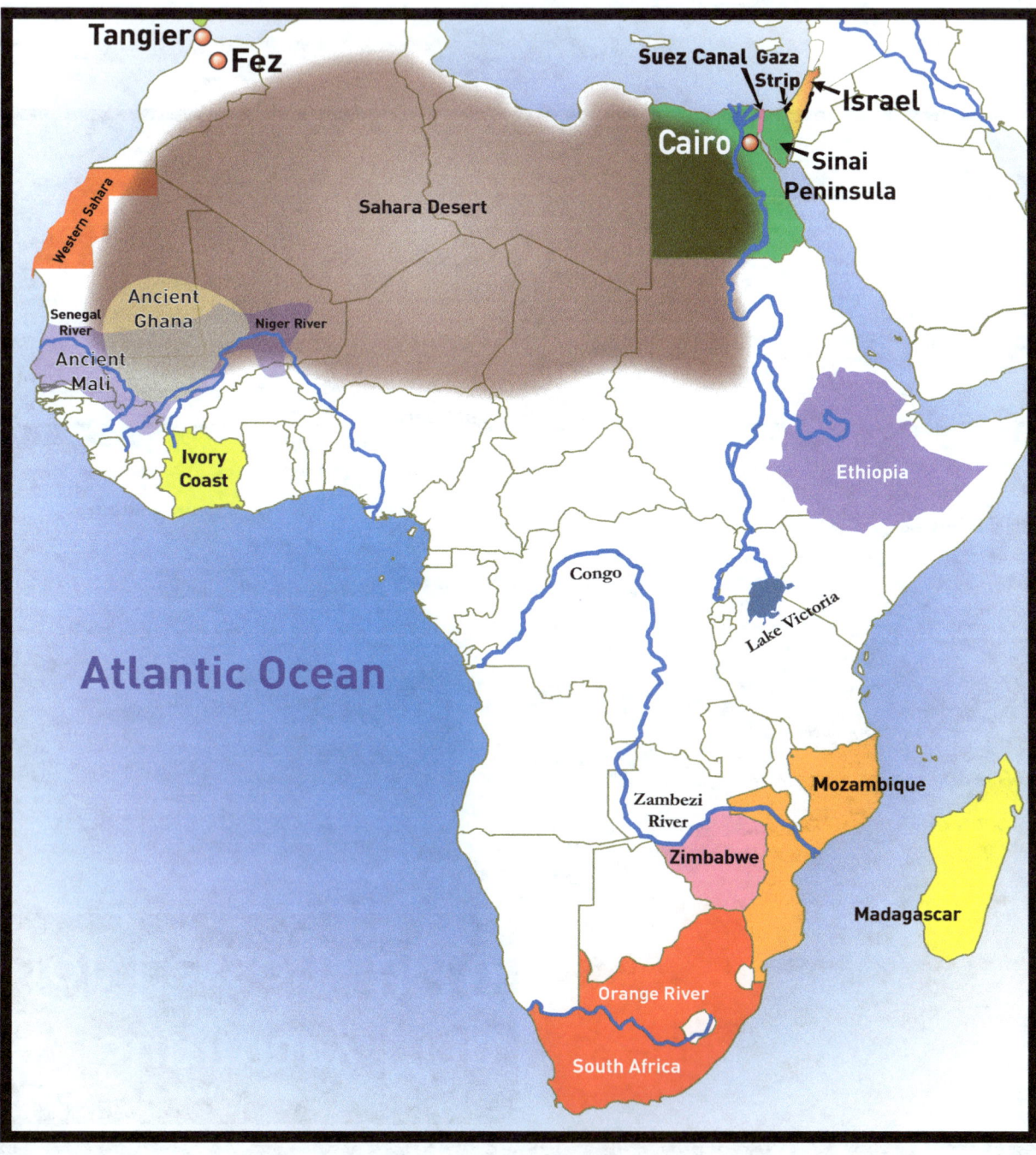

Summary Map for Lessons 13-17

Lesson 13
Western Africa
Atlantic Ocean
Senegal River
Niger River
Sahara Desert
Ivory Coast

Lesson 14
Ancient Africa
Ancient Ghana
Ancient Mali
Western Sahara
Fez
Tangier

Lesson 15
Middle East
Israel
Sinai Peninsula
Suez Canal
Cairo
Gaza Strip

Lesson 16
African Waters
Congo River
Lake Victoria
Zambezi River
Orange River

Lesson 17
African Countries
Ethiopia
Mozambique
Zimbabwe
South Africa
Madagascar

Summary Map for Lessons 18-19, 22-23

Lesson 18
Mesoamerica Regions
  Gulf of Mexico
  Yucatan Peninsula
  Olmec Civilization
  Maya Civilization
  Aztec Civilization

Lesson 19
Mesoamerica
  Mexico City
  Chichen Itza
  Lake Texcoco
  Mayapan
  Oaxaca

Lesson 22
South America (West)
  Venezuela
  Columbia
  Ecuador
  Peru
  Bolivia
  Chile

Lesson 23
South America (East)
  Argentina
  Uruguay
  Paraguay
  Brazil
  French Guiana
  Suriname
  Guyana

Summary Map for Lessons 20-21, 24

Lesson 20
Dominion of Canada
Ontario
Quebec
New Brunswick
Nova Scotia
Ontario Boundary of 1867
Quebec Boundary of 1867

Lesson 21
Canadian Waters
Great Bear Lake
Great Slave Lake
Hudson Bay
Baffin Bay
Labrador Sea

Lesson 24
North Atlantic
Greenland
Iceland
Denmark Strait
Davis Strait

Fertile Crescent

Mediterranean Sea
Mesopotamia
Euphrates River
Tigris River
Sumer

Where in the World?

Lesson 1

15

A Closer Look & Zoom Me In!

Lesson 1

This Lesson's Geography
The Fertile Crescent
Fertile Crescent
Mediterranean Sea
Mesopotamia
Euphrates River
Tigris River
Sumer

Use this sheet as a reference for this lesson's worksheets - be sure to practice until you don't have to look!

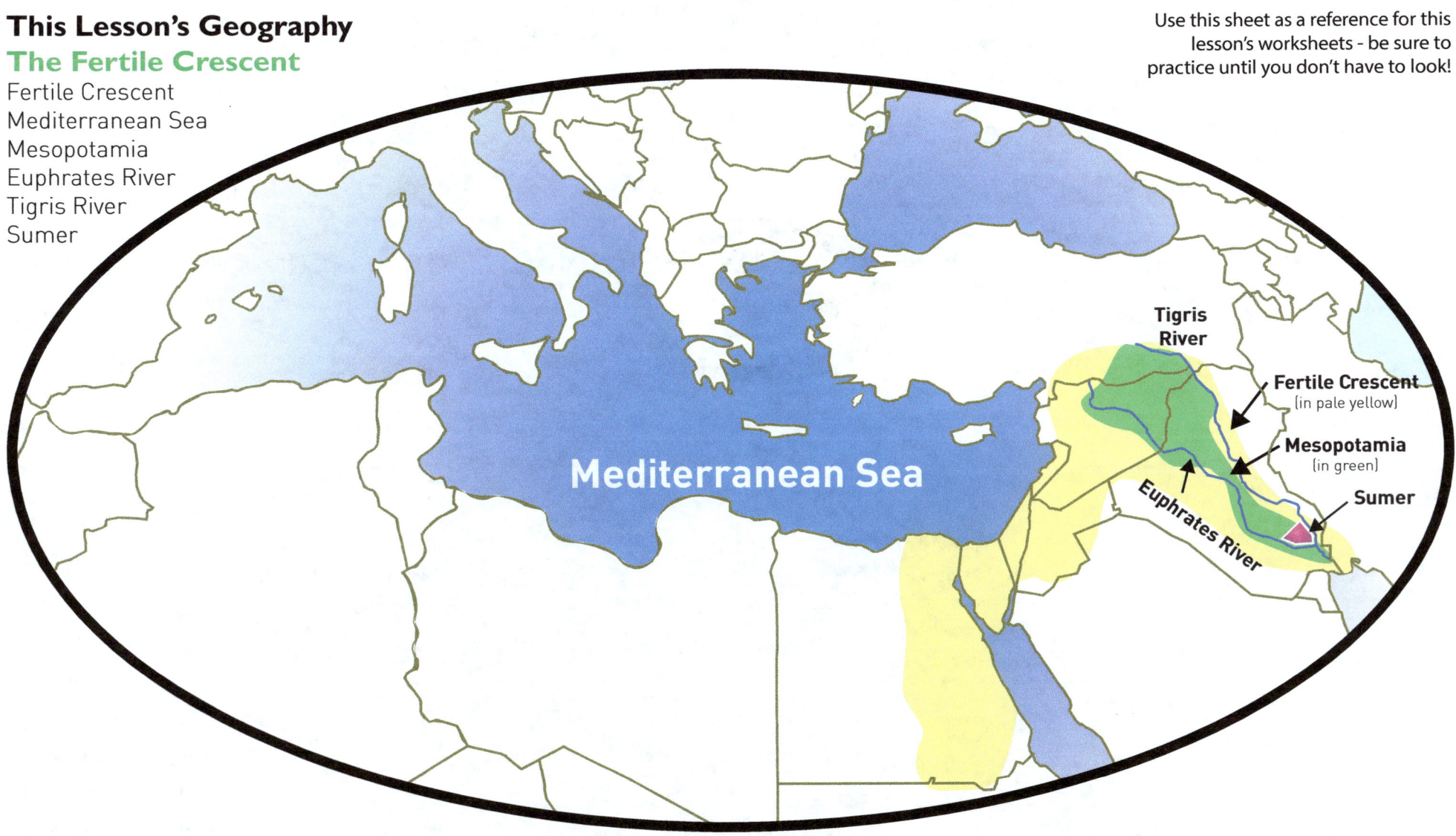

Parent/Teacher: The "A Closer Look" page is intended to show students the accumulated geographic areas being learned in this portion of the world. However, Lesson 1 is the first map in this area of the world and therefore this page doubles with "Zoom Me In!" For Teaching Tips on how to utilize these two teaching aides for the different learning levels please refer to page 1.

Lesson 1 Geography
Fertile Crescent
Fertile Crescent
Mesopotamia
Euphrates River
Tigris River
Sumer

Tid-Bits

Fertile Crescent: View from Tehran - Isfahan road, Iran, Middle East, Western Asia.

The Fertile Crescent area encapsulates Mesopotamia, Sumer, the Tigris and Euphrates rivers, and the great Mediterranean Sea. It is believed by many that somewhere within the Fertile Crescent lies the most ancient Garden of Eden, where Adam and Eve were created and walked with the Lord.

Historically referred to as the Fertile Crescent, the area gets its name from the shape of a crescent moon. Likewise, ancient civilizations thrived here with rich, fertile soil that made planting crops and reaping the benefits possible! Spanning from the north Nile River in Egypt to the southern fringe of Turkey. It goes west by the Mediterranean Sea and on the East alongside the Persian Gulf. Through the heart, the Tigris and Euphrates rivers flow.

In addition to containing remarkably fertile soil, there was freshwater along with salty wetlands. The combination of these elements produced a bounty of edible plants. It was here that people first began to experiment with farming grains as they transitioned from hunter-gatherer groups to agricultural civilizations.

A historical area of Western Asia situated within the Tigris–Euphrates river system was called Mesopotamia, found in the northern part of the Fertile Crescent. Within, the first known civilization lived. An ancient people referred to as the Sumer civilization lived in circular homes made of brick bounded together with mud. They referred to themselves as the Sag-giga, or "black-headed ones." Sumer was located in the lower area valleys of the Euphrates and Tigris rivers, where they kept sheep and pigs and farmed plants like wheat, lentils, flax, and barley. Do you eat any of these types of food that the Sumer people grew? These ancient grains are still enjoyed today throughout the world.

Maybe there are other things we have in common or have benefited from early civilizations within Mesopotamia. Well, if you like running water and freshly grown fruits and vegetables, you may want to know that the people of Mesopotamia came up with the idea to innovate irrigation through levees and canals. For drinking water, they created aqueduct systems. They also designed and formed pottery, early forms of banking and credit, and ownership of personal property. Additionally, they invented the cuneiform script, which is one of the earliest forms of writing. Another noteworthy accomplishment is the engineering and construction of large stepped pyramids called ziggurats.

Sumerians celebrated art and literature, such as the 3,000-line poem, the "Epic of Gilgamesh," which tells of

A Sumer civilization Ziggurat, found in modern-day Iraq. Image by Abdulmomn Kadhim from Pixabay

Sadly, today's Fertile Crescent is no longer as fertile as ancient times. In the 1950s, a series of large-scale irrigation projects diverted water away from the Mesopotamian marshes of the Tigris-Euphrates rivers. This caused them to dry up.

Later, in 1991, Saddam Hussein's reign built a series of dikes and dams to drain the marshes as a punishment to Arabs that cultivated rice and raised water buffalo. By 1992 approximately 90 percent of the marshland had disappeared, turning more than a thousand square miles into desert. Today, people are working to restore the wetlands, but stressed relationships between Iraq and Turkey have slowed progress.

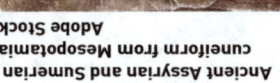

Ancient Assyrian and Sumerian cuneiform from Mesopotamia
Adobe Stock

the adventures of a Sumer king battling a forest monster and chasing after the secrets of eternal life.

Topographical view of the Euphrates River with desert surrounding. Image by Pexels from Pixabay

Ancient City Hasankeyf along the Tigris River in Mesopotamia - Adobe Stock

Where in the World?

Lesson 2

Assyrian Empire
Red Sea
Persian Gulf
Caspian Sea
Black Sea
Babylon

19

A Closer Look
at what you have learned so far!

PLUS+
This Lesson's Geography

The Assyrian Empire
Red Sea
Persian Gulf
Caspian Sea
Black Sea
Babylon

Lesson 2

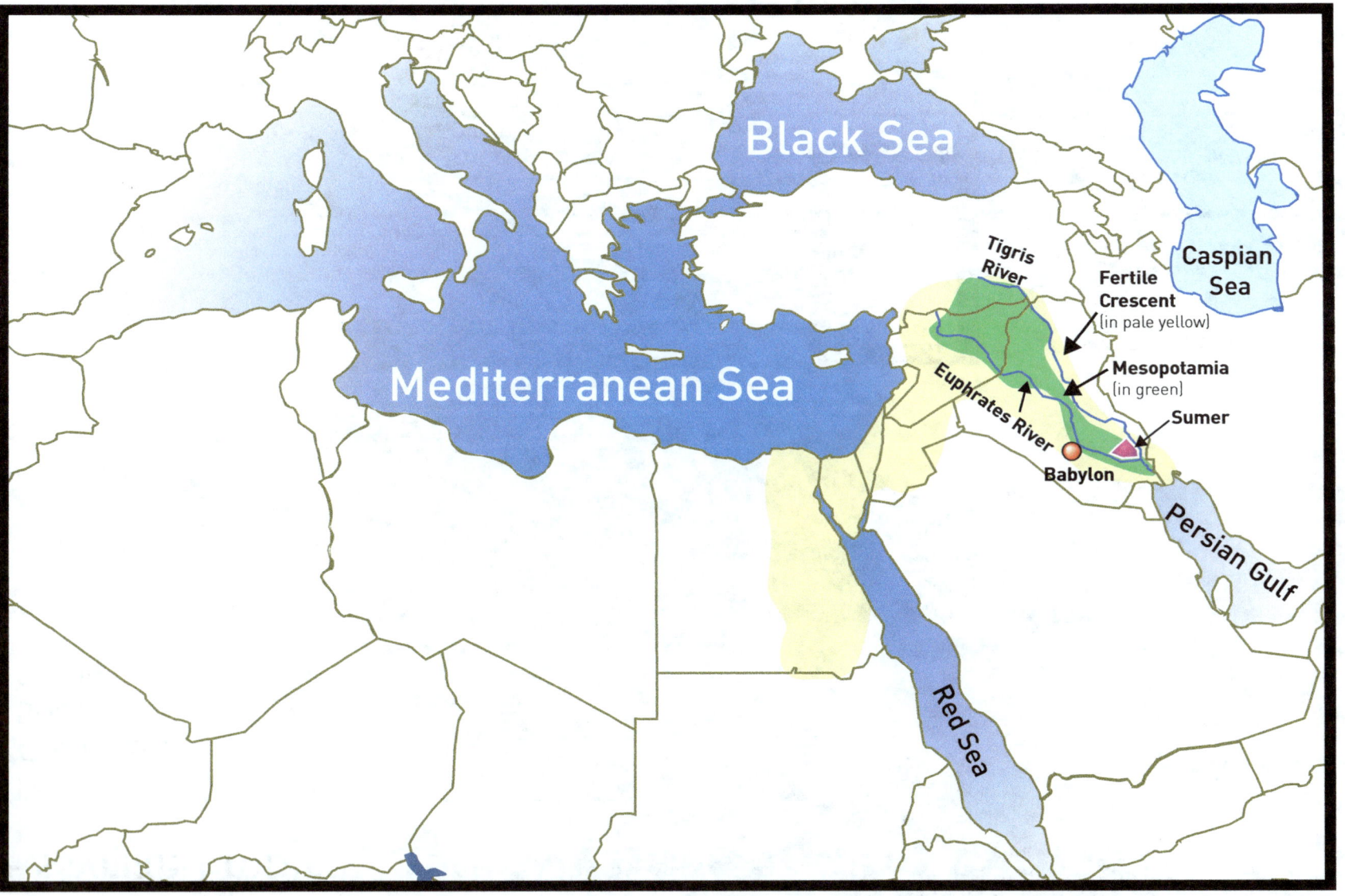

Previous Learned Geography:

Lesson 1
Fertile Crescent
Mediterranean Sea
Mesopotamia
Euphrates River
Tigris River
Sumer

Hint: The geography found on this page, is also the geography that you will be reviewing this week. Refer to this map as needed when doing your "Memorization Through Repetition" worksheets.

Parent/Teacher: The "A Closer Look" page is intended to show students the accumulated geographic areas taught within their 6-week review period. For additional teaching tips on how to utilize this teaching aide for the different learning levels, please refer to page 1.

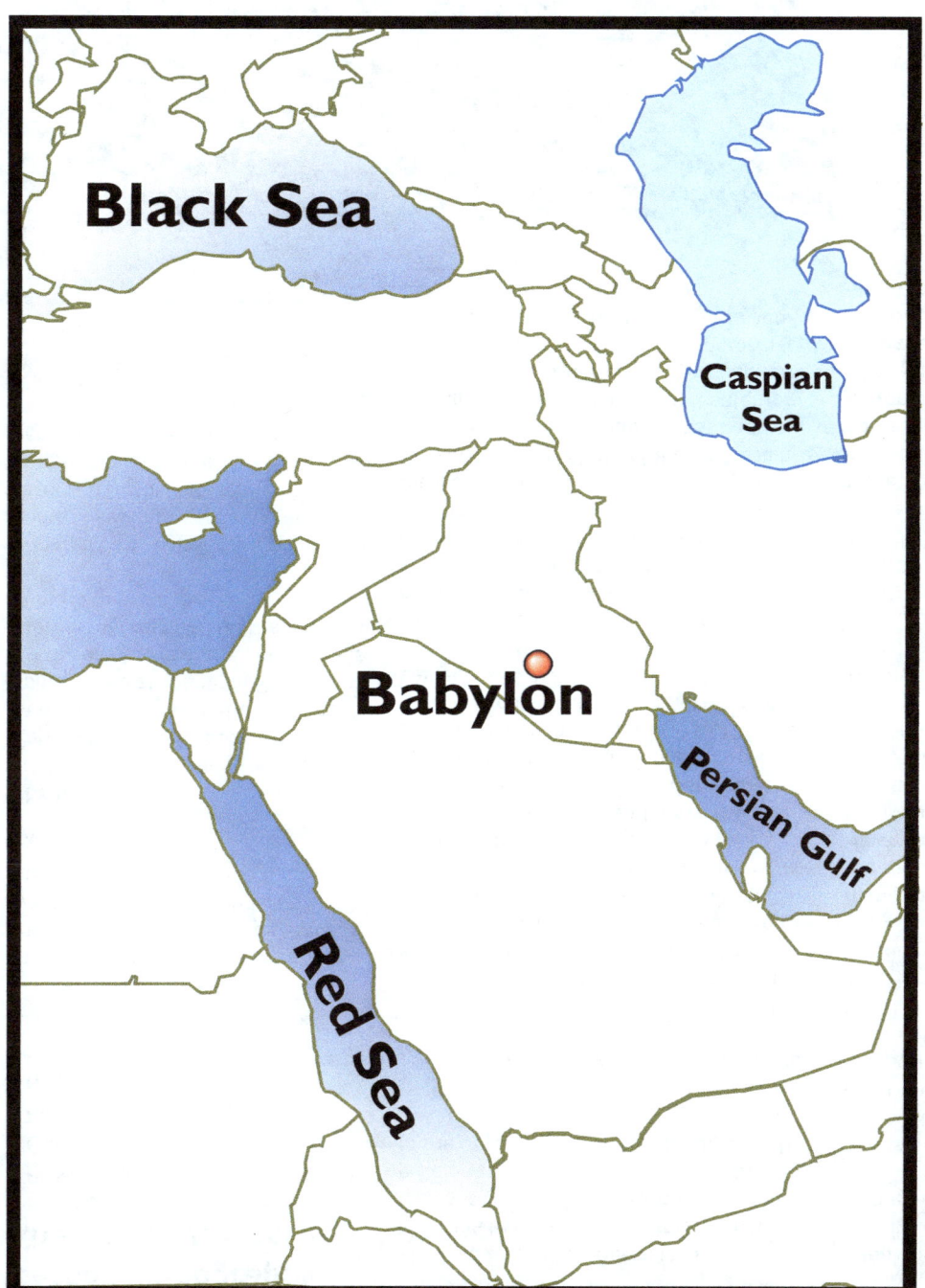

Zoom Me In!

Lesson 2

Use this sheet as a reference for this lesson's "Now, let's trace, shade & label" worksheet.

This Lesson's Geography
The Assyrian Empire
Red Sea
Persian Gulf
Caspian Sea
Black Sea
Babylon

Lesson 2 Geography
The Assyrian Empire
Red Sea
Persian Gulf
Caspian Sea
Black Sea
Babylon

Tid-Bits

In this lesson you will learn about the ancient Assyrian Empire which went from the Black and Caspian Seas all the way down to the Red Sea and Persian Gulf.

The Red Sea parts two major continents, separating the Arabian Peninsula from northeastern Africa. At the northern end, the Red Sea splits in two at the Sinai Peninsula. On the west side of the peninsula is the Gulf of Suez and on the east side is the Gulf of Aqaba.

The Red Sea is one of the first large bodies of water mentioned in recorded history. Moses led the Israelites across the Red Sea; it was necessary for early Egyptian maritime trading about 2000 BC. The sea was used as a route to India by about 1000 BCE. In about 600 BC the Phoenicians recorded their exploration of the Red Sea's shores.

The Red Sea got its name from the color it changes to from time to time. Usually, the Red Sea is an intense turqoise, but occasionally, it is full of extensive blooms of the algae. When the algae dies off, the sea turns reddish-brown!

The narrow strip of water goes from Suez, Egypt, for about 1,200 miles and is 190 miles at its widest. Its greatest depth is 9,974 feet, which is shy of 2 miles deep! Within the banks of the Red Sea are some of the hottest and saltiest seawater in the world. With ships traveling between Europe and Asia, this waterway is one of the most heavily traveled. Ships carry people and goods up and down the sea, traveling through the Suez Canal that opened in 1869. This landmark construction project changed how the world traded for it made trade and transportation much easier.

However, if you were a ship captain, you might not like passing through the Red Sea because navigation is difficult. There are few harbors because the natural growth of coral reefs has restricted the navigable channel and blocked some harbor facilities. Parts of the Red Sea are only open because people blast and dredge the sea open making it safer for ships to travel. Additionally, atmospheric distortion (heat shimmer), sandstorms, and crazy irregular water currents add to the navigational uncertainties.

Speaking of coral reefs, most "islands" of the Red Sea are just exposed reefs. With a few exceptions... Just south of Dahlak Archipelago is a island group of active volcanoes, as well as an extinct volcano located on the island of Jabal.

In this area of the world, there isn't a lot of rain. Being outside is great in the Autumn, Winter, and Spring, but come Summer, not so much. Temperatures in the summer soar high, up to 104 °F with all other seasons varying between 46 and 82 °F. During the the cooler months it does get windy! The Red Sea some experiences what is best knows as the "Egyptian winds." These winds blow with violent force and are accompanied by fog and sand storms.

The Persian Gulf is a shallow sea found between the Arabian Peninsula and southwestern Iran. Running for 615 miles, at its widest, it is 210 miles.

Along the Iran shoreline, there are mountains with many cliffs. However, there is the Musandam Peninsula, where many enjoy spectacular sandy beaches and many islands enclosing small lagoons.

The gulf is shallow, meaning not very deep. Rarely is the Persian Gulf deeper than about 300 feet, with some areas getting only as deep as 360 feet. There are many islands here. Mostly are salt dome islands, while others are mere accumulations of coral and skeletal debris. What is a salt dome, you may ask? A salt dome is where salty water is trapped, where the in-flow of salt-rich seawater is not balanced by outflow. In this case, the Indian Ocean pushes its saltwater into the Persian Gulf but never makes it out. When the water evaporates, all of the salt is left behind and layered up, making an island!

United Arab Emirates - Dubai coastline off the waters of the Persian Gulf. Image by Irina Art from Pixabay

When going to the shore, we can experience soft sandy beaches and sometimes rocky beaches. The shores of the Persian Gulf are different. Often, the seafloor has been hardened and turned to rock by calcium carbonate deposits from the warm, salty waters.

The gulf has an incredibly bothersome climate. With exception to the most northern portion in the winter, temperatures are high. When the rain comes, which it rarely does, it is a sharp downpour. And oh the winds! The "shamal," as it is called, is a wind that sometimes blows at speeds of 95 miles per hour within as short a time as five minutes. Humidity is high with little

The Red Sea meets Egypt - Image by Sabine Zierer from Pixabay

cloud cover. While thunderstorms and fog are rare, dust storms and haze frequently occur in summer.

The discovery of oil in Iran in 1908 changed the economy of the whole country. Once upon a time, the Persian Gulf was important for fishing, pearling, the building of dhows (lateen-rigged boats that are standard in the region), sailcloth making, camel breeding, the making of reed mats, and date growing. Economically, this supported a small number of people in this arid region surrounding the gulf, for little else could be produced.

Since World War II, the Persian Gulf and the surrounding countries have accounted for a significant proportion of the world's oil production. Being leaders in oil production has led the region to acquire strategic relationships with industrialized countries. Oil exploration has remained active, and new reserves are continually being discovered, both on land and offshore.

The Caspian Sea is the world's largest inland body of water. It lies to the east of the Caucasus Mountains and the west of the vast steppe of Central Asia. The sea's name arises from the ancient Kaspi peoples, who once lived in the south Caucasus region. Like most other geographical regions, the Caspian Sea had different names, mainly from other people living in the area. One of these was the name Girkansk, which meant "Country of the Wolves."

Aerial of the Caspian Sea - Adobe Stock

As the largest salt lake globally, this sea stretches for nearly 750 miles from north to south. While its average width is only 200 miles, it is larger than the area of Japan. The Caspian's surface is interestingly 90 feet below sea level and has a maximum depth of 3,360 feet.

As you might guess, the Caspian serves as both a busy trade route for ships coming and going out from the Mediterranean Sea. The surrounding countries benefit from all the fish that the Caspian offers up and the beautiful sandy beaches that welcome visitors from all over.

Overall, the Caspian Sea is an excellent place to be! The summer air is warm from July to August with a slight fluctuation between 75 to 79 °F. However, high temperatures sneak in from time to time on the eastern shore, where it can get as hot as 111 °F. When winter comes, the temperatures dip down. Depending on where you are, it could be as low as 14 °F outside. The more north you go, the colder it gets. In fact, it gets so frigid that ice forms and the sea usually freezes completely over by January. Now, if you are in the southern portion, the weather outside is far more comfortable at around 50 °F

As you now know, the Caspian Sea is salty. When you look at the map, you can plainly see that the entire body of water is not connected to any other sea or ocean water. So why is it called a sea when it looks like a lake? When the Ancient Romans first found that it was salty, they determined it to be a sea. It is thought that there was a connection between the Caspian Sea and another body of saltwater. This theory is based on the commonality between the seafloor of the Caspian and other standard oceanic basalt floors. The salinity (the water's salty level) is far more concentrated in the south than in the north, where freshwater pours in many large rivers, including the great Volga.

With this unique makeup of brackish water (partly fresh and partly salty water) and salty seawater, about 850 animals and more than 500 plant species live in the Caspian. That may sound like a lot, but it is pretty low for a large body of water like the Caspain. However, the remarkable thing about these animals and plants is that many are endemic to this area. Endemic means that the type of animal or plant is only found only there. A cute example of one of these animals is the Caspian Seal.

Caspian Seal, endemic to the Caspian Sea - Adobe Stock

The Black Sea straddles the boundary between Europe and Asia, with many large rivers adding freshwater to its' depths. These rivers include the Don, Danube, and Dnieper rivers.

Unlike the Caspian Sea, the Black Sea connects to the Mediterranean and Aegean Seas and many straits that all lead to the Atlantic Ocean.

Now here is a science-e term, but don't fear, you will learn something very cool! The Black Sea is the world's largest body of water, with a meromictic basin. Well, we got the big word done; now, what is a meromictic basin? A meromictic basin is created when deep waters do not mix with the upper layers of water. The upper layers of the Black Sea receive oxygen from the atmosphere. The surface water is less salty and not as dense as the waters below. The water temperature is close to that of air: warm in the summer and freezing in the winter. This is the Black Sea familiar to most people: swimming and diving, fishermen and dolphins catching fish. However, because the

Satellite image of the black sea with swirls of algae bloom. - NASA

waters don't mix, over 90% of the deep Black Sea water is without oxygen! So, how does the Black Sea support life in its depths? Well, the short answer is that it doesn't. But the better explanation is that only the top layer, 10% or 660 feet, supports life. Beyond 660 feet, there is a sole inhabitant,

anaerobic bacteria. The job of this bacteria disintegrates the sinking remains of the marine life above. When this bacteria does its job, a gas is released (sulfuric hydride (H2S) that is colorless, smelly like rotten eggs, poisonous, corrosive, and flammable. It doesn't sound very good. However, there is a silver lining that some people find impressive.

This deep layer of dense water without oxygen is called anoxic water. While this anoxic water lacks life, it preserves artifacts such as boat hulls. As a result, marine archaeologists "dig" the Black Sea for its' shipwrecks! Ancient shipwrecks in the Black Sea are remarkably preserved. One such discovery was a Byzantine-era wreck referred to as "Sinop D." This 700-foot ship was discovered almost 1.24 miles below the surface, where it is thought to have been situated for more than 2,400 years.
"This will change our understanding of shipbuilding and seafaring in the ancient world," stated Professor Jon Adams, the principal investigator of the team that found the wreck.

Babylon was a city-state of ancient Mesopotamia, located in present-day Iraq, about 55 miles south of Baghdad. All that remains of this ancient city are mounds of broken mud-brick buildings in the Mesopotamian plain between the Tigris and Euphrates rivers.
These mounds cover about 1.24 miles by 0.62 miles along the Euphrates west bank. Back then, the Euphrates had a slightly different route that split the city in two. Since then, the river course shifted, locating many remains of Babylon underwater, except portions of the city wall that remain.

History recorded in Genesis 10:10 in the Bible describes the founder of Babylon as Nimrod. He built Babylon in the land of Shinar and was one of eight

Sinop D Shipwreck found at the bottom of the Black Sea. Public Domain

Babylon ruins, Hillah, Iraq - Adobe Stock

kingdoms he made. Another account is given in Genesis 11, which tells how Babylon (called "Babel" in the Bible) got its' name:

"Now the whole earth had one language and the same words. And as people migrated from the east, they found a plain in the land of Shinar and settled there. And they said to one another, "Come, let us make bricks, and burn them thoroughly." And they had brick for stone, and bitumen for mortar. Then they said, "Come, let us build ourselves a city and a tower with its top in the heavens, and let us make a name for ourselves, lest we be dispersed over the face of the whole earth." And the LORD came down to see the city and the tower, which the children of man had built. And the LORD said, "Behold, they are one people, and they have all one language, and this is only the beginning of what they will do. And nothing that they propose to do will now be impossible for them. Come, let us go down and there confuse their language, so that they may not understand one another's speech." So the LORD dispersed them from there over the face of all the earth, and they left off building the city. Therefore its name was called Babel, because there the LORD confused the language of all the earth. And from there the LORD dispersed them over the face of all the earth."

This account is commonly referred to as the "Tower of Babel."

Additionally, Babylon appears throughout the Hebrew Bible, including descriptions of the Babylonian Captivity, and is featured in several prophecies. The New Testament Book of Revelation refers to Babylon many centuries after it ceased to be a major political center.

What remains of Babylon include "Kasr," a palace or possibly a castle that was a ziggurat. The Kasr is in the center of all of the remains. In another mound referred to as "Amran Ibn Ali" is the highest mound and is believed to have been the site of "Esagila," a temple of Marduk - the god of the Babylonians. This site also contained shrines to Ea and Nabu. Next is a reddish colored mound called "Homera" where most Hellenistic remains are found. "Hellenistic" relates to Greek history, language, and culture from the time of Alexander the Great's death to the defeat of Mark Antony and Cleopatra by Octavian in 31 BC. In this period, Greek culture flourished, spreading through the Mediterranean, the Near East, and Asia, including Mesopotamia. Lastly is the mound named "Babil." It is believed that these remains are of Nebuchadnezzar's palace.

While Babylon existed, they had various rulers and empires govern them. There was the Assyrian Empire, Neo-Babylonian Chaldean Empire, and then Persia captured Babylon.

During the Assyrian period, the people of Babylon were in a constant state of revolt alleviated only by the city's complete destruction. In 689 BC, the city walls, temples, and palaces were all destroyed, and their leader Sennacherib was murdered by two of his sons. Following this, the Assyrian successor, Esarhaddon, hurried to rebuild the city. The Assyrians continued to rule until the Babylonians threw off the Assyrians in 612 BC, becoming the capital of the Neo-Babylonian Chaldean Empire and gaining their independence. Soon after, a new era of prosperity followed with Nebuchadnezzar II, who made Babylon beautiful. Nebuchadnezzar had the people reconstruct the imperial grounds, including rebuilding the Etemenanki ziggurat and the Ishtar Gate, the most magnificent of eight gates that ringed the perimeter of Babylon.

Nebuchadnezzar also constructed the Hanging Gardens of Babylon, one of the seven wonders of the ancient world. These gardens are said to have been built for his homesick wife, Amyitis. She missed her homeland's green hills and valleys. In the writings of the Babylonian priest Berossus, in about 290 BC, a description that Josephus later quoted described these gardens as a remarkable feat of engineering. It had ascending tiered gardens containing trees of many kinds, shrubs, and vines. The garden resembled a lush green mountain constructed of mud bricks.

"The Tower of Babel" (1563) by Pieter Bruegel (also Brueghel or Breughel) the Elder (1525/30-1569). Kunsthistorisches Museum (Art History Museum) in Vienna, Austria - Adobe Stock

Then came along Persia, today that same country is called Iran. In 539 BC, in the Battle of Opis, the Neo-Babylonian Empire fell to Cyrus the Great, king of Persia. As the story goes, the walls of Babylon were very high and thick. The only way into the city was through its many gates. Since that couldn't happen, they devised another plan. The Euphrates River flowed next to the Babylonian walls, and Cyrus decided to use the river to get into the city. Cyrus' troops diverted the Euphrates river causing the level of the water to drop. Next, the soldiers entered the city to conquer.

While the Babylonians were busy with a celebration that evening, the Persian Army took over most of the city before they even knew that the Persians were there. This account was reported by Herodotus and mentioned in the Bible. Cyrus took the city by simply walking through the gates of Babylon with no resistance.

King Cyrus later allowed Babylonian people, including the Jews, to return to their land and gave the Jewish people the ability to rebuild their temple in Jerusalem.

Under Cyrus and the following Persian king, Darius the Great, Babylon became the capital city. It was a center of learning and scientific advancement, including the Babylonian arts of astronomy and mathematics. Scholars from Babylon made maps of constellations. This city was the capital of the Persian Empire, and the empire was the most powerful in the known world.

Assyrian and Babylonian relief carving, ancient history of Mesopotamia - Adobe Stock

The early Persian kings attempted to abide in the religious ceremonies of Marduk, the Babylonian god. By the time Darius III reigned, over-taxation and numerous wars had led to a deterioration of Babylon's main shrines and canals. The people of Babylon were no longer unified. Despite rebellions in 522 BCE, 521 BCE, and 482 BCE, Babylon remained under Persian rule for two centuries. Until 331 BC.

In 331 BC, Alexander the Great set his sights on the Persian Empire. After he had conquered Egypt, Alexander went east to face Darius and his massive troops. Following fierce battles and many lives lost, Darius fled. His troops assassinated him. Alexander was sad when he found Darius's body and gave him a royal burial.

After being rid of Darius, Alexander proclaimed himself King of Persia. But he wasn't the only one. Another Persian leader, Bessus, who was Darius's murderer, had also claimed the Persian throne. Alexander couldn't let the claim stand. Bessus' troops handed him over, and he was no more. With Bessus out of the way, Alexander had complete control of Persia.

With this tremendous change, Babylon was no longer the center of what was the great Persian Empire. Under Alexander the Great's control, Babylon shrunk and lost importance until it disappeared.

The main entrance to the ruins of the ancient Babylon. It is a replica of the original Ishtar gate which was situated in the ancient city. It is about a third of the size of the original Ishtar gate. - Adobe Stock

A Closer Look
at what you have learned so far!

PLUS+
This Lesson's Geography:

The Hebrew Empire
Judah
Israel
Jordan River
Dead Sea
Phoenicia
Sea of Galilee

Hint: The geography found on this page, is also the geography that you will be reviewing this week. Refer to this map as needed when doing your "Memorization Through Repetition" worksheets.

Lesson 3

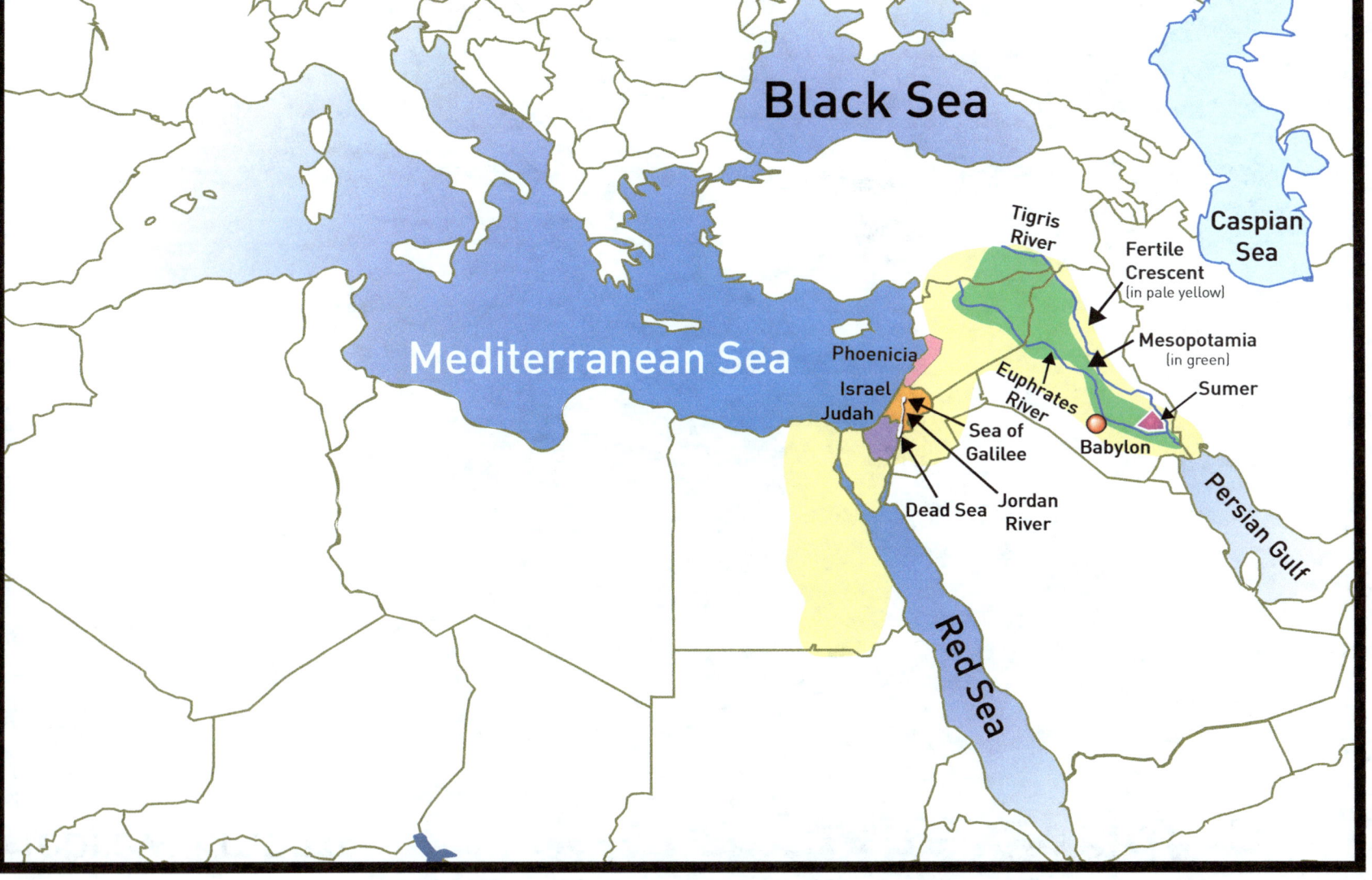

Previous Learned Geography:

Lesson 1
Fertile Crescent
Mediterranean Sea
Mesopotamia
Euphrates River
Tigris River
Sumer

Lesson 2
Red Sea
Persian Gulf
Caspian Sea
Black Sea
Babylon

Parent/Teacher: The "A Closer Look" page is intended to show students the accumulated geographic areas taught within their 6-week review period. For additional teaching tips on how to utilize this teaching aide for the different learning levels, please refer to page 1.

Zoom Me In!

Lesson 3

Use this sheet as a reference for this lesson's "Now, let's trace, shade & label" worksheet.

This Lesson's Geography
The Hebrew Empire
Judah
Israel
Jordan River
Dead Sea
Phoenicia
Sea of Galilee

Lesson 3 Geography
The Hebrew Empire
Judah
Israel
Jordan River
Dead Sea
Phoenicia
Sea of Galilee

Tid-Bits

In this lesson you will learn

about you are learning about the ancient Hebrew Empire which went from Phoenicia down to the Sinai Peninsula and beyond the Jordan River.

Israel is the only nation that lives on the same land, communicates in the same language, has the same name, and worships the same God that it did over 3,300 years ago. If you were to dig down into this land, you might uncover pottery from the time of David's reign, or what is sometimes referred to as the Davidic times.

DEAD SEA SCROLLS: The Isaiah Scroll which contains almost the entire book of Isaiah. This was one of 25,000 fragments found in the Qumran caves near the Dead Sea. Photographs by Ardon Bar Hama, Public Domain

You may discover coins from the times of Bar Kokhba, who was the Jewish leader that led the third revolt against the Roman Empire in circa 132–136 AD. Or, maybe you'll be lucky enough to find more 5,000-year-old scrolls like that of the Dead Sea scrolls, which most were written in a script very much like the Hebrew writings of today. This ancient Hebrew Empire was made up of people who share an incredible family line (or lineage). Today, that family line continues, and they are referred to as the Nation of Israel.

This extensive family line is referred to by many different names. This may be confusing, with each name holding intertwined history. If you ever hear someone talking about the Hebrews, the Israelites, the children of Israel, the Jewish people, or simply, the Jews, well, these are all the same people.

Today the Jews enjoy their land that their people govern. They have not always had this privilege. They have been independent and ruled by other empires. And, in 70 AD, the Roman Empire exiled the Jews from their land; their Temple was destroyed for the second time. The Jews scattered outside of Israel's land, migrating to different parts of Europe and North Africa.

Coins from the Bar Kokhba times: Palm tree with seven branches and two clusters of fruit; below it, a paleo-Hebrew inscription Shimon which means "Hearkening," meaning "heed" or "pay attention. On the reverse a bunch of grapes with small branch and leaf, surrounded by the inscription "for the freedom of Jerusalem." Coin dated to circa 132-135 AD with The Bar Kokhba Revolt that broke out seventy years after the destruction of the Second Temple. Photo credit: Winner's Auctions, Public Domain

DEAD SEA SCROLLS: Qumran cave 4, where ninety percent of the scrolls were found. By Effi Schweizer - Own work, Public Domain

Wall relief on arch of titus depicting Menorah taken from temple in Jerusalem in 70 AD when the Roman Empire destroyed Jerusalem, the Jewish Temple and scattered the Jewish people - Adobe Stock

Map of the division made in the Nation of Israel or "Holy Land" by the 12 tribes of Israel. Adobe Stock

Becoming, once again, a united independent nation was a long road for the Jewish people. They would not unite again on their land until 1,878 years later. The year was 1948, three years after the conclusion of World War II and the atrocities of the holocaust.

The history of the Hebrews is deep, spanning thousands of years and all known history. The earliest record of this family line begins with a man named Abraham, who was called a Hebrew. Abraham's clan was from Ur under the Babylonian empire within Mesopotamia. At one time, Abraham and his clan migrated to the land of Canaan (which would become Israel, the promised land). Abraham and his wife had a son named Isaac. Isaac had a son named Jacob. These three Hebrew men are referred to as the patriarchs of the Hebrews. All three lived in the Land of Canaan, which later became known as the Nation of Israel. The name Israel comes from the name change that was given to the third patriarch, Jacob. Israel had 12 sons. These sons' descendants became the 12 tribes of Israel that developed into the Jewish nation, or what you can call the "Hebrew Empire."

This family line became the Jewish nation in 1300 BC after their Exodus from Egypt under the leadership of Moses. After 40 long years wandering the Sinai desert, Moses led them to the Land of Israel, formerly known as Canaan. As history from the Bible communicates, this land was promised by God to the descendants of the patriarchs, Abraham, Isaac, and Jacob.

Before Moses died, he made Joshua the new leader of the 12 tribes of Israel. Joshua's first order of business was to lead the Hebrews into the land to conquer and settle. After, the land was split up between the tribes. From 1000-587 BC was the

"Period of the Kings" where noteworthy kings ruled. King David ruled from 1010-970 BC, making Jerusalem the Capital of Israel. King David's successor and son was King Solomon, who ruled from 970-931 BC. He built the first Temple in Jerusalem and was considered the wisest of all men.

In 587 BC, the Babylonian Empire's leader, Nebuchadnezzar, had his army capture Jerusalem and destroy the Temple. The Jews were exiled until Persia, led by Cyrus, invaded and took Babylon.

This latest take over by the Persian Empire served as a turning point for the Middle East. From the year 587 BC, the area was ruled by various superpowers. In order: Babylonian, Persian, Greek Hellenistic, Roman and Byzantine Empires, Islamic and Christian crusaders, Ottoman Empire, and the British Empire.

City of Jerusalem, the capital of the Nation of Israel at sunset - Adobe Stock

Jewish men at the whaling wall in Jerusalem - Image by Richard van Liessum from Pixabay

Where in the World?

Lesson 4

Hittite Empire
Hattusa
Asia Minor
Arabian Desert
Cyprus

A Closer Look at what you have learned so far!

PLUS+ This Lesson's Geography

The Hittite Empire
Hattusa
Asia Minor
Arabian Desert
Cyprus

Hint: All geography found on this page, is also the geography that you will be reviewing this week. Refer to this map as needed when doing your "Memorization Through Repetition" worksheets.

Lesson 4

Previous Learned Geography:

Lesson 1
Fertile Crescent
Mediterranean Sea
Mesopotamia
Euphrates River
Tigris River
Sumer

Lesson 2
Red Sea
Persian Gulf
Caspian Sea
Black Sea
Babylon

Lesson 3
Judah
Israel
Jordan River
Dead Sea
Phoenicia

Parent/Teacher: The "A Closer Look" page is intended to show students the accumulated geographic areas taught within their 6-week review period. For additional teaching tips on how to utilize this teaching aide for the different learning levels, please refer to page 1.

Zoom Me In!

Use this sheet as a reference for this lesson's "Now, let's trace, shade & label" worksheet.

Lesson 4

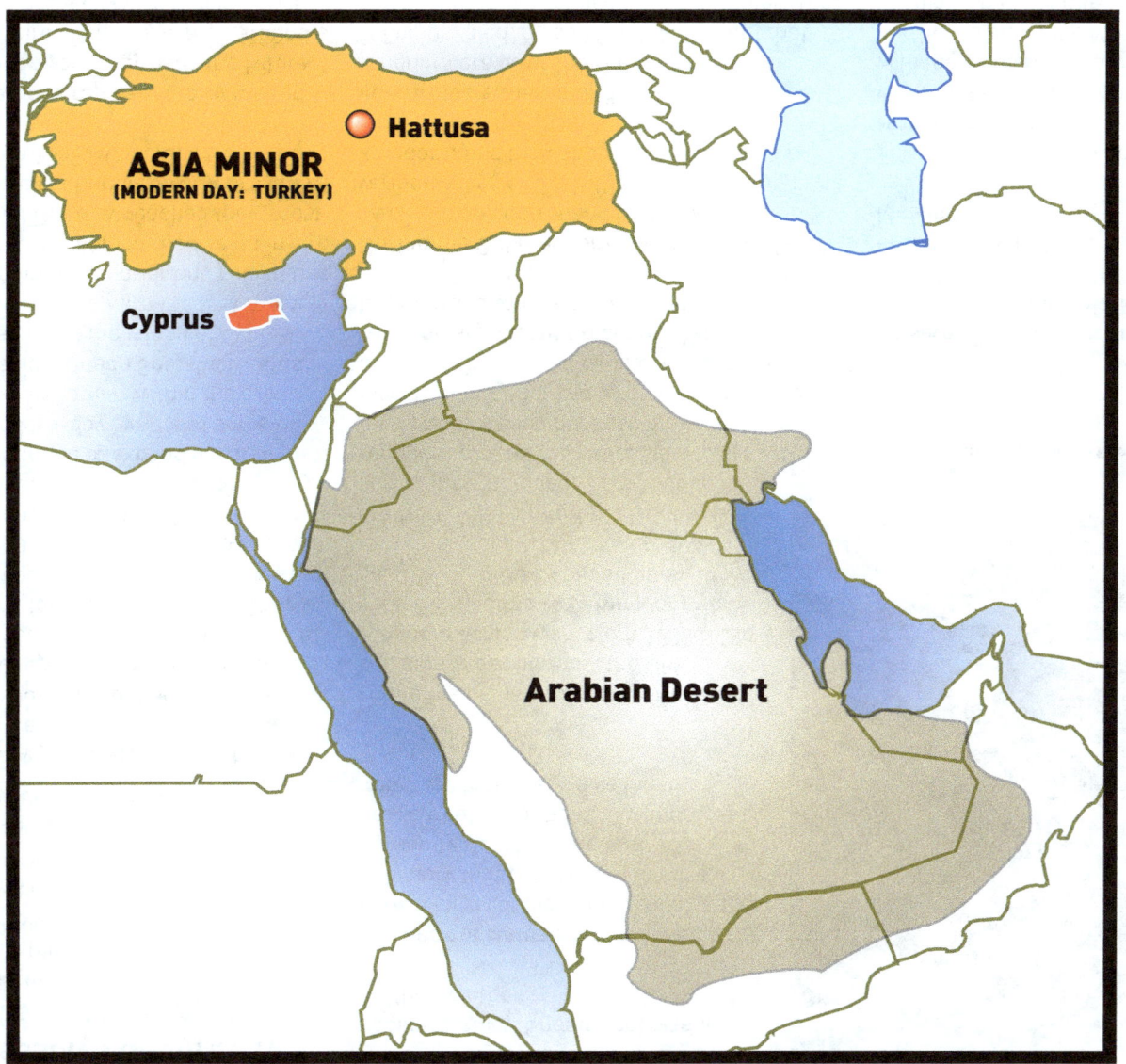

This Lesson's Geography
The Hittite Empire
Hattusa
Asia Minor
Arabian Desert
Cyprus

Lesson 4 Geography
The Hittite Empire
Hattusa
Asia Minor
Arabian Desert
Cyprus

Tid-Bits

Many years ago, various tribes shared a common language and resources in a land now called Turkey. Over time, these tribes joined together to conquer more land for more resources. They called themselves the Hittites and began their conquests in Anatolia, a land area within Asia Minor (most modern-day Turkey). They continued to expand down to modern-day Syria and some of Mesopotamia. Within the great Mediterranean Sea, the Hittites also ruled the island of Cyprus. The Hittites were the first major empire to conquer and rule in this land. Beginning their reign in circa 1700 BC, they reached their most powerful hundreds of years later, from 1350 BC to 1250 BC.

Hattusa, represented by the red dot on your map, was the Hittite Empire capital. The area around this great city was rich in agricultural fields and many hilly lands that served as pastures and forests. In ancient times, these forests were a plentiful supply of lumber for building city structures and homes. The fields produced

wheat, barley, flax, and lentils for people to enjoy. Sheep wool was woven for their clothes.

The ancient Hittite Empire is well known for a couple of influential pieces of history that contributed to advancing humanity. Namely, the first-ever peace treaty and the ability to process iron into steel. Let's dive into the history!

Hittite history is commonly divided into two significant periods: the Old Kingdom, which went from 1700 BC to 1500 BC, and the New Kingdom from 1400 BC to 1180 BC. In addition, there is an overlapping one-hundred-year era from 1500 BC to 1400 BC that is sometimes included. This Middle Kingdom era, as it is called, is a mysterious period because archaeologically, there are few written findings to give us clues about these people in that period, with one significant exception. We'll circle back around to this in a moment.

During the Old Kingdom, the rulers' goals were to gain control and bring together the various tribes of the Hittites into a singular kingdom; this took about 200 years.

Few artifacts were found for the Middle Kingdom era after the Old Kingdom's ruler, Telipinus, died in 1500 BC. It is thought that few documents exist because the Hittites were likely under attack continually, for they were not the only empire that wanted the same land and resources. Many researchers look to the Old and New Kingdoms for answers and surrounding empires during this time to find clues.

Ruins of old Hittite capital Hattusa - Photo by Mathas Rehak, Adobe

However, a critical occurrence during this time was an alliance formed with Egypt. Unfortunately, this relationship between the two superpower empires began to crumble when Egypt allied with a new enemy of the Hittites: the Mitanni.

This alliance between Egypt and Mitanni led to more than 200 years of tension and conflict with the Hittites. Egypt moved northward along the Mediterranean coast; the Hittite Empire moved southward. The two clashed in what was called the battle of Kadesh. Both sides suffered heavy losses, and both sides declared victory.

Dead warriors, Battle of Kadesh, Ramesseum, by: BasPhoto, Adobe

In 1258 BC, fifteen years after this battle, the first known peace treaty was signed to end this long war between the Hittite Empire and the Egyptians, who had fought for over two centuries to gain dominance over the lands of the eastern Mediterranean. This peace treaty is referred to as the "Treaty of Kadesh," which was ratified in the 21st year of Ramesses II's reign and continued until the Hittite Empire collapsed eighty years later.

Metallurgy: The process of making steel from iron. Image by kepinator from Pixabay

The Egyptian-Hittite peace treaty between Ramesses II and Hattušili III, mid-13th century BC. Neues Museum, Berlin, By Osama Shukir Muhammed Amin

As you may know, all of history is split up into "ages." Each "age" is a period that is characterized by something significant. For example, scientifically, artistically, culturally, industrially, and more.

The New Kingdom period was considered the Bronze Age, as the advanced civilizations utilized bronze for creating weapons, art, architecture, and more. That is until the Hittites discovered how to process iron into steel. Hittites relied on trade routes for their growth and to obtain resources like iron. Iron is a shiny metal that is commonly found all over the world. When the Hittites learned how to process iron into steel, it gave them an advantage over other empires in battle with superior weaponry and chariots. Steel is lighter than bronze, making their weapons easier to wield and their chariots faster.

After the Battle of Kadesh, the Hittites saw their power begin to decline as the Assyrians became more powerful. The success of the empirical movement of the Assyrians and other groups led to the fall of the Hittite empire. As their kingdom fell, the Hittites scattered to surrounding lands, including Hittites knowledgeable in iron metallurgy, which spread this unique experience from the Hittites to the whole Middle East. Like that of the Hittites, Steel revolutionized weaponry, but now for many more civilizations. It was no longer the Bronze Age; it was now The Iron Age.

The Hittite Empire was followed by the Assyrians and then the Greeks, who began to settle around 1100 BC. The Greeks founded vibrant cities in the area, including Byzantium, which after the split of the Roman Empire, would be ruled by Constantine, and he renamed it Constantinople. Later, this same city would be renamed once again to Istanbul by the Ottoman Empire.

The land of ancient Asia Minor is located in the southwestern part of Asia, making up most present-day Turkey. First described as 'The Land of the Hatti" by the Akkadian Dynasty (2334-2083 BCE) was inhabited by the Hittites. The Hittites referred to the land as 'Assuwa' or Aswiya. This name is considered the Bronze Age origin for the name 'Asia' as the Romans designated the area. It was called, by the Greeks, 'Anatolia,' which means 'place of the rising sun' for the lands east of Greece where the sun rises.

The name 'Asia Minor' is from the Greek 'Mikra Asia,' meaning 'Little Asia.' Coined to distinguish the main of Asia from that region which had been evangelized by Paul the Apostle. Sites included are known from Paul's Epistles in the Bible, such as Ephesus and Galicia.

Traveling by camel in the Arabian Desert, Image from Pixabay

The Arabian Desert is a vast dry wilderness in western Asia, stretching from Yemen to the Persian

Arabian Desert Image by Ivan Ghazal from Pixabay

Gulf, from Oman to Jordan and Iraq. It occupies most of the Arabian Peninsula. Average low temperatures during the summer nights remain high at over 68 °F. Record high temperatures are above 122 °F in much of the desert. This hot and dry climate experiences plenty of sunshine throughout the year with only about 4 inches of rainfall per year, with some areas having the least at just 1 inch per year!

We usually think of camels, scorpions, and snakes when we think of the desert - but cats? Yes! Meet this cute and cuddly (well, maybe not!) Arabian Desert Cat. This cat, also known as the Sand Cat, is a unique breed that looks similar in many ways to kitties we may have in our homes - but these cats have enhanced features. The Arabian Desert Cat has a wider, flatter face and larger ears than the domestic cat. With a solid body structure and short fur, this cat can cope with the intense heat and high temperatures of the Arabian Desert. Its legs are slender with oval paws and fur between its toes to protect it from the hot sand. This cat may look like our cuddly creatures, but this desert version is tough and survives on various prey, including reptiles, birds, rodents, and insects.

The island of Cyprus in the eastern Mediterranean Sea is the third largest and the third most populated island in the Mediterranean. The Mycenaean Greeks initially settled Cyprus in the 2nd millennium BC. This island has a strategic location that

Cobblestone streets in Cyprus - Image by Dimitris Vetsikas from Pixabay

had many empires desiring to rule over it. Over the centuries, several significant powers have inhabited the island, including the Hittites, Assyrians, Egyptians, and Persians, from whom the island was seized in 333 BC by Alexander the Great. Then Egypt again, the Classical and Eastern Roman Empires, Arab caliphates for a short period, the French and the Venetians, followed by over three centuries of Ottoman rule.

Today, the island shares the occupancy of two countries. Turkey and Greece. The people on the island call themselves Cypriots. There are Greek Cypriots and Turkish Cypriots, and they both enjoy the tropical paradise of Cyprus. In Greek Mythologie, Cyprus is known as the playground of the Gods and where Aphrodite was born, the Greek Goddess of Love. The most famous landmark is Mount Olympus, along with the pristine beaches. And while the Gods don't play here, Cyprus is quite a destination spot today!

An ocean view from the island of Cyprus - Image by Dimitris Vetsikas from Pixabay

Arabian Desert Cat, Adobe Stock

Where in the World?

Lesson 5

Egyptian Empire
Egypt
Nile River
Upper/Lower Egypt
Nile River Delta

39

A Closer Look
at what you have learned so far!

PLUS+
This Lesson's Geography

The Egyptian Empire
Egypt
Nile River
Upper/Lower Egypt
Nile River Delta

Lesson 5

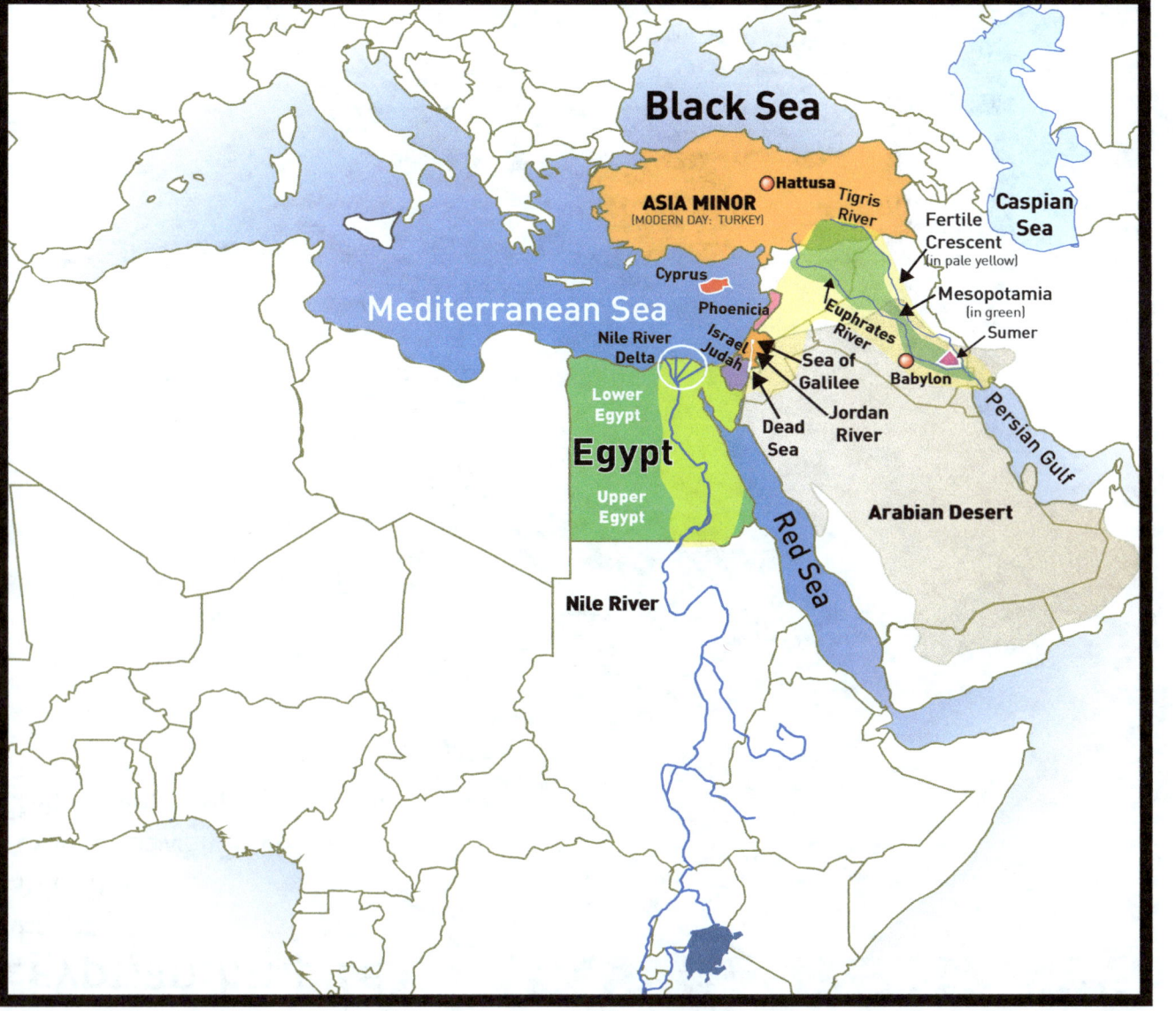

Previous Learned Geography:

Lesson 1
Fertile Crescent
Mediterranean Sea
Mesopotamia
Euphrates River
Tigris River
Sumer

Lesson 2
Red Sea
Persian Gulf
Caspian Sea
Black Sea
Babylon

Lesson 3
Judah
Israel
Jordan River
Dead Sea
Phoenicia
Sea of Galilee

Lesson 4
Hattusa
Asia Minor
Arabian Desert
Cyprus

Hint: All geography found on this page, is also the geography that you will be reviewing this week. Refer to this map as needed when doing your "Memorization Through Repetition" worksheets.

Parent/Teacher: The "A Closer Look" page is intended to show students the accumulated geographic areas taught within their 6-week review period. For additional teaching tips on how to utilize this teaching aide for the different learning levels, please refer to page 1.

Zoom Me In!

Lesson 5

Use this sheet as a reference for this lesson's "Now, let's trace, shade & label" worksheet.

This Lesson's Geography
The Egyptian Empire
Egypt
Nile River
Upper/Lower Egypt
Nile River Delta

Lesson 5 Geography
The Egyptian Empire
Egypt
Nile River
Upper/Lower Egypt
Nile River Delta

Tid-Bits

The Ancient Egyptian Empire brings to mind images of pyramids, statues, and artwork unique to this culture and thousands of years old. But, while the Sphinx, the Great Pyramid, or the Egyptian hieroglyphics are impressive to see, it also tells a tale. Egyptian history is a tangible gift from the past that allows a glimpse of the Egyptian culture

Replica of the burial mask of Pharaoh Tutankhamun. By Petre Bonek, Adobe Stock

rooted in a pluralistic faith in many gods with a heavy focus on life after death. This civilization survived from 3100 to 332 BC.

The Egyptians had a leader called "Pharaoh," and whoever was Pharaoh was believed to be a descendant of one of their many gods. Located in northeast Africa along the longest river in all the world, the Nile provided fertile land to grow many types of crops by flooding fresh minerals from the river's bed every year. These crops included wheat, barley, figs, vegetables, and fruits. Grain was the most abundant crop, which was used as money. All the food was harvested and given to the government, who gave each person what they needed.

Their architecture was mainly made out of stone and mud bricks. Houses were built with mud bricks, while temples and pyramids were built with stone. Buildings had high walls with columns and flat roofs. Walls and columns were covered in ancient Egyptian writing, known as hieroglyphics, which were pictures instead of letters. As Egyptian

The Nile River in Egypt, by Daylight Photo, Adobe Stock

Pharaoh stone sarcophagus tomb, by PhotoSpirit, Adobe Stock

civilization progressed, it is thought that there were about seventeen cities and twenty-four towns along with the national capital. While the population varied over time, it has been estimated at between 100,000 and 200,000 people.

Temples, pyramids, and other architecture of ancient Egypt were astonishing back then, but they still amaze us today. Temples and pyramids were absolutely massive and highly detailed. They were able to construct these vast buildings because they had very advanced technology for their time. Most Ancient Egyptian pyramids were built to be tombs for the Pharaoh and their family. The afterlife was so crucial to the Egyptians that they spent much of their time and resources preparing for it. They believed that life on earth is temporary and the afterlife is permanent. The tombs (pyramids) were built to house their afterlife bodies. So they were created to be beautiful, with all of their favorite things safely placed, most notably their body, which was preserved through a process called mummification. There have been 130 pyramids discovered so far in Egypt, the most prominent being the Pyramid of Khufu at Giza, also simply referred to as the Pyramid of Giza. The Great Pyramid of Giza is in the desert near Cairo in Egypt. The pyramid aligns perfectly with the compass points, meaning the

Above & Below: Photographs to show the size of the stones used to construct the pyramids. Look to see if you can find the people. Do you think each stone is bigger or smaller than a person? How do you think the ancient Egyptians moved these into place?

Giza Pyramid complex in Egypt - Adobe Stock

43

north side of the pyramid face exactly north, the west side faces exactly west, and so on...

The Great Pyramid of Giza is the only one of the Seven Wonders of the Ancient World to still exist. Nearby, the great Sphinx guards the way to all the pyramids in this area, a total of six. The Sphinx is a limestone statue of a lion with a human head. It is believed that the Great Pyramid of Giza took over 20 years to build and was smooth versus having steps, making this pyramid unique. It is made with over 2 million pieces of granite, with the exterior finished off in a polished limestone that, in its time, made it sparkle! Each of these stones weighed a whopping 5-6 thousand pounds each! So how did they build the pyramid without the heavy lifting equipment of our modern times? We still don't know!

Egypt Edfu temple, Aswan. Passage flanked by two glowing walls full of Egyptian hieroglyphs, by Konstantin, Adobe Stock

Egyptian mythology is fascinating, like many ancient cultures, they believed in magical beings. A half-cat with a snake neck was called a Serpopard and lived in a world beyond the Nile. It was a symbol of violence. With a lion body, the head and wings of an eagle, the Griffins were seen as the hunters and protectors of the Egyptian people. The Sphinx were the protectors of tombs and were depicted in many ways; they could have the head of a woman, cat, sheep, or falcon with the body of a lion and falcon wings. Ancient Greece documented stories of the Sphinx, but the imagery comes from Egypt.

Tied into mythology, the Egyptians are known for their artwork, all kinds of art, including painting, relief carvings in ivory, sculpting, glazed ceramics, and jewelry, to name a few. If you don't know what a relief carving is, which was an essential art for the Egyptians, it is a carving made on flat surfaces made to look separate from the background. And if it stood still, it was decorated with Egyptian art. Their art was about realism and showing the power of Pharaoh, the gods, and the afterlife. The Egyptians believed that the spirits enjoyed art.

Temple of Medinet Habu. Egypt, Luxor. The Mortuary Temple of Ramesses III at Medinet Habu is an important New Kingdom period structure in the West Bank of Luxor in Egypt. By Konstantin Adobe Stock

A page of papryus from The Papyrus of Ani, more commonly known as the Egyptian Book of the Dead, is a papyrus manuscript and illustrated with color miniatures created in the 1240s BCE. It contains declarations and spells to help the deceased in the afterlife. By francescodemarco, Adobe Stock

Ancient Egyptian hieroglyphs and relief drawings on one of the walls of the Edfu complex. Temple of Edfu, Nubia, Egypt. By Konstantin, Adobe Stock

They wanted to represent life as it was in their craft, depicting war, religion, government, and daily life. It was a way of glorifying Pharaoh's power after his death for those alive and dead. Art reflected realism; the artists would make Pharaohs bigger than everyone else, displaying their importance. Differing colors were used to show a person's class or job.

In art, the Egyptian pose is famous. But, did the Egyptians walk around with their one arm in front and bent up with the hand pointed straight, bent at the wrist at 90 degrees, with the other arm doing the same thing, but behind and turned down? No, not really! The artists' unique approach to drawing people was to show several sides of the person's body at once. It may look strange to us, but it was an essential part of ancient Egyptian art, to which the style changed little over time.

The Egyptian language is no longer written or spoken and is called a "dead language."

For centuries, it was impossible to read or understand writings in ancient Egyptian. Then, in 1799, the Rosetta Stone was discovered. It is a stone with a royal decree carved into it in three different languages: hieroglyphics, demotic (an alphabet), and Greek. Because researchers knew ancient Greek, they were able to translate the other two Egyptian scripts. Once the Rosetta Stone was solved, the other ancient Egyptian documents were also able to be translated. In total, the Egyptian alphabet contains more than 700 hieroglyphs!

We have a few things to be thankful for that the Ancient Egyptians invented. Namely paper, pens, locks, keys, and – believe it or not – toothpaste!

RIGHT: Rosetta Stone, discovered in 1799. Image by djorenstein from Pixabay
BELOW: Close-up of the Rosetta Stone heiroglyphics. By Guillermo, Adobe Stock

Where in the World?

Lesson 6

Ancient Greece
Greece
Aegean Sea
Macedonia
Crete
Rhodes

Arctic Ocean

Greenland

Baffin Bay

Great Bear Lake

Great Slave Lake

Hudson Bay

Labrador Sea

Iceland

Faroe Islands

North Pacific Ocean

North Atlantic Ocean

Gulf of Mexico

Hawaii

Germany

Gaul

Mongolia

China

Sea of Japan

Korea

Japan

Mt. Fuji

Yellow Sea

Himalayas

Arabian Desert

Arabian Sea

Bay of Bengal

North Pacific Ocean

Venezuela

Colombia

Ecuador

Peru

Bolivia

Brazil

Chile

Argentina

Sahara Desert

Ivory Coast

Sao Tome & Principe

Ethiopia

Mozambique

Zimbabwe

Madagascar

South Africa

South Atlantic Ocean

South Pacific Ocean

Indian Ocean

A Closer Look at what you have learned so far!

PLUS+ This Lesson's Geography

Ancient Greece
Greece
Aegean Sea
Macedonia
Crete
Rhodes

Lesson 6

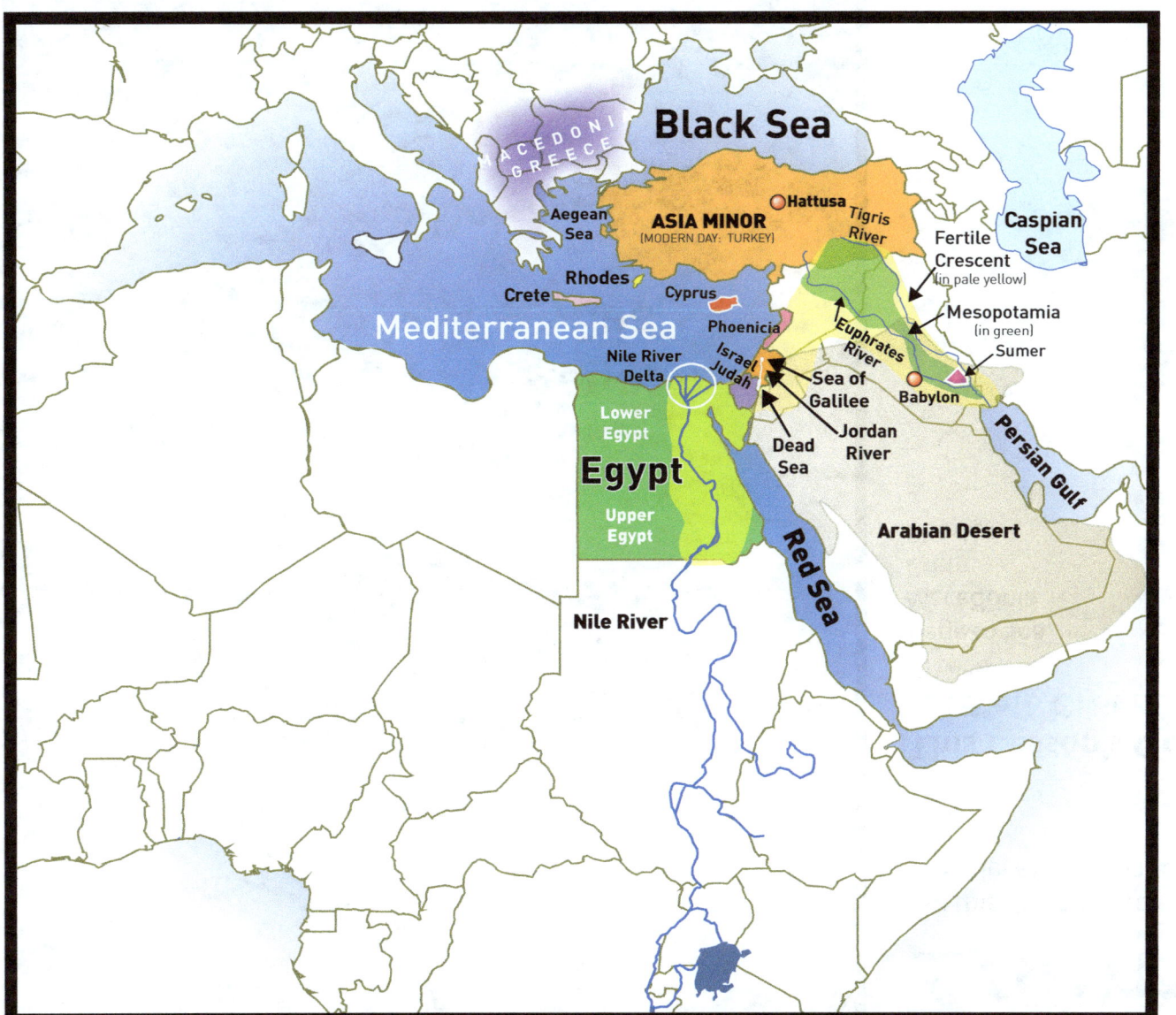

Previous Learned Geography:

Lesson 1
Fertile Crescent
Mediterranean Sea
Mesopotamia
Euphrates River
Tigris River
Sumer

Lesson 2
Red Sea
Persian Gulf
Caspian Sea
Black Sea
Babylon

Lesson 3
Judah
Israel
Jordan River
Dead Sea
Phoenicia
Sea of Galilee

Lesson 4
Hattusa
Asia Minor
Arabian Desert
Cyprus

Lesson 5
Egypt
Nile River
Upper/Lower Egypt
Nile River Delta

Hint: All geography found on this page, is also the geography that you will be reviewing this week. Refer to this map as needed when doing your "Memorization Through Repetition" worksheets.

Parent/Teacher: The "A Closer Look" page is intended to show students the accumulated geographic areas taught within their 6-week review period. For additional teaching tips on how to utilize this teaching aide for the different learning levels, please refer to page 1.

Zoom Me In! **Lesson 6**

Use this sheet as a reference for this lesson's "Now, let's trace, shade & label" worksheet.

This Lesson's Geography
Ancient Greece
Greece
Aegean Sea
Macedonia
Crete
Rhodes

Lesson 6 Geography
Ancient Greece
Greece
Aegean Sea
Macedonia
Crete
Rhodes

Tid-Bits

Greece was one of the most remarkable civilizations of the ancient world. They were forward thinkers and mighty warriors, along with writers, actors, athletes, artists, architects, and politicians that set the stage for much of our modern world.

Initially, this civilization called themselves Hellenes, and their land was Hellas. Later, the Romans renamed the land Greece, and their people were thereafter referred to as 'Greeks.' They lived in mainland Greece and the Greek islands and colonies scattered around the Mediterranean Sea.

Reaching back... The earliest 'Greek' settlers who mostly lived a simple hunter-gatherer or farming lifestyle were called Minoans after their king, Minos. This was the first Greek civilization that lived on the island of Crete. Then came the Mycenaean civilization from mainland Greece, bringing their fine builders, traders, and warriors. They fought in the famous battle of Troy. Homer, an essential Greek author, wrote stories of the Mycenaean age in his books "The Iliad" and "The Odyssey" that are still published and read today.

Circa 1100 BC, the Mycenaean age came to a close, and Greece went dark. Nobody knows much about what happened to this civilization, for all written language and art have never been found. This is known as the Greek Dark Ages, which lasted for about 300 years.

In 800 BC, the Greek's began to trade and slowly emerge, communicating with the rest of the known world. The Greeks held the first Olympic Games and fought off the invading Persian army. Historians have named this stretch of time the Archaic period of Greek history.

During the Archaic period, city-states began to emerge. Villages came together in part for protection and also for organized trade. There was no central government because of the geography of Greece; that is, there were no roads connecting the city-states and lots and lots of mountains and winding coastlines, altogether making travel by land incredibly difficult. Mostly, people traveled by waterways, namely the seas surrounding Greece: Mediterranean, Aegean, Sea of Crete, Thracian, and the Ionian Sea. The Greek city-states did not know each other. Grecians were allowed to visit or even move to a different city-state. However, each city-state was independent.

There grew to be somewhere between one to two thousand city-states in Ancient Greece. Some were relatively small, while others were large and powerful. Noteworthy examples are Athens, Sparta, Corinth, Thebes, Syracuse, Aegina, Rhodes, Árgos, Erétria, and Elis.

They differed significantly from each other in governing philosophies and interests. Sparta was ruled by two kings and a council of elders. It emphasized maintaining a strong military, while Athens valued education and art.

Interestingly, Greeks that lived in these different city-states were loyal first to their own. For example, a citizen of Sparta considered themselves a Spartan first and then a Greek. The city-states didn't always get along and often fought with each other; their battles are famous. However, sometimes they joined forces to fight against a bigger enemy, like the Persian Empire.

The people of Greece sincerely believed that their minds and bodies should be at their best. Therefore, children were taught to strive for excellence in education, studying math, music, and sports from age 7 to 18. They made gyms and created sporting games. The city-states loved competition in just about everything! So much so that they created the Olympics, figuring that it would satisfy the need to compete and honor their gods every four years. And, if any were currently at war, they would put aside their differences to compete.

On the shores of Greece. Image by DanaTentis from Pixabay

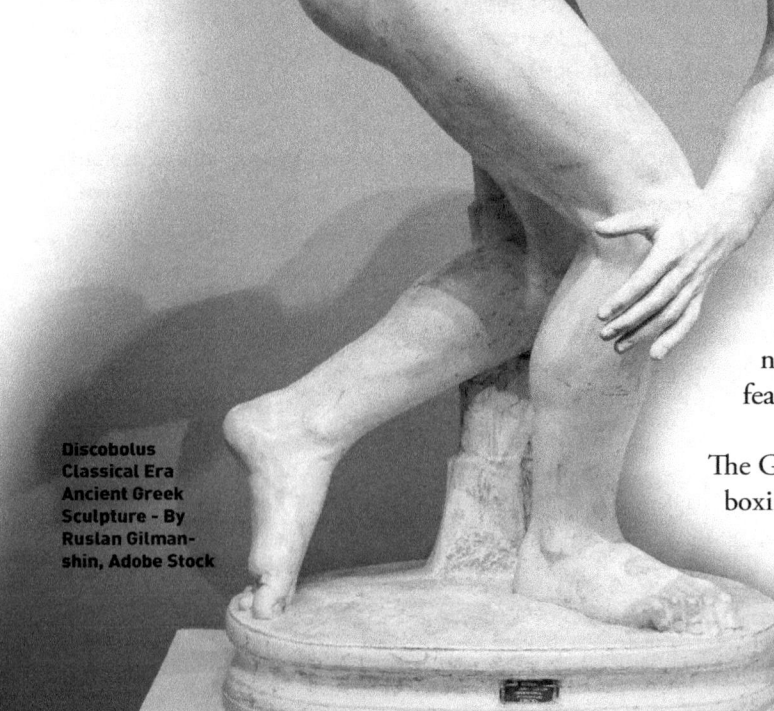

"*Full of blood, passion, and extraordinary feats of athletic endeavor, the Olympic Games were the sporting, social and cultural highlight of the Ancient Greek calendar for almost 12 centuries.*

"It is hard for us to exaggerate how important the Olympics were for the Greeks," Paul Christesen, Professor of Ancient Greek History at Dartmouth College, USA, said.

"The classic example is that when the Persians invaded Greece in the summer of 480 (BC), a lot of the Greek city-states agreed that they would put together an allied army, but they had a very hard time getting one together because so many people wanted to go to the Olympics. So, they actually had to delay putting the army together to defend the country against the Persians."

The threat of invasion or not, the Games took place every four years from 776BC to at least 392AD. All free Greek males were allowed to take part, from farmhands to royal heirs, although the majority of Olympians were soldiers. Women could not compete or even attend. There was, however, a loophole to this rule – chariot owners, not riders, were declared

LET'S LEARN MORE ABOUT THE ANCIENT OLYMPIC GAMES!

Olympic champions, and anyone could own a chariot. Kyniska, daughter of a Spartan king, took advantage of this, claiming victory wreaths in 396BC and 392BC.

At their heart, the Games were a religious festival and a good excuse for Greeks from all over the Mediterranean basin to gather for a riotous barbeque. On the middle day of the festival, a vast number of cows were slaughtered in honor of Zeus, King of the Greek Gods – once he had been given a small taste, the rest was for the people.

For the first 250-plus years, all the action took place in the sanctuary of Olympia, situated in the north-western Peloponnese. Pock-marked by olive trees, from which the victory wreaths were cut, and featuring an altar to Zeus, it was a hugely sacred spot.

The Games lasted a full five days by the fifth century BC and saw running, jumping, and throwing events plus boxing, wrestling, pankration, and chariot racing. At least 40,000 spectators would have packed the stadium each day at the height of the Games' popularity, in the second century AD, with many more selling their wares outside.

Discobolus
Classical Era
Ancient Greek
Sculpture - By
Ruslan Gilman-
shin, Adobe Stock

INTERESTING, FUNNY, AND POSSIBLY BIZARRE FACTS ABOUT THE ANCIENT OLYMPIC GAMES!

All athletes competed naked.

Wrestlers and pankration (a sort of mixed martial art which combined boxing and wrestling) competitors fought covered in oil.

Corporal punishment awaited those guilty of a false start on the track.

There were only two rules in the pankration – no biting and no gouging.

Boxers were urged to avoid attacking the on-display male genitals.

There were no points, no time limits, and no weight classifications in boxing.

Athletes in combat sports had to indicate their surrender by raising their index fingers – at times, they died before they could do this.

Boxers could not be separated and could opt for "climax," a system whereby one fighter was granted a free hit and vice-versa – a coin toss decided who went first."

Olympic Article Source: olympics.com
Kharkiv, Ukraine. May 23, 2021. A male athlete holding the Olympic flag against the sky. Olympic Games Tokyo 2020-2021 - By syhin_stas

THE OLYMPICS HAVE CHANGED DRAMATICALLY OVER TIME. EXPANDING THE TYPES OF COMPETITION, ALLOWING WOMEN TO COMPETE, THE RULES OF THE GAMES, AND NOW THE WHOLE WORLD IS INVITED, NOT JUST THE CITY-STATES OF GREECE.

"The Olympic torch incorporates both an important symbol and an important tradition for the Olympic games. The flame is symbolic of the positive values that man has typically associated with fire. The ancient Greeks believed that fire was a gift from Prometheus, who stole it from the gods and gave it to man. This gave fire a revered and respected role in Greek history.

In the Ancient Olympic Games in Olympia, a flame burned throughout the games at an altar to the goddess Hestia, whose Roman name was Vesta. Romans believed that Vestals were guardians of fire.

In modern times, a similar tradition has been observed in every Olympics since 1928, when a flame is lit in the opening ceremony and remains lit until the closing ceremony."

**Composite image of the Olympic Fire
By vectorfusionart, Adobe Stock**

Around 480 BC, Greece entered the Golden Age. When fantastic temples were built, people made scientific discoveries, wrote plays, and founded the first proper democracy. This period is referred to as Classical Greece that lasted for 200 years.

During the Classical Age, in celebration of love and beauty, the ancient Greeks made fantastic art. Some of the most famous pieces of art are statues, vases, and jewelry from ancient Greece. Greek artists used mathematical proportions to make their art realistic. It is called the golden ratio in geometry and art, and it happens in nature all around us. There is a similar term called the Fibonacci Sequence, which is closely related.

Circa 450 BC, an Athens' general named Pericles gave public money for paid artisans to build temples and other public buildings to support the city-state's artists and thinkers.

source quoted: brighthubeducation.com

Parthenon on Acropolis of Athens, Greece. Panoramic view on sky background. By scaliger, Adobe Stock   Marble statue of Greek Olympic god with cornucopia in his hands. By Magryt, Adobe Stock

He believed that this would win the support of the Athenian people by employing many through the construction process. When finished, Athens would have created many magnificent monuments that people would come from all over to see, increasing Athens' prestige and his own.

Today, the ancient Parthenon still stands and is perhaps the most outstanding result of Pericles' public-works campaign. The Parthenon was a temple built in honor of the city's patron goddess Athena.

With a rectangular stone platform, front and back porches, and rows of columns, the Parthenon was a powerful example of Greek architecture. The Ancient Grecians did not worship within their temples as we do today. Instead, the interior room was small, with only a statue of the god that the temple was created to honor. People would gather outside, entering only to bring offerings to the statue.

Like the Parthenon, most temples of Ancient Greece shared the same general look. There are rows of columns that supported a horizontal architecture finished off with a triangular roof. At each end of the top, above the columns, was a triangular space known as the pediment, into which sculptors created beautifully detailed scenes. For example, the Parthenon scenes play out the birth of Athena on one end and a battle between Athena and Poseidon on the other.

In addition, well known is the Ancient art of Greek Sculpture. Not many classical sculptures or statues survive today because stone statues broke easily, and often the

metal sculptures were melted and re-used. However, a few notable exceptions have been found and preserved for us to enjoy! One of the most well-known Greek sculptures is the Venus de Milo, carved in 100 BC. She was uncovered in 1820 on the Greek island, Melos.

Lastly, there is the most practical type of art that has been found from Ancient Greece: Pottery. Classical Greek pottery was perhaps the most diverse and helpful art form that people created. They offered terra-cotta figurines as gifts to gods and goddesses; they would bury them with the dead and give them to their children for playtime. They also used clay pots, jars, and vases for similar things that we do today. These were painted with religious or mythological scenes that grew more sophisticated and realistic over time. The final period of Ancient Greek history is

Amphoras in Greece - By Gelia, Adobe Stock - An Amphora is a tall ancient Greek or Roman jar with two handles and a narrow neck.

the Hellenistic period that lasted from 323 BC to 30 BC. As you learned, Ancient Greece was not one country, but city-states. For a brief time, however, it was an empire. For 13 years, Alexander the Great of Macedonia (A Greek City-State) rose to power, conquering all the Greek city-states. He then enlarged his empire by conquering Egypt, Mesopotamia, parts of India, and more. After his death, the Greek city-states went back to ruling themselves.

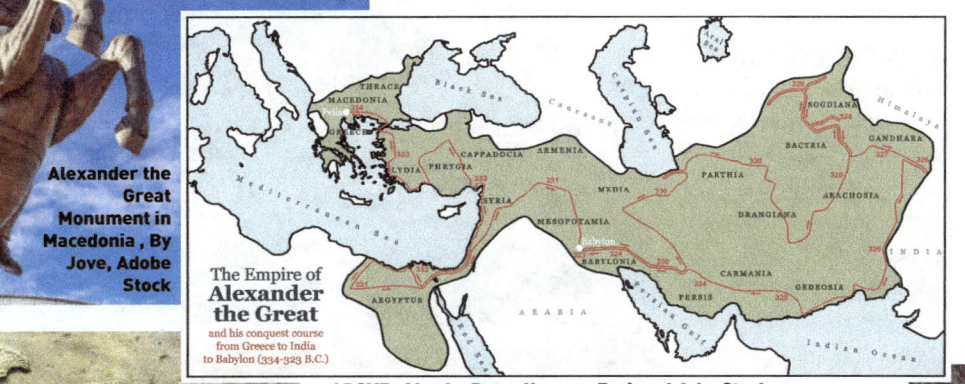

Alexander the Great Monument in Macedonia, By Jove, Adobe Stock

The Empire of Alexander the Great and his conquest course from Greece to India to Babylon (334-323 B.C.)

ABOVE: Map by Peter Hermes Furian, Adobe Stock

Alexander the Great Image By Brigida Soriano, Adobe Stock

The geography of the land prevented many types of crops from growing well. That is, with a couple of exceptions. Up in the mountains, they were able to grow olives for olive oil and grapes for wine. In addition, Greece enjoyed the booming seafood industry that the various seas provided along its shores and had access to many Mediterranean trade routes, allowing Ancient Greece to trade with people worldwide.

The Greeks put the earliest form of democracy and trial-by-jury into action in Athens, a city-state, in 600 BC. Democracy allowed men to

Later during the Hellenistic period, the Romans took over the Hellenes (as they called themselves). Thankfully, the Romans didn't destroy their way of life. On the contrary, they respected them and copied many things about their culture, including their buildings, beliefs, and clothes. At this time, they also renamed them the 'Greeks.' Greece is hilly with lots of mountains, including Mount Olympus, the famous mythological home of the Greek gods, throne of Zeus.

As you can imagine, mountains are a challenging place to live. So, back then, most people lived near the Mediterranean Sea in the south on the Balkan Peninsula and along the Aegean Sea in the east. Off the shore of the mainland are many islands. On the upwards of 227 of the approximate 6,000 islands are inhabited. The biggest island co-inhabited today by Greece and Turkey is Crete. In addition, the island of Rhodes serves as the historical capital of a group of Grecian islands referred to as the Dodecanese Islands of Greece.

Navagio Beach (Shipwreck Beach), Zakynthos Island, Greece. Image by Julius Silver from Pixabay

Sunset over Mount Olympus, by Dimitris - Adobe Stock

vote and be a part of making laws. Democracy is a part of many countries today, including the United States of America.

The Greek language is spoken in Greece today as it was in ancient times. The language was so crucial that writings were saved for thousands of years, passed from generation to generation to study the language. Ancient Greek writers created new ways of telling stories that laid the foundation of how we write today. They wrote about history, art, philosophy, medicine, science, comedy, drama, poetry, and theater, the last of which had never been done before! They are well-known for epic poems. These are long stories about a hero. The most famous are "The Iliad" and "The Odyssey" by Homer. Herodotus wrote the first history book that was researched and written for people to read. Before Herodotus, everything was recorded but not written to read, learn, and enjoy.

The invention of the theater was for entertainment but also honored their mythical gods and celebrated important events. There were two types of theater: tragedy with a sad ending and comedy with a happy one.

In Ancient Greece, only wealthy families could send their boys to school. Other boys and girls of the poorer classes were taught at home or by unpaid teachers. Upper-class Greeks were rulers and owned land. Middle-class people were farmers. Thetes were poor

LEFT: Scenic view of Crete landscape at sunset. Typical for much of Greece, olive tree groves, vineyards and narrow roads up to the hills. By GIORGOS, Adobe Stock. TOP RIGHT: Olive Oil - Image by Pexels from Pixabay. BOTTOM RIGHT: Wine made from grapes. Image by Oldiefan from Pixabay.

people who were craftsmen that made weapons and furniture out of wood or leather. People wore clothes made out of linen or wool. They usually had one or two pieces of clothing and wore sandals made of leather.

The Greeks gave many gifts! Democracy, trial-by-jury, the theatre, advances in medicine and science, architectural feats with ancient Greek columns, heroic tales, to name a few. In a significant part, these gifts result from good competition between all the Ancient Greek city-states. They desired to be the best at everything. Of course, ancient Greece is very different from today's world. But what they did more than two thousand years ago impacts us today.

Coastal town on Greece mainland overlooking the Mediterranean Sea. Image by Russell_Yan from Pixabay

Sculpture portrait head (bust) of Hippocrates Image by blackboard1965 – Adobe Stock

"The greatest medicine of all is teaching people how not to need it"

-Hippocrates

Where in the World?

Lesson 7

Roman Empire
Hispania
Gaul
Germania
Alexandria
Carthage

55

A Closer Look

Lesson 7

at what you have learned so far!

PLUS+
This Lesson's Geography:

The Roman Empire
Hispania
Gaul
Germania
Alexandria
Carthage

Previous Learned Geography:

Lesson 1
Fertile Crescent
Mediterranean Sea
Mesopotamia
Euphrates River
Tigris River
Sumer

Lesson 2
Red Sea
Persian Gulf
Caspian Sea
Black Sea
Babylon

Lesson 3
Judah
Israel
Jordan River
Dead Sea
Phoenicia
Sea of Galilee

Lesson 4
Hattusa
Asia Minor
Arabian Desert
Cyprus

Lesson 5
Egypt
Nile River
Upper/Lower Egypt
Nile River Delta

Lesson 6
Greece
Aegean Sea
Macedonia
Crete
Rhodes

Hint: All geography found on this page, is also the geography that you will be reviewing this week. Refer to this map as needed when doing your "Memorization Through Repetition" worksheets.

Parent/Teacher: The "A Closer Look" page is intended to show students the accumulated geographic areas taught within their 6-week review period. For additional teaching tips on how to utilize this teaching aide for the different learning levels, please refer to page 1.

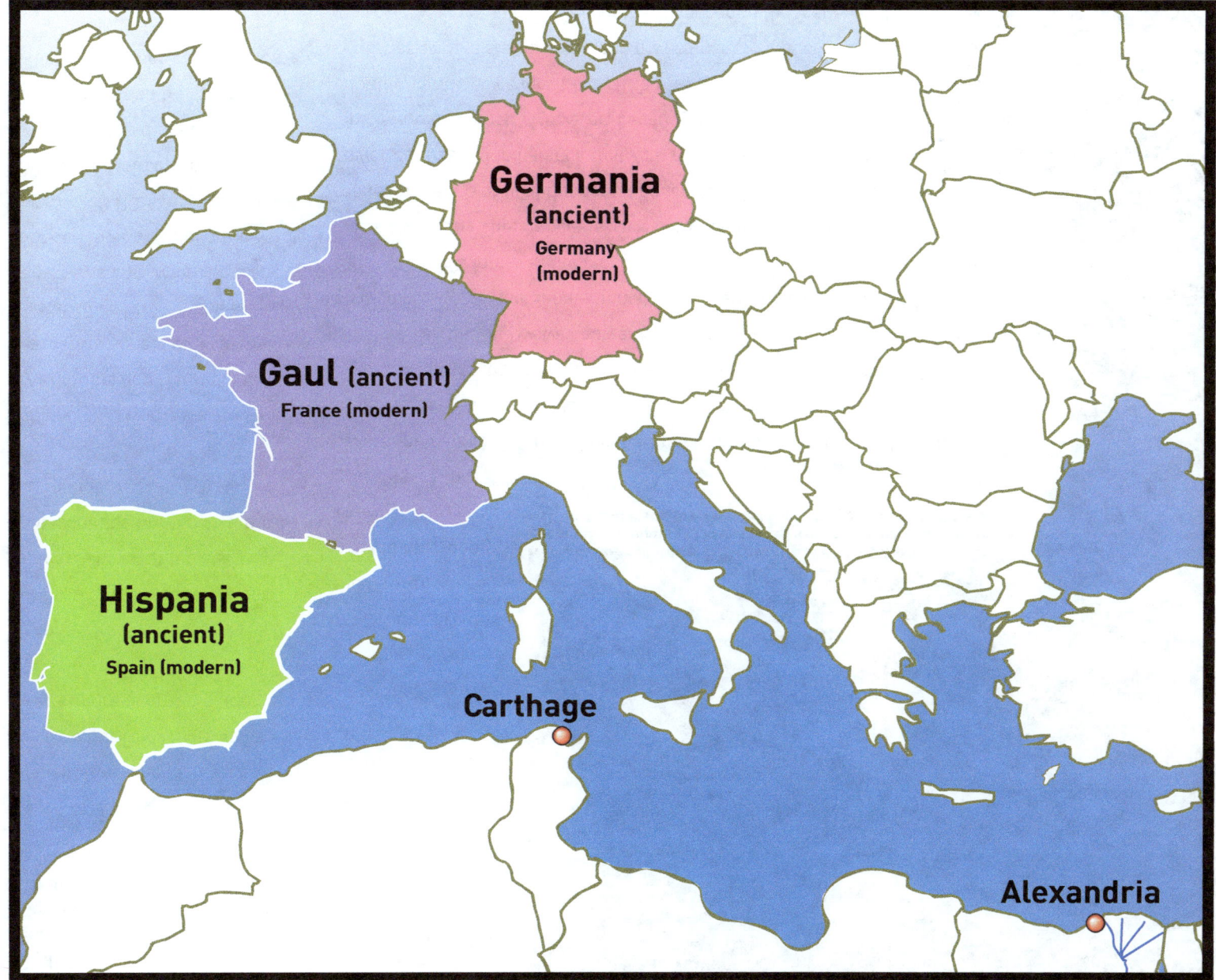

Lesson 7

Zoom Me In!

This Lesson's Geography
The Roman Empire
Hispania
Gaul
Germania
Alexandria
Carthage

Use this sheet as a reference for this lesson's "Now, let's trace, shade & label" worksheet.

Lesson 7 Geography
Roman Empire
Hispania
Gaul
Germania
Alexandria
Carthage

Tid-Bits

Ancient Rome began as a small town on the Tiber River in Italy. Over hundreds of years, the city became an empire that ruled Europe, Britain, West and North Africa, and the Mediterranean islands. They created a legacy that would be Europe's cultural foundation.

Legend says Rome was founded by Romulus and Remus, the God Mars' twin sons. Left in a basket, on the Tiber River, found and raised by a she-wolf. The twins founded their city along the same river in 753 BC. Who shall rule this land? Both brothers said, "I." Well, both could not be King. So, Romulus settled the matter by killing his brother, naming Rome after himself.

Thus, Rome began as a monarchy. This means that there is a King or a Queen ruling over the land and people. The monarchy of Rome lasted 244 years, ending in 509 BC when the King was overthrown. After that, Rome created the Forum, which housed the Senate. This was the ruling government that

Public stone sculpture of Romulus and Remus drinking milk from the female wolf on Grand Place, Brussels, Belgium – By reodejongh, Adobe Stock

served the people as a Republic. A Republic nation's power is held by the citizens that elect representatives to govern and has either an elected or nominated president rather than a King or Queen. Rome's Republic established laws that were written on the Twelve Tables, which were twelve bronze tablets. To run for an elected position in the Senate, initially, a citizen would need to be a Patrician. A Patrician was a family in the bloodline of Romulus. Anyone that wasn't a Patrician was a Plebeian. The Plebeians were common folk; however, they made up the majority of the population. Patricians wanted the power but needed to balance that with respect toward the Plebeians to avoid conflict. However, because of the lack of true equality, conflict was inevitable. The Plebeians struggled for centuries to gain status within the government to influence laws for society. Eventually, all offices were opened to the Plebeians for

The Citizens of Rome Reviewing the Publicly Displayed Twelve Tables, the cornerstone of Roman Law. By Unknown Artist, sourced from Wikipedia – Public Domain

Wealthy Patrician Family at Home, Image of Ancient Engraving by: By Erica Guilane-Nachez, Adobe Stock

Peasant Plebeian Family
Image of Ancient Engraving by: By Erica Guilane-Nachez, Adobe Stock

the Punic Wars, Rome learned a valuable lesson at the Battle of Allia River, which Gaul (France) won. After their victory, Gaul's forces marched on to Rome. In late July 390 BC, the undefended city fell to the invaders to be burnt and sacked. Only on Capitol Hill did a small number of Romans put up a valiant defense, holding out until hunger forced them to surrender. To be freed from their captors, they had to pay a sizeable amount of gold to Gaul. The Romans improved their military and strengthened the city wall to prevent them from being sacked ever again.

As Rome took on new territories, they came to experience different cultures, which led to adopting some for themselves. Most notably, they grew accustomed to Greek religion, art, and philosophy.

election. This development helped transform the Senate from a body of Patricians into a body of Plebeians and Patrician aristocrats.

Rome was a vast empire that became large and powerful, but it came at the cost of many wars. They fought hundreds of battles through the centuries to conquer land and defend the Empire they had built. They were not satisfied by growing to neighboring lands; they desired to capture more and more. This desire was partly fueled by their victory in the three Punic wars with Carthage, a city-state of Greece, making them the most powerful Empire in the Mediterranean region. The First Punic War was fought from 264-241 BC, the Second Punic War was fought from 218-201 BC; lastly, the Third Punic War was fought from 149-146 BC. Together with many other wars, the Roman Empire, at its greatest extent, included much of Europe, western Asia, and northern Africa.

Although Rome was a powerful force, they were not always triumphant. Far before

Map By Peter Hermes Furian - Adobe Stock

The acclaimed Julius Caesar is one of the more fascinating historical figures of Rome's ancient leaders. He was the world's most talented military leader, the most impressive politician, and a member of the First Triumvirate. Caesar led the Roman armies in the Gallic Wars before governing the Roman Republic from 49 BC until his assassination in 44 BC. He also was well known for his complicated love life, which included an affair with the renowned Egyptian Queen Cleopatra.

After winning many wars, Caesar became governor over three Gaul provinces. Together with a man named Pompey, he formed the First Triumvirate. The two had different territories to rule, but both wanted the entire region. Pompey was another Roman politician and military leader. Both were worthy adversaries, and both were held in high esteem by the people. To fight Caesar for the position, Pompey invaded Italy and started a civil war. Pompey was defeated and sought refuge in Egypt, where he was assassinated. Caesar became Rome's dictator. However, there was political unrest in Rome, and Caesar's time in power was brief. He was murdered by several of his

Julius Caesar, Image of bust statue by Ruslan Gilmanshin, Adobe Stock

The Death of Julius Caesar, as depicted by Vincenzo Camuccini. Caesar was assassinated on the Ides of March (15 March) 44 BC. Public Domain, Wikipedia

A Roman bust of Mark Antony, late 1st century AD, Vatican Museums, Unknown Artist, Wikipedia

42 BC Denarius, Military mint with Lepidus in Italy. Marcus Aemilius Lepidus, Image by Classical Numismatic Group, Inc., Wikipedia

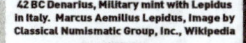

own nobles.

Not everyone was against Caesar. On the contrary, those that were his closest supporters were angry and vengeful after his assassination. Namely, a man named Mark Antony, a relative of Julius Caesar that also served as one of his generals. Then there was Marcus Aemilius Lepidus, another of Caesar's generals, and lastly, Octavian, Caesar's great-nephew and adopted son. These three men formed a dictatorship known to historians as the Second Triumvirate. The Triumvirs defeated Caesar's murderers and divided the government of the Republic between themselves.

Lepidus lost his leverage and power in his territory through a series of actions supporting Antony and Octavian. Then there were two. Octavian and Antony. While they weren't the best of buds and almost went to war, they committed to peace by sealing their relationship politically with the marriage of Octavian's sister Octavia to Antony.

Octavian, Julius Caesar's adopted son. Antony would struggle with Octavian for leadership of the Caesarian party following Caesar's assassination. Unknown Artist, Wikipedia

Unfortunately, the relationship became sour once again. Both wanted more of Rome to rule - just like Caesar and Pompey. As Antony sought greater political power, he had a love affair with Cleopatra,

Antony and Cleopatra (1883) by Lawrence Alma-Tadema depicting Antony's meeting with Cleopatra in 41 BC., By Lawrence Alma-Tadema - Public Domain, Wikipedia

Cleopatra VII bust in the Altes Museum, Antikensammlung Berlin, Roman artwork, 1st century BC, By Anagoria - Own work, Public Domain, Wikipedia

With Antony dead, Octavian became the unchallenged ruler of the Roman world. Then, in 27 BC, Octavian was granted the title of Augustus, marking the shift from a Republic to an empire, with himself as the first Roman emperor. He ruled for 56 years.

Hundreds of years later, Rome was having difficulty surviving because of political turmoil, violence, and the sheer size of the Empire with too few leaders to oversee. The Emperor Diocletian attempted to reunite the Empire and bring a period of peace and prosperity by dividing up power, allowing others to rule over specific areas. Those he chose were Galerius, Maximian, Constantius I Chlorus, and himself - four in total. To Maximian, he shared the title of Augustus, and Galerius and Chlorus were entitled Caesars. Interestingly, to strengthen the colleagues' union, each Augustus adopted his Caesar. To further cement the relationships, Galerius married Diocletian's daughter, and Chlorus married Maximian's stepdaughter. This combination of shared power in the Roman Empire is referred to as the tetrarchy.

Queen of Egypt. This is the same Cleopatra that Caesar fell for! She provided military strength in Antony's quest for territory and bore him three children.

Antony divorced Octavia in favor of Cleopatra. He also declared that Caesarion, the alleged son of Cleopatra and Julius Caesar, was the rightful heir to the Roman Empire. In reaction to this, rumors quickly spread that Antony was to make Cleopatra the Queen of Rome and that Alexandria would be the new Roman capital. Rome's people didn't think highly of this and turned against Marc Antony, and the Senate was on Octavian's side. With the support of both the Senate and the citizens of Rome, Octavian declared war on Cleopatra instead of attacking Antony directly. Antony's troops were defeated, with many of his soldiers switching to Octavian's side. After this defeat, Marc Antony took his own life. Cleopatra, following his example, allowed herself to be bitten by a venomous snake. The two were buried side by side.

The Battle of Actium (1672) by Lorenzo A. Castro. This is where Mark Antony lost to Octavian. National Maritime Museum, London - Public Domain, Wikipedia

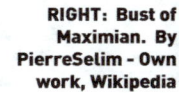
LEFT: Head from a statue of Diocletian at the Istanbul Archaeological Museum - By G.dallorto - Own work, Wikipedia

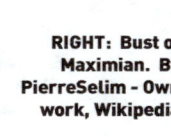
RIGHT: Bust of Maximian. By PierreSelim - Own work, Wikipedia

61

Map of the Roman Empire under the tetrarchy, showing the dioceses and the four tetrarchs' zones of influence post-299, after Diocletian and Galerius had exchanged their allocated provinces. - By Coppermine Photo Gallery, Wikipedia

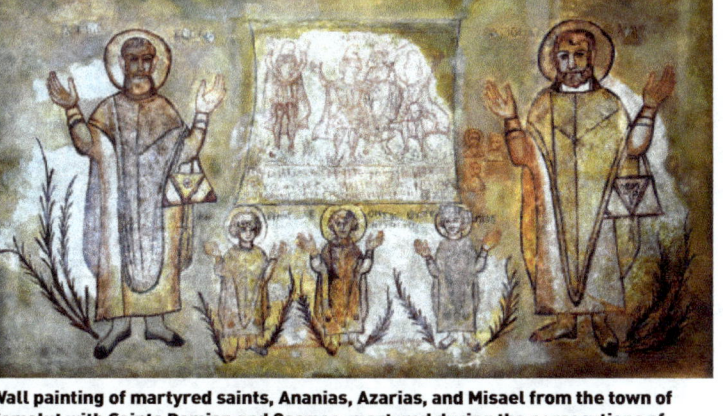

Wall painting of martyred saints, Ananias, Azarias, and Misael from the town of Samalut with Saints Damian and Cosmas; martyred during the persecutions of Diocletian in the late 3rd century AD. Stucco. 6th century AD. From Wadi Sarga, Egypt. British Museum - Image By Osama Shukir Muhammed Amin, Wikipedia

Diocletian believed in the traditional Roman religion that worshiped many gods, including Jupiter, Mars, Apollo, and others. He associated himself and his co-Augustus, Maximian, with Jupiter and Hercules, respectively. In this, there was not just disregard, but fear possibly leading to the disdain of the rising Christian population. Although Diocletian successfully brought stability, security, and efficient government to Rome after 50 years of chaos, however, the end of Diocletian's reign was darkened by the last significant persecution of the Christians.

The reasons for this persecution are not completely clear. However, a few explanations have been formed. Firstly, the influence of Galerius, a fanatic follower of the traditional Roman religion. Secondly, Diocletian wanted to restore complete unity, and Christians couldn't be a part of that unity based on their beliefs. Therefore, they were seen as agitators and separatists. Also, it was thought that Christians were forming a kind of state within the state that could lead to conflict. Some or all of these explanations led Diocletian to publish the four edicts of 303–304, promising all the while that he would not spill blood. His vow went unheeded. The persecutions spread through the Empire with extreme violence that did not succeed in wiping out Christianity. Instead, it caused the faith to blaze forth.

The four edicts were recorded in various historical texts, as quoted:

First Edict: "It was in the nineteenth year of the reign of Diocletian, in the month Dystrus, called March by the Romans, when the feast of the Saviour's passion was near at

The Christian Martyrs' Last Prayer, by Jean-Léon Gérôme (1883) Walters Art Museum, Public Domain, Wikipedia

hand, that royal edicts were published everywhere, commanding that the churches be leveled to the ground, and the Scriptures be destroyed by fire, and ordering that those who held places of honor be degraded, and that the household servants if they persisted in the profession of Christianity, be deprived of freedom. (by Eusebius in his Church History) **Second Edict:** Not long after... a royal edict directed that the rulers of the churches everywhere should be thrown into prison and bonds. (by Eusebius in his Church History) **Third Edict:** Other decrees followed the first, directing that those in prison if they would sacrifice (to the Roman gods) should be permitted to depart in freedom, but that those who refused should be harassed with many tortures. (by Eusebius in his Church History) **Fourth Edict:** In the course of the second year [304 AD], the persecution against us increased greatly. And at that time Urbanus being governor of the province, imperial edicts were first issued to him, commanding by a general decree that all the people should sacrifice at once in the different cities, and offer libations to the idols. (Martyrs of Palestine 3)

Any peace that Diocletian brought forth through the division of power had lost its foothold. So, after 20 years of being Emporer, Diocletian retired.

Next came Constantine, the son of Caesar Constantius I Chlorus. Constantine became emperor in 306 AD. Years later, in 324 AD, he moved Rome's capital to Byzantium (a Greek city) to save the Empire, renaming the city to Constantinople, after himself. It was the perfect city for trading, for it was located between Europe and Asia between the Black and Aegean Seas and had been structurally updated with roads and various water systems. With this move, the Roman Empire was split into West and East. The Eastern Roman Empire stayed in place for centuries and became known as the Byzantine Empire. The new capital did not have religious persecution, for the majority were Christians. In light of this, Constantine made Christianity the official religion. After this move, Western Rome and Eastern Rome never reunited.

Germanic tribes were constantly attacking the Western Roman Empire. The Empire was too big and too expensive to control as attacks continued to come in from all over Rome.

TOP LEFT & RIGHT: Statue and bust of antiquity of Constantine. By Unknown, Public Domain

The Split of the Roman Empire

Original Map By Peter Hermes Furian - Adobe Stock - Altered by Amanda Predmore

Soon provinces were gaining their independence. Britain left first, then Spain and North Africa. Finally, Attila and his Huns invaded Gaul and Italy, making it even harder for Rome to maintain control. Western Rome fell in 476 when Odovacar, a German prince, attacked Rome and made himself King of Italy. Eastern Rome, now called the Byzantine Empire, fell to the Ottoman Empire in 1453.

Although the expression *"The Fall of Rome"* suggests that some sudden event was the Roman Empire's demise, this is far from true. Rather, the great Empire that stretched from the British Isles to Egypt and Iraq fell slowly, resulting from challenges that came from within and without. Not over 20 years, 50 years, or even 150 years, but over hundreds of years until Rome was unrecognizable.

Old Rome cobblestone road. Adobe Stock

Pictured: Roman Coleseum and Constantine's Arch. Adobe Stock

"All Roads Lead to Rome"

There's a saying that "all roads lead to Rome." Back then, it was true! Around 300 BC, the Roman Republic began building long routed and straight roads. These roadways are considered by some to be one of the reasons the Roman Empire became so strong. They made 29 roads that connected 113 provinces, with Rome at the center. Hence, "all roads lead to Rome!" Today, this idiom (or saying) means "many routes lead to the same destination, outcome, or result." *Source: theidioms.com*

For entertainment, the Romans would flood the whole Colosseum for boat battles! Big boats topped with warriors fought it out in the alligator filled water. Eek! In the famous Colosseum building in the center of Rome, when not flooded, was used to watch sporting events including battles between Gladiators!

Ancient Rome is underground. In Rome, you can go underground two layers at Basilica San Clemente and you can go three layers down in the ancient Roman houses, which gives you an understanding of how Rome built on top of old structures, many times over!

Have you ever tried eating dinner lying down on a couch? If ever invited to dine in Ancient Rome, you would be shown to a room lined with couches without tables or chairs. They would prop themselves on their left arm and use their right to bring food to their mouth. Occasionally they would use spoons, but would never use knives or forks. Wealthy Romans at exotic foods including stork, roast parrot, and even flamingo!

Romans washed their clothes in urine. Ewe! Urine contains ammonia, which is a powerful bleaching agent. At many street corners, there were public urinals where urine was collected and brought to public laundries. Also in Ancient Rome, there were public bath houses, where people bathed together. Civilization sure has come a long way!

A Closer Look

at what you have learned so far!

Lesson 8

PLUS+
This Lesson's Geography

Indus River Valley Civilization
Indus River
Ganges River
Himalayas
Arabian Sea
Bay of Bengal
Great Indian Desert

Previously Learned Geography a TRUE REVIEW - 6 week review

Lesson 2
Red Sea
Persian Gulf
Caspian Sea
Black Sea
Babylon

Lesson 3
Judah
Israel
Jordan River
Dead Sea
Phoenicia
Sea of Galilee

Lesson 4
Hattusa
Asia Minor
Arabian Desert
Cyprus

Lesson 5
Egypt
Nile River
Upper/Lower Egypt
Nile River Delta

Lesson 6
Greece
Aegean Sea
Macedonia
Crete
Rhodes

Lesson 7
Hispania
Gaul
Germania
Alexandria
Carthage

> **Lesson 1** has dropped off of your six week TRUE REVIEW. You have new geography, plus 6 weeks of review as shown on this sheet.

Map labels (main map): Germania (ancient) Germany (modern), Gaul (ancient) France (modern), Hispania (ancient) Spain (modern), Carthage, Black Sea, MACEDONIA GREECE, Aegean Sea, ASIA MINOR (MODERN DAY TURKEY), Hattusa, Caspian Sea, Rhodes, Cyprus, Crete, Nile River Delta, Phoenicia, Israel, Judah, Mesopotamia (in green), Alexandria, Sea of Galilee, Babylon, Dead Sea, Jordan River, Persian Gulf, Lower Egypt, Egypt, Upper Egypt, Arabian Desert, Nile River, Red Sea

Hint: All geography found on this page, is also the geography that you will be reviewing this week. Refer to these maps as needed when doing your "Memorization Through Repetition" worksheets.

Parent/Teacher/Student:

We have switched places in the world! The "A Closer Look" page is intended to show students the accumulated geographic areas taught within the 6-week review period plus new geography. For additional teaching tips on how to utilize this teaching aide for the different learning levels, please refer to page 1.

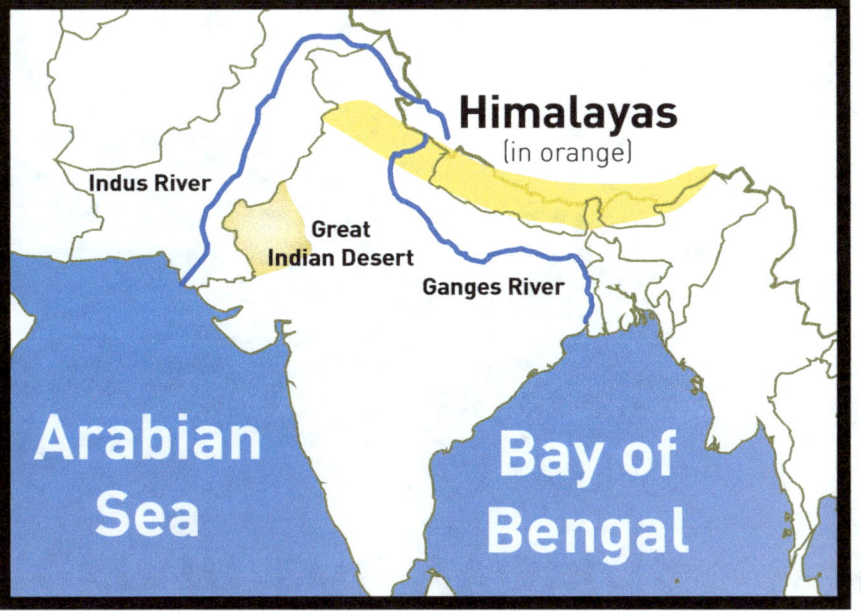

Map labels (inset map): Indus River, Himalayas (in orange), Great Indian Desert, Ganges River, Arabian Sea, Bay of Bengal

Lesson 8

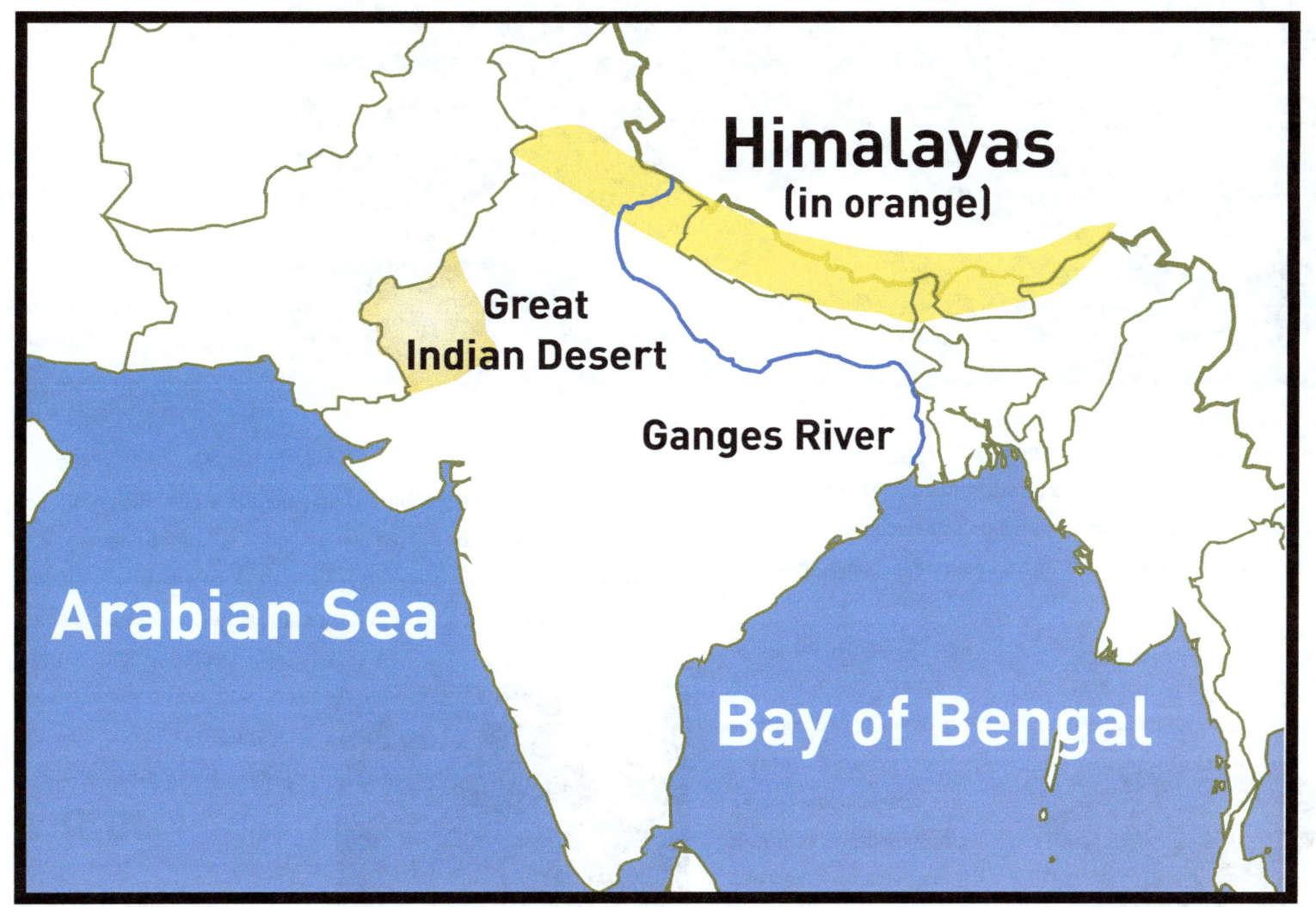

Zoom Me In!

This Lesson's Geography
Indus River Valley Civilization
Ganges River
Himalayas
Arabian Sea
Bay of Bengal
Great Indian Desert

Use this sheet as a reference for this lesson's "Now, let's trace, shade & label" worksheet.

Lesson 8 Geography
Indus River Valley
Indus River
Ganges River
Arabian Sea
Bay of Bengal
Great Indian Desert

Tid-Bits

The Indus River Valley Civilization was the biggest of all six great ancient civilizations. It covered most of modern-day Pakistan, a significant part of India, and parts of Afghanistan. It is thought to have lasted for at least 1600 years, with an area around the size of Western Europe. Its beginning date is not yet confirmed, but it collapsed somewhere around 16th century BC due to unknown reasons.

settlements have been found! The Indus River Valley Civilization flourished in the basins of two major rivers: the Indus River and Ghaggar-Hakra River, which is a river that flowed only during the monsoon season.

Harappa and Mohenjo-Daro are the two big cities. There were public buildings for bathing, storing grains, processing food, and more. These two cities were very advanced and wanted people to have clean and healthy lives.

They were planning and architectural geniuses! The Indus River Valley Civilization created their cities and neighborhoods on a grid system cut with right angles, which are used to this day. They also built upon giant platforms on elevated grounds to protect the people from seasonal floods and polluted waters. The houses had connected outer walls that led to a shared courtyard.

The Indus River Valley Civilization is famous for its advanced engineering, well-planned grid-based cities, and a drainage system that wouldn't be improved upon for many centuries.

As mentioned, they were the BIGGEST! A staggering 1,056 cities and

Toilets? Yes! Every day we use our toilets and showers and enjoy this luxury that some parts of the developing world still don't have today. We need to thank the Indus River Valley Civilization, for they set the stage with fantastic innovation with the first sophisticated water management

system ever. The average home in this ancient civilization had indoor plumbing of toilets and bathrooms with sewage drains that emptied into wider public drains, ultimately depositing the fertile sludge on surrounding agricultural fields. Some homes were even equipped with the world's earliest known flush toilets! Most houses had private wells, and there was a sophisticated water management system with numerous reservoirs. Before the twentieth century, this ancient civilization's sewage and drainage systems were more advanced than most western cities!

It's a mysterious civilization because it was buried and lost for centuries. In the 19th century, the Indus River Valley Civilization was discovered while Britain was building a railroad. In the 1920s, archaeologists worked hard to unearth a village to find another one until they found an entire network of villages. Historians say it began in 3300 BC as a farming region but grew into a sophisticated civilization and peaked between 2500 and 1900 BC, but disappeared entirely around 1500 BC. Everything known about the Indus Valley is from the buried remains. So much is known, but there are still many mysteries.

There is very little evidence of violence and war, so they probably enjoyed a long period of peace and prosperity. Nevertheless, they left clues of agriculture, trade, and administration.

Most people were farmers in small communities, growing wheat, peas, lentils, barley, dates, grapes, melons, and more with an advanced irrigation system while raising cattle, pigs, goats, sheep, chickens, and maybe even elephants! They also hunted and fished. There were also tradespeople in the cities making pottery, cloth, beads, and more, traded throughout the civilization. They also traded with outside cultures like China, Afghanistan, Persia, and Mesopotamia as goods from these different cultures were found in the cities. They traveled by land, by river, and by sea. They even kept track of trade activities because writing samples have been found. Translations have not been done, but between 400 and 600 unique symbols

have been found in the writings. Stone seals with pictures of animals marked these writings to keep records of many different types of documents. Archaeologists have found more than 3500 seals.

No one knows for sure why the Indus Valley civilization disappeared. Historians agree that they stopped prospering around 1900 BC. Some believe Aryans invaded and attacked. While others believe there was a natural disaster, like a big flood, drought, or earthquake, which made it impossible to farm and trade for the Indus Valley people. With more and more Aryans in the area, it would have been challenging to produce enough food and goods for everyone to survive. By 1500 BC, the Indus Valley people had all disappeared. The Aryans had arrived, settled, and created their civilization on top of the Indus Valley civilization, quite literally burying it until it was discovered thousands of years later.

Где in the World? Lesson 9

China
Mongolia
Yellow Sea
Yellow River
Yangtze River
Beijing

A Closer Look

at what you have learned so far!

PLUS+

This Lesson's Geography

China
Mongolia
Yellow Sea
Yellow River
Yangtze River
Beijing

Lesson 9

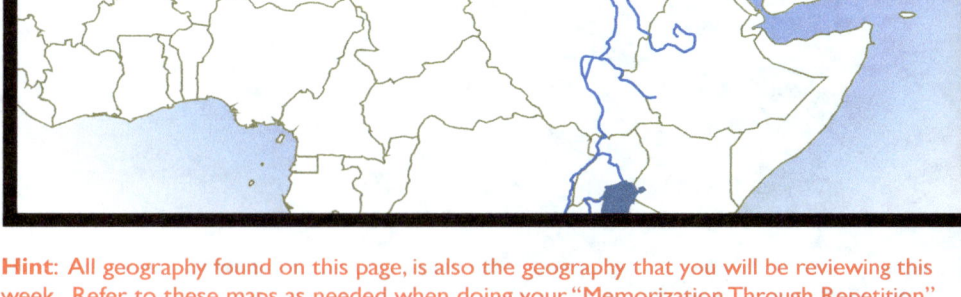

Previously Learned Geography a TRUE REVIEW - 6 week review

Lesson 3
Judah
Israel
Jordan River
Dead Sea
Phoenicia
Sea of Galilee

Lesson 4
Hattusa
Asia Minor
Arabian Desert
Cyprus

Lesson 5
Egypt
Nile River
Upper/Lower Egypt
Nile River Delta

Lesson 6
Greece
Aegean Sea
Macedonia
Crete
Rhodes

Lesson 7
Hispania
Gaul
Germania
Alexandria
Carthage

Lesson 8
Indus River
Ganges River
Himalayas
Arabian Sea
Bay of Bengal
Great Indian Desert

Hint: All geography found on this page, is also the geography that you will be reviewing this week. Refer to these maps as needed when doing your "Memorization Through Repetition" worksheets.

Parent/Teacher: The "A Closer Look" page is intended to show students the accumulated geographic areas taught within their 6-week review period plus new geography. For additional teaching tips on how to utilize this teaching aide for the different learning levels, please refer to page 1.

Lesson 9

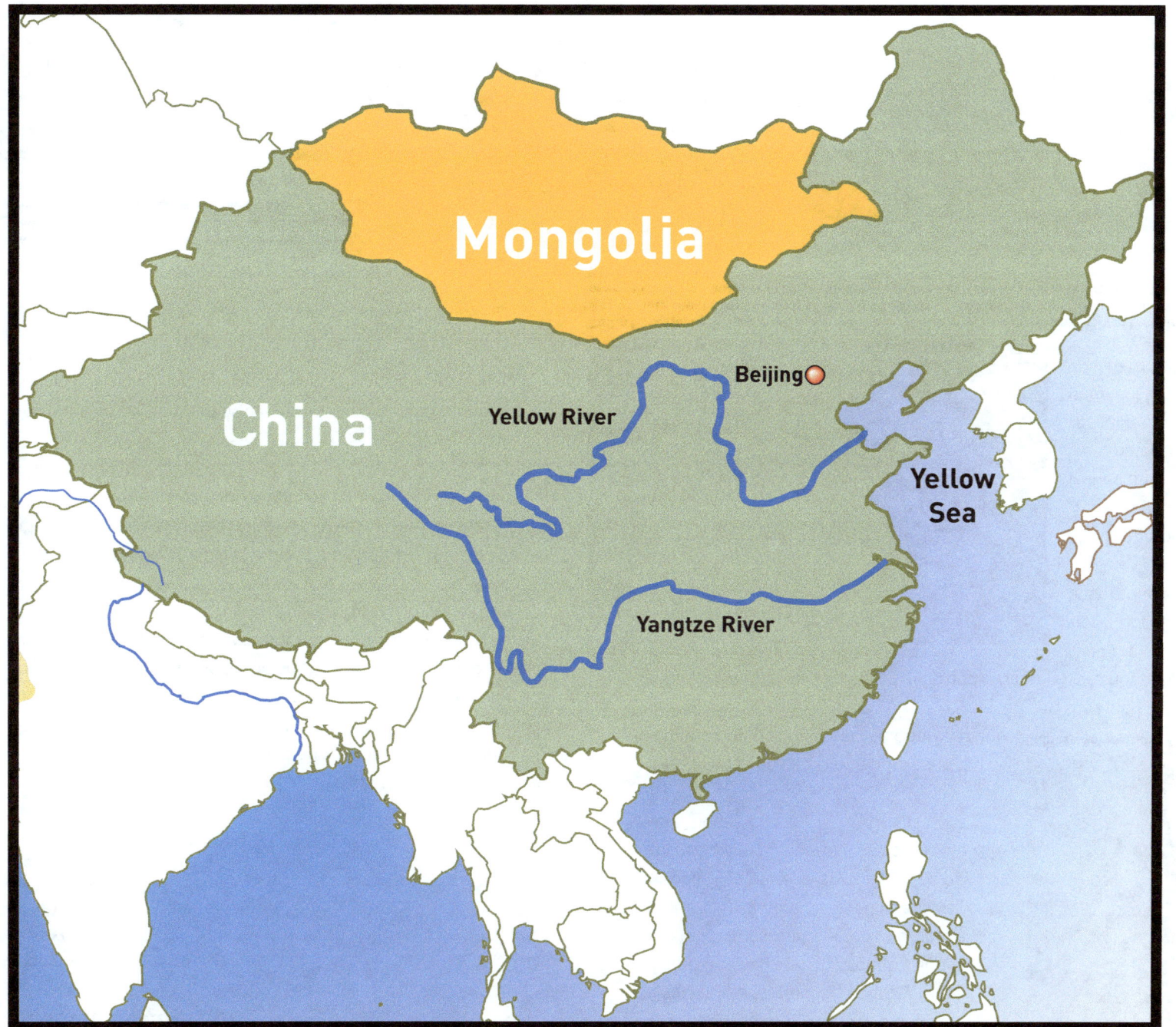

Zoom Me In!

This Lesson's Geography
China
Mongolia
Yellow Sea
Yellow River
Yangtze River
Beijing

Use this sheet as a reference for this lesson's "Now, let's trace, shade & label" worksheet.

Lesson 9 Geography
China
Mongolia
Yellow Sea
Yellow River
Yangtze River
Beijing

Tid-Bits

The location of China determined how the culture developed. This country was isolated, separated from most of the world by desolate deserts on the north and west, the vast Pacific Ocean on the east, and the forbidden mountains to the south. Thus, this remote culture developed independently, without influence from other civilizations.

Ancient China is a civilization with a long and exciting history ruled by dynasties lasting hundreds of years. They made significant advancements and contributions in architecture, art, religion, and government.

Ancient China was ruled by dynasties. A dynasty comprises a family that makes decisions politically, socially, economically, militarily, and more for the country's people. These dynasties lasted hundreds of years and shaped China into a fascinating country. The Emperor ruled over the country and was the most important person in Chinese culture. They were believed to answer only to God. Therefore, everyone had to pay respect to the Emperor. His son would rule after he died.

The Chinese people lived and died in the same social position that their parents and grandparents had. If a person was born a farmer, they died as a farmer, and so did their children. Men and women were treated differently. Women were not allowed to get an education, and they lived their lives in their homes doing domestic work. Society had a very rigid structure that was believed to keep the country in harmony.

The Emperor was at the top of the social chain. Below the Emperor were the aristocrats. They owned and rented their land to tenants. Farmers were below the aristocrats and were highly respected because they provided food to the people. Many farmers owned their land. Farming was hard but respected work. After the farmers,

Chinese Agricultural Farm Worker - By Kadmy, Adobe Stock

Guilin fisherman - By gnomeandi, Adobe Stock. Guilin is a prefecture-level city in the northeast of China's Guangxi Zhuang Autonomous Region. It is situated on the west bank of the Li River and borders Hunan to the north. Its name means "forest of sweet osmanthus", owing to the large number of fragrant sweet osmanthus trees located in the region. The city has long been renowned for its scenery of karst topography.

Landscape of Mount Huangshan (Yellow Mountains). UNESCO World Heritage Site. Located in Huangshan, Anhui, China. - By aphotostory, Adobe Stock

the artists and craftsmen were next in the social hierarchy. They were not permitted to own land or even the tools they used, but they were respected for their skill. Merchants and traders were the lowest class. Some made more money than farmers and artisans, but they did not produce what they sold, so there was little respect for the work they did. They were often seen as lazy and greedy.

There have been many different dynasties throughout China's history. Each Dynasty brought something unique to the culture. The first recorded Dynasty in history was The Shang Dynasty, which made advancements in math, astronomy, art, and the military. The Han dynasty made Confucianism a vital part of Chinese philosophy. The Qin dynasty established the first Chinese empire, started constructing The Great Wall of China, and moved the capital to Xianyang. Finally, the Ming dynasty created porcelain.

Statue of Confucius at Temple in Shanghai, China - By philipus, Adobe Stock

Religion has always played an essential role in China's history, culture, and philosophy. The three main religions in ancient China were Confucianism, Taoism, and Buddhism.

Confucius wanted to preserve the ancient culture by influencing society to behave well. For example, treat others in ways you want to be treated, and always treat parents, elders, and ancestors with respect. These ideals are still a big part of Chinese culture today.

Taoism is a belief in balance and nature. Yin and Yang is a well-known symbol that comes from this religion that represents everything having balance. Where there is good, there is evil. Where there is light, there is darkness. Where there is chaos, there is peace. It is the belief that one thing cannot exist without its opposite.

Octagonal Symbol of Taoism, Yin Yang - By Yali Shi, Adobe Stock

Buddhism began in northern India, but it arrived in China and is still practiced today. The most important belief is in karma, whereas a person who does good will have good fortune and a bright future. Likewise, a person who does bad will have bad fortune and future suffering. Buddhists

Large Temple Stutue of Buddha, Image by Christel SAGNIEZ from Pixabay

also believe that the mind never stops existing. It is reborn into a god or human if they have good karma but reborn into an animal if they have bad karma.

Ancient Chinese architecture varied depending on the Dynasty in power, but there are general similarities throughout. Wood was used instead of stone as it was lighter and more versatile. China used internal columns and the dougong system to disperse the weight in their architecture. The dougong is a system of brackets and crossbeams between the columns. This type of architecture is

Typical Chinese Traditional Architecture. Image by happypixel19 from Pixabay

Silk was first developed in ancient China. Legend gives credit for developing silk to a Chinese empress, Leizu. Silk was initially reserved for the Emperors of China for their own use and gifts to others but spread gradually through Chinese culture and trade. Eventually, silk was in great demand throughout Asia and became a staple of pre-industrial international trade. With the demand for silk, there came what history calls the Silk Road, which was an ancient network of trade routes that connected the East and West.

Chinese trade silk road - By Maxim P, Adobe Stock

The two most important geographical features of ancient China were two major rivers: the Yellow River and the Yangtze River. They were the source of freshwater, food, fertile soil, and transportation. They also were the subjects of poetry, art, literature, and folklore.

A famous bend of yangtze river in Yunnan Province, China, first curve of yangtze river, Lijiang
By martinhosmat083, Adobe Stock

Buildings were not tall and often had curved roofs with overhanging eaves. Often Buildings and cities were designed to have every part mirrored on the opposite side. With a vibrancy of color, everything was decorated. Ornamental carvings in beams and columns, along with paintings of Chinese culture and nature, hung on the walls.

Curvy roads, Silk trading route between China and India.
By mitrarudra, Adobe Stock

prevalent from the ancient times of China and reflects Taoism, their philosophy of balanced living. Everything in their architecture is about balance, symmetry, and emphasizing horizontal traits.

Qiankun Bay of Yellow River in Shanxi, China - By Jack, Adobe Stock

The Great Wall of China, Image by jl w from Pixabay

with chariots, horses, archers, and so much more. Ancient China created art out of bronze, tin, and copper. They even carved jade, a green stone. To ancient Chinese, jade was the most valuable symbol of wisdom, bravery, and purity. It was very hard to carve. Calligraphy is an old and beloved art form that is still practiced today. It is the art of writing with a brush and ink.

Closeup of the ancient Terracotta Army, Image by Christel SAGNIEZ from Pixabay

The Great Wall of China is made of stone, brick, pressed earth, wood, and other materials. It is built along an east-to-west line across the historical northern borders of China to protect the Chinese states and empires against the raids and invasions of the various enemy countries. The defensive characteristics of the Great Wall were enhanced by the construction of watchtowers, troop barracks, and garrison stations, with signaling capabilities through the means of smoke or fire. Apart from defense, other purposes of the Great Wall have included border controls, collection of duties on goods transported along the Silk Road, and control of immigration and emigration. Lastly, the Great Wall served as a transportation corridor.

Who built this Great Wall, and how great is it really? Various Dynasties built the Great Wall of China, dating from the Zhou Dynasty in 771 BC to the Sui Dynasty that ended in 617 AD. Notably, the last Dynasty to work on the Great Wall, the Sui Dynasty, had over 1 million forced laborers. An archaeological survey found that the entire wall measures 13,171 miles and can be seen from outer space! Today, the Great Wall is recognized as one of the most impressive architectural feats in history. That is really great!

China has a long history of creating beautiful art out of metal, pottery, and jade. During ancient times, art reflected a person's status in society. Pottery is some of the oldest known Chinese art. Different dynasties had different styles. Yangshao had red-painted pottery, Shang had an early dark brown glaze. The Terracotta Army is the most famous, with 8,000 human-sized warriors complete

The ancient Terracotta Army, Image by Allan Lee from Pixabay

Chinese Calligraphy - By Marco Balaz, Adobe Stock

Ancient jade carving of terracotta soldier By bbbar, Adobe Stock

Beijing is in northeast China and is the current capital. It used to be known as Peking and Beiping. More than fifteen million people live there. People from all over China and the world go to Beijing to work and live. It hosted the Summer Olympics in 2008 and the Winter Olympics in 2022; no other city has done that! Beijing is rich in ancient history. The name means "the northern capital." Some of the most well-known historical places include Tiananmen Square, The Forbidden City, Temple of Heaven, Summer Palace, and the Great Wall. It's been the capital of several dynasties and was given the name "Beijing" by the Ming dynasty.

Mongolia is a country between Russia and China. It is entirely landlocked and has no access to seas or oceans. Their government is the Parliamentary Republic, and most of their people

Beijing at Twilight - Image by 立重立 (Anthony Chong) from Pixabay

practice Buddhism. Ulaanbaatar is the capital and largest city; over a third of the entire population lives there. There are mountains and dessert there.

A nomadic way of life has always been and continues to be a large part of Mongolian society. They move around without one specific place to live. In 1206, Genghis Khan created the Mongol Empire, but it collapsed, and the people went back to living a nomadic life. For a time, they lived under Chinese rule. But in 1911, Mongolia fought for its independence for ten long years; in the end, they were successful!

Goats Surrounding a yurt in Western Mongolia, By katiekk2 - Adobe Stock

Mongolian Eagle Hunter with His Eagle, Bayan-Olgii, West Mongolia, By R.M. Nunes - Adobe Stock

A Closer Look

at what you have learned so far!

PLUS+

This Lesson's Geography

Japan
Kyoto
Tokyo
Mt. Fuji
Pacific Ocean
Sea of Japan

Lesson 10

Previously Learned Geography a TRUE REVIEW - 6 week review

Lesson 4
Hattusa
Asia Minor
Arabian Desert
Cyprus

Lesson 5
Egypt
Nile River
Upper/Lower Egypt
Nile River Delta

Lesson 6
Greece
Aegean Sea
Macedonia
Crete
Rhodes

Lesson 7
Hispania
Gaul
Germania
Alexandria
Carthage

Lesson 8
Indus River
Ganges River
Himalayas
Arabian Sea
Bay of Bengal
Great Indian Desert

Lesson 9
China
Mongolia
Yellow Sea
Yellow River
Yangtze River
Beijing

Hint: All geography found on this page, is also the geography that you will be reviewing this week. Refer to these maps as needed when doing your "Memorization Through Repetition" worksheets.

Parent/Teacher: The "A Closer Look" page is intended to show students the accumulated geographic areas taught within their 6-week review period plus new geography. For additional teaching tips on how to utilize this teaching aide for the different learning levels, please refer to page 1.

Lesson 10

Zoom Me In!

This Lesson's Geography
Japan
Kyoto
Tokyo
Mt. Fuji
Pacific Ocean
Sea of Japan

Use this sheet as a reference for this lesson's "Now, let's trace, shade & label" worksheet.

Lesson 10 Geography
Japan

Kyoto
Tokyo
Mt. Fuji
Pacific Ocean
Sea of Japan

Tid-Bits

Japan is made up of thousands of islands in the Pacific Ocean that are actually the tops of mountains. Only 400-600 of these islands have people living on them. The four main islands are called Hokkaido, Honshu, Shikoku, and Kyushu from north to south. Japan is mainly covered with mountains and forests, with only 11.6% of the land is suitable for growing crops. The highest point is Mt. Fuji, at 12,385 feet. The lowest point in Japan is Lake Hachirogata, at 12 feet below sea level. Though it is

separate from continental Asia, ancient Japan made many unique and essential contributions to Asian and global cultures. Initially, the Japanese culture was influenced by China and Korea, but they were never ruled over by any foreign country.

Positioned astride the Pacific Ring of Fire, Japan has a number of hydrothermal features such as geysers and hot springs. It also suffers frequent earthquakes, tsunamis, and volcanic eruptions.

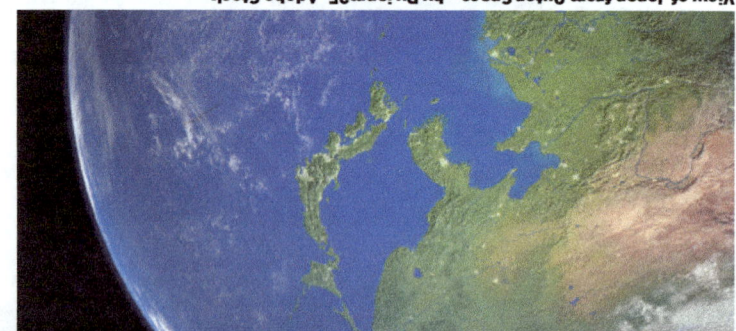
View of Japan from Outer Space - by By ianm35, Adobe Stock

In case you were wondering, "What is the Pacific Ring of Fire?" here is your answer! The Ring of Fire is a major area in the basin of the Pacific Ocean where many earthquakes and volcanic eruptions occur. In a 25,000 mile horseshoe shape, it is associated with a nearly continuous series of oceanic trenches, volcanic arcs, and volcanic belts and plate movements. It has 452 volcanoes, which is more than 75% of the world's active and dormant volcanoes. About 90% of the world's earthquakes and 81% of the world's largest earthquakes occur along the Ring of Fire.

Stretching 2,174 miles from North to South, Japan includes a number of different climate zones. It has a temperate climate overall, with four seasons.

First an earthquake, then a tsunami, leveled this oceanside town in Japan in 2011 - By Fly_and_Dive, Adobe Stock

Heavy snowfall is the 970, the town of Kutchan received over 10 feet of snow in a single day! The total snowfall for that winter was more than 66 feet!

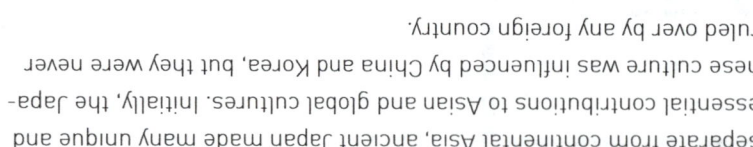
Bamboo Grove in Japan, By rabbit75_fot - Adobe Stock

The southern island of Okinawa, in contrast, has a semi-tropical climate with an average annual temperature of 72 degrees Fahrenheit. The island receives about 80 inches of rain per year.

Here is an interesting tid-bit: Starting in the mid-seventh century, the Japanese government placed a ban on eating meat which lasted on and off for over 1,200 years. Probably influenced by the Buddhist precept that forbids the taking of life. Emperor Tenmu issued an edict in 675 AD that banned the eating of beef, monkeys, and domestic animals under penalty of death!

The original law was only meant to be observed between April and September. Later laws and religious practices essentially made eating most meat, especially beef, illegal or taboo. Contact with Christian missionaries began to popularize meat eating again in the 16th century. Although another ban was proclaimed in 1687, but some Japanese continued to eat meat.
By 1872, the Japanese authorities had officially lifted the ban and even the emperor had become a meat eater. While not everybody was immediately enthused, particularly monks, the centuries-old taboo on eating meat soon faded away.

Shinto religion and its architecture play a vital role in Japan's ancient history. In Shintoism, the belief is that the gods Izanami and Izanagi created the Japanese Islands by dipping a jeweled spear into the sea. Along with the islands, these gods created 800 kami, or spirits.

The Jomon Period is the earliest documented period lasting until about 300 BC. Agriculture began to appear in Japan around 5000 BC. Sannai-Maruyama was the earliest Japanese settlement dating from 3500-2000 BC. Evidence of rice being grown in wet fields shows up around 600 BCE. This period is known for distinctive pottery with rope-like decoration.

From 300 BC-200 AD, the Yayoi Period flourished and is named for the reddish pottery found. Migrants from Asia and the Korean peninsula emigrated to Japan, bringing their own culture to the indigenous people. They brought better farming tools, weaponry, and armor with them, and the people blended and flourished. As a result, they had over 4.5 million people living on the islands. During this period, Japan started sending people to communicate and trade with China.

The Kofun Period was named for the large burial mounds and lasted between 250-538 AD. More than 20,000 of these mounds have been found throughout Japan. During this period, people continued to come from the Korean peninsula, bringing iron, weaving, and irrigation. They also expressed new ways of thinking. For example, teachers, scholars, and artists shared Chinese writing, Confucian texts, and Buddhism. In addition, they explored international diplomacy even more.

The Asuka Period spanned 538-710 AD and is named for the capital of that time. Prince Shotoku was the most prominent ruler and reformed the government by centralizing it like the Chinese had. He also created the

Colorful Autumn Season and Mountain Fuji with morning fog and red leaves at lake Kawaguchiko is one of the best places in Japan - By Travel mania - Adobe Stock

Seventeen Article Constitution to get rid of corruption and create a relationship with China. In 645, the Fujiwara clan took over the government and made it even more like China's. They established the Taika Reforms. These laws made all the land belong to the Emperor. The people were taxed more, social rank was made, and laws were passed, giving the Emperor absolute power.

Entrance of kofun, ByMumura Heng - Adobe Stock

Between 710-794 AD, the Nara Period gave the Emperor even more power by centralizing the government through the military. Buddhism continued to spread throughout Japan, and Emperor Shomu built a temple in every province. More Japanese people were sent to Korea and China to construct solid foreign relationships. It was also a time of outstanding artistic achievement. Kohiki and Nihon Shoki told Shinto stories. Manyoshu was the first collection of poetry. "Manyoshu" means "collection to be handed down throughout ten thousand eras" or the "collection of ten thousand leaves." The Manyoshu is the oldest existing collection of Japanese poetry. The finding of this poetry is highly revered in Japan and contains 4,500 poems spread among 20 volumes. Also, in the Nara Period, there were frequent food shortages because agricultural tools were primitive,

and there were not enough crops to feed Japan. Smallpox also broke out, and it is thought that the population decreased by 35%.

The Heian Period spanned 794-1185 AD. The capital, Heiankyo, was laid out on a grid pattern with wide central avenues. Japan didn't communicate as much with continental Asia because they didn't feel they needed to defend their borders and had no desire to expand their empire. However, they did some trading with China for goods. This period also saw the creation of kana or Japanese writing.

The Kamakura Period lasted from 1185-1333 AD. During this time, Japan saw a reform in their government with military families in power. Although there was an Emporer, they were appointed by the Shoguns, who ruled in the name of the Emporer. It was called a Shogunate. Sakoku, which means "closed country," was the policy of the Japanese shogunate under which, for 214 years, relations and trade between Japan and other countries were severely limited. This timeperiod is commonly referred to as "Japan's Isolation." Nearly all foreign nationals were barred from entering Japan, while ordinary Japanese people were kept from leaving. During this era, Buddhism and the Samurai were an essential part of daily life and culture.

Samurai were fierce warriors that were placed in power by inheriting the

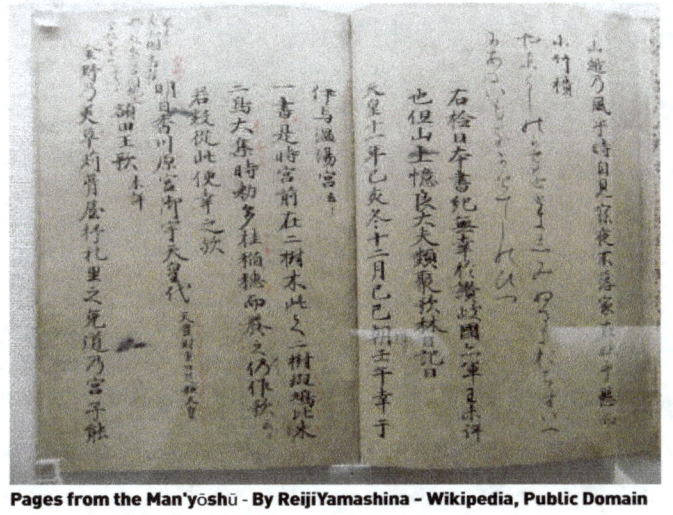

Pages from the Man'yōshū - By ReijiYamashina - Wikipedia, Public Domain

position. The Samurai were part of an officer caste that fought for land-owning lords and the Emperor. They were known as intellectual masters of war. They lived by Bushido, a code of honor, meaning "the way of the warrior." They were indifferent to pain, held unflinching loyalty, and engaged in many battles. With high prestige, they had special rights, such as wearing two swords - a long and a short. Whereas commoners were unable to wear or own

Medieval Japanese Classical Engraving Art. Kabuki actors portraying Japanese samurai intimidating the commoners, dragon,red sun . Ancient illustration. – By Matrioshka, Adobe Stock

any weaponry. They also had the right to execute by beheading any individual that offended them. The memory of the Samurai and their weaponry remain prominent in Japanese popular culture. During this period, artwork continued to evolve and consisted of religious paintings, wood sculptures, and military weapons.

From 1336-1573 AD, the Muromachi Period grew. There were a lot of military conflicts. Castles were built. Art continued to be influenced by Chinese culture and began to depict life outside of religion and included birds, cities, and animals.

From 1603-1868, Japan experienced stability in the Edo Period with very little foreign influence. As a result, art evolved into strictly Japanese styles. After the Edo Period, the periods were named after the reigning Emperor.

Some unique traditions that the Japanese people have include Koinobori. These are kites shaped like carp, specifically a freshwater and beautiful type of carp called koi. Koi are an important symbol of strength, energy, and courage for the Japanese. Koinobori is flown on May 5th for Kodomo-no-Hi, or Children's Day, as a way to celebrate and hope children grow up strong and healthy. In addition, Koi flags were flown on poles in front of a home to tell friends and family a baby was born.

Pagodas are an essential part of Japanese culture and architecture. They came from China and India as Buddhism spread. Though they are similar to Chinese pagodas, they are very different too. Japanese pagodas are built out of wood to survive earthquakes which Japan is prone to have. They have a square shape with twelve pillars. Each floor is smaller than the one below it. There are five roofs to symbolize the elements: earth, water, fire, wind, and space.

Japanese Koinobori - Carp shaped kites. - Photographer Unknown: Public Domain

Japanese painting of a peacock and roses, from the Muromachi Period - Artist: Unknown, Public Domain

Japanese Temple Pogoda - Image by Pexels from Pixabay

85

Byzantine Empire

Constantinople
Rome
Athens
Ephesus
Antioch

Where in the World?

Lesson 11

A Closer Look at what you have learned so far!

Lesson 11

PLUS+ This Lesson's Geography

Byzantine Empire
Constantinople
Rome
Athens
Ephesus
Antioch

Previously Learned Geography a TRUE REVIEW - 6 week review

Lesson 5
Egypt
Nile River
Upper/Lower Egypt
Nile River Delta

Lesson 6
Greece
Aegean Sea
Macedonia
Crete
Rhodes

Lesson 7
Hispania
Gaul
Germania
Alexandria
Carthage

Lesson 8
Indus River
Ganges River
Himalayas
Arabian Sea
Bay of Bengal
Great Indian Desert

Lesson 9
China
Mongolia
Yellow Sea
Yellow River
Yangtze River
Beijing

Lesson 10
Japan
Kyoto
Tokyo
Mt. Fuji
Pacific Ocean
Sea of Japan

Hint: All geography found on this page, is also the geography that you will be reviewing this week. Refer to these maps as needed when doing your "Memorization Through Repetition" worksheets.

Parent/Teacher: The "A Closer Look" page is intended to show students the accumulated geographic areas taught within their 6-week review period plus new geography. For additional teaching tips on how to utilize this teaching aide for the different learning levels, please refer to page 1.

Zoom Me In!

Use this sheet as a reference for this lesson's "Now, let's trace, shade & label" worksheet.

Lesson 11

This Lesson's Geography

Byzantine Empire

Constantinople
Rome
Athens
Ephesus
Antioch

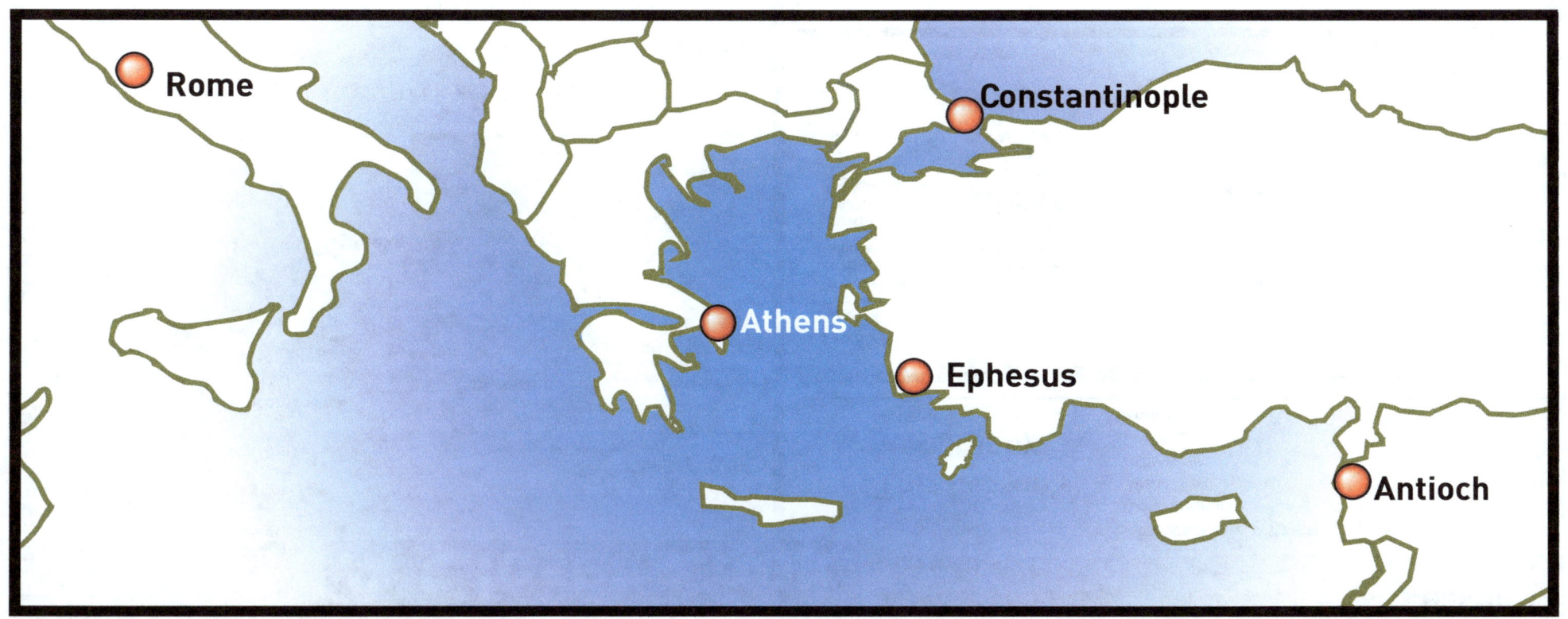

Lesson 11 Geography
The Byzantine Empire
Constantinople
Rome
Athens
Ephesus
Antioch

555 AD

This map reflects the Byzantine Empire at its greatest extent under Justinian the Great. Map procured thanks to Dr. Paul H. Freedman, Chester D. Tripp, Professor of History, Chair, History of Science and Medicine Program, Yale University

Tid-Bits

The Byzantine Empire, named for the ancient Greek city Byzantium, included Italy, Greece, the Levant, Asia Minor, North Africa, and the Balkans. Greek was the official language, with Christianity as its official religion. During their 1,123 years, they created their own political system that set the stage for much of the western world. In addition, they created art and architecture that was heavily influenced by Greek and Roman culture. The Byzantine Empire was the longest-lasting medieval Empire.

The Byzantine Empire lasted from 330-1453 AD and was founded by Constantine I. Sometimes called the Eastern Roman Empire, for it was created when the Roman Empire split. Constantine moved the capital of Rome to Byzantium and renamed it for himself "Constantinople."
Emperor Constantine I came to power as a Roman Emperor in 306 AD and saw the split of the Roman Empire. He ruled the Eastern portion that became known as the Byzantine Empire for 30 years. Under his rule, the Empire thrived and became powerful.

Christians were sporadically persecuted under Roman rule for over two and a half centuries because they refused to believe that the Emperors were gods. Treason was punishable by execution. The most notable, widespread persecution was carried out by Diocletian. When Constantine came into power, he issued the Edict of Milan, which made the worship of Christians lawful. This shift, called "Peace of the Church," reaffirmed the importance of religious worship to the Empire's welfare. It was also a turning point that brought many to believe in Christ, and the Church became a large part of the Roman Empire for more than 1,000 years. Constantine died at 61 years of age and was buried in the Temple of the Holy Apostles. Just a few days before his death, he was baptized.

Constantinople was founded where modern-day Istanbul is; it had a natural harbor and supplied access between Europe and Asia, which was very important for trade. In 410, they built the Theodosian Wall across the harbor entrance that protected them from attacks. Constantinople, in its time, was the most extensive and wealthiest Christian city in Europe.

Byzantine emperors were called Basileus and lived in the Great Palace, ruling as an Absolute Monarch over the Church and the government.

Statue of Constantine I Image by Public Domain Pictures from Pixabay

They were expected to lead with wisdom and good judgment and also proven military success. Their image was put on coins. When a Basileus made poor choices, military generals would remove them to prevent ruin. There were no rules of succession, so the Basileus could name their son or someone else to succeed them. There was a Senate that helped counsel the Basileus; it was made up of well-connected men. Eunuchs worked for the Basileus and had great control over who saw him. The most important official was the Praetorian Prefect of the East. He managed all the regional governors to make sure the Empire continued to run smoothly; only the Basileus was more powerful.

Among the many accomplishments of the Byzantine Empire, one of the most influential for today's world was called "Corpus juris civilis" or what is more commonly referred to as the "Justinian Code."

Imagine trying to run an empire but not having a strict set of laws to enforce. Or imagine that there are laws, but most of them are not even written down! Would that be difficult? Well, Justinian "the Great" sure thought so!

Mosaic depicting a crowned Justinian, By Petar Milošević , Wikicommons

Justinian ruled in the year 527 AD. He was a strong leader, influential, powerful, yet fair. As he came into power, there was one fundamental problem that his people were facing. Inconsistent laws. His goal was to protect the people, but he couldn't very well do that when the laws were scattered and unclear. Even worse, the Empire was so large, some laws were enforced in one area but not another. How confusing!

So, Justinian had heads of government, judges, and lawyers write down all of the laws in one place. Then they carefully went through all of the old rules, cutting out unnecessary laws, adding new laws, and changing the existing laws to make more sense.

Over time, four books of law were created, and together they made up the Justinian Code. Two of the four books individually had 12 and 50 volumes each! One of the books was an introductory textbook for beginning law students. The last book was a publication that was a collection of new laws added by Justinian to protect the people, giving rights to women and slaves, like the ability to buy land. This significantly helped widowed mothers. These two groups had not had many rights in the past.

The Justinian Code also discussed marriage, property, crime, adoption, slavery, business, and trade laws. Phew! Pretty much everything an empire might need was included in those laws. Other countries were influenced by the Byzantine Empire to utilize their hard work of compiling thousands of years of law into an organized format that could be understood and taught.

A page from the Archaic Justinian Code

Many laws found in the Justinian Code still make sense even today. For example, the code stated that all ports and rivers were public areas. Therefore everyone had the right to fish in those waters. It also talked about how the price of something you are selling has to be honest and fair; otherwise, you could be charged with stealing.

Some laws written in the Justinian Code may seem silly to us today. For example, if you grow fruit on your land, you do not own that fruit until you pick it off of the tree! Another says that if someone steals, then you are allowed to kill them! And those who committed crimes could be kicked out of the city and sent to a remote island. Wow!

While many modern laws and governments are based on the Justinian Code, many laws would be found unjust by some in today's society. Some believe that the men who wrote the Bill of Rights for the United States used the

Justinian Code for guidance. Latin was the official language of the Justinian Code, although much of it was written or translated into Greek. As time marched on, the code was translated into Italian, English, and more.

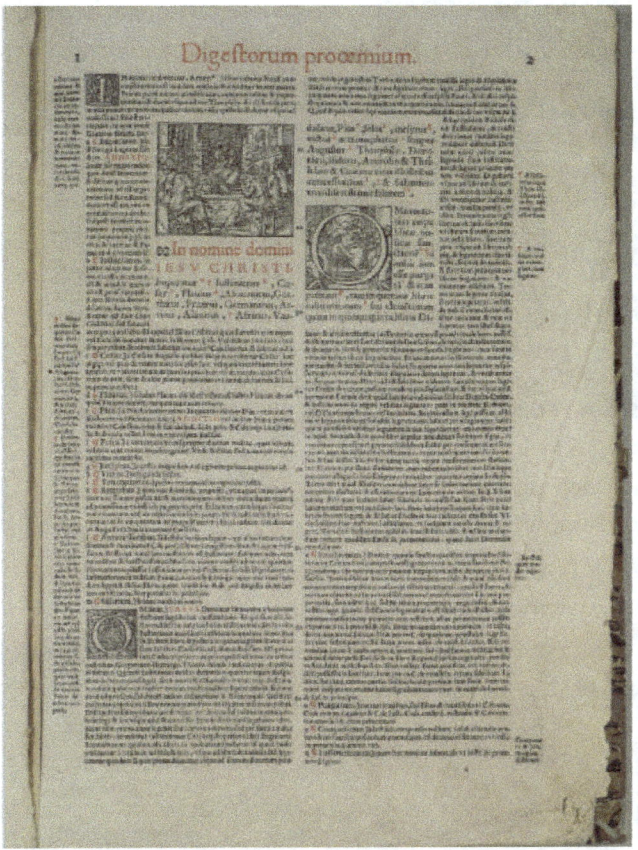

A page from the Justinian Code, translated into Italian and published in 1558-1560. Public Domain, sourced from digitized Italian archives.

Under Justinian, the Empire gained more and more land and reached the pinnacle of its power and wealth. During his reign, there were many reforms. The most noteworthy was the law. But beyond organizing the law, Justinian also encouraged the arts, including music and drama. In addition, he funded many public works projects like bridges, roads, aqueducts, and churches. Perhaps his best-known project was the Hagia Sophia, a beautiful and massive church built in Constantinople; it still stands today in Istanbul, Turkey.

In the Byzantine Empire, family names were significant to the people. There wasn't a noble class like in other cultures. But a wealthy person who owned or controlled land was at the highest level of society. Through patronage and education, a person could gain a higher social standing. The Basileus could give out land, titles, and favors, but he could also take them away. It was easy to see a person's rank through titles, seals, clothing, and jewelry. Lower classes of people passed down their profession from parent to child. People working in law, administration, and commerce were a higher class than artisans and farmers who owned little land. Most people were in the lowest class and worked the ground for a landowner. Slaves were at the bottom of society. A person became a slave as a prisoner of war or because they were indebted to the landowner.

Women and men had different roles depending on their rank. Women of the higher class managed their homes and cared for children. Women of the lower class worked in agriculture, manufacturing, and food services. Thanks to Justinian, women were allowed to own property and businesses and inherit wealth, but they could not hold public office. Many improved their social standing through marriage. Widows were guardians of their children. In their free time, they would weave, go to Church, shop, and those who could, would read.

Justinian the Great (center) and his retinue, Basilica of San Vitale, Ravenna, 527-457 CE, mosaic / Wikimedia Commons

Christianity had a massive impact on Byzantine culture, from art and politics to law and war. A person called the "Patriarch of Constantinople" also went by "Bishop." He was in charge of the Church and was put in his position by the Basileus. There were less important Bishops in cities and towns around the Empire. They acted on behalf of the Patriarch of Constantinople and the Basileus. Christianity helped unite the Empire, but people were allowed to practice whatever their religion was, so Jews, Muslims, Pagans, and more were among the population.

Byzantine art is an important part of their history, but artists did not have a high social standing. Most of the art was two-dimensional and revolved around religious messages. Salvation and faith were the most critical artistic themes. Most of the art created was wall mosaics, wall paintings, and icons.

Architecture combined classical design with that found in the Near East. It was eclectic. The insides were more beautiful than the outsides. The people built amphitheaters, hippodromes, baths, villas, aqueducts, and more like those found in Rome. They also created domed

The Byzantine Empire's geography changed throughout its history. From 600-800 AD, the Muslim Empire took many territories away. Arab forces tried to take over Constantinople

Byzantine Empire era mosaic art. Image by Gerhard Bögner from Pixabay

between 674-678 AD and again in 717-718 AD, but they were never able to. The Basileus, Basil I, reconquered parts of Italy, Cyprus, and Greece in the late 800s. The Basileus, Basil II,

churches, walled monasteries, and fortified walls. As we've learned, the Hagia Sophia, built in Constantinople, is one of the most beautiful and well-known Byzantine-era churches. It has incredible architecture and fantastic mosaic art throughout; people come from all over to see it. Byzantine architecture has influenced builders and designers around the world throughout history and even today.

fought Vikings from Kiev in the eleventh century and doubled the size of the Empire. Unfortunately, it was the beginning of the end of the Byzantine Empire. They had too many enemies throughout their territories to fight them all and maintain the land. In 1204, Crusaders from Europe sacked Constantinople. By the time the Byzantine Empire fell for good, it had controlled part of southern Greece and the area around Constantinople.

On May 29, 1453, the Byzantine Empire fell when Sultan Mehmed II of the Ottoman Empire conquered Constantinople. However, the Byzantine Empire lasted for more than twelve centuries, and its legacy endures even today.

Within the Hagia Sophia. Image by mostafa meraji from Pixabay

Hagia Sophia at dusk. Image by Claudia Beyli from Pixabay

Jesus Christ Mosaic in Hagia Sophia. Image by Günther Simmermacher from Pixabay

Where in the World?

Lesson 12

Muslim Empire
Mecca
Medina
Baghdad
Damascus
Tours
Syria

93

A Closer Look

at what you have learned so far!

PLUS+

This Lesson's Geography

Lesson 12

Muslim Empire
Mecca
Medina
Baghdad
Damascus
Tours
Syria

Previously Learned Geography a TRUE REVIEW - 6 week review

Lesson 6
Greece
Aegean Sea
Macedonia
Crete
Rhodes

Lesson 7
Hispania
Gaul
Germania
Alexandria
Carthage

Lesson 8
Indus River
Ganges River
Himalayas
Arabian Sea
Bay of Bengal
Great Indian Desert

Lesson 9
China
Mongolia
Yellow Sea
Yellow River
Yangtze River
Beijing

Lesson 10
Japan
Kyoto
Tokyo
Mt. Fuji
Pacific Ocean
Sea of Japan

Lesson 11
Constantinople
Rome
Athens
Ephesus
Antioch

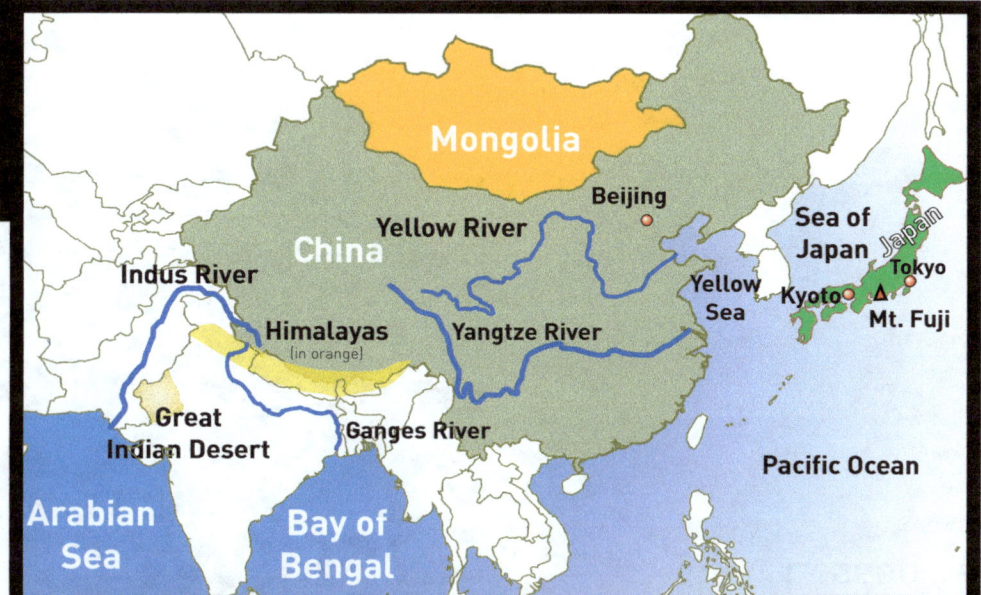

Hint: All geography found on this page, is also the geography that you will be reviewing this week. Refer to these maps as needed when doing your "Memorization Through Repetition" worksheets.

Parent/Teacher: The "A Closer Look" page is intended to show students the accumulated geographic areas taught within their 6-week review period plus new geography. For additional teaching tips on how to utilize this teaching aide for the different learning levels, please refer to page 1.

Lesson 12

Zoom Me In!

This Lesson's Geography
Muslim Empire
Mecca
Medina
Baghdad
Damascus
Tours
Syria

> Use this sheet as a reference for this lesson's "Now, let's trace, shade & label" worksheet.

Lesson 12 Geography
The Muslim Empire
Mecca
Medina
Baghdad
Damascus
Tours
Syria

Tid-Bits

Muslim Empire is also referred to as the Islamic Empire. Islam began with the founder, Mohammed, who was born in Mecca in 570 AD. At 40 years old (610 AD), he claimed to have had communication from God, receiving the first revelations of the Quran.

In 622 AD, Mohammad's flight from Mecca to Medina, due to persecution, was the beginning of the rise of Islam and also marks the beginning of the Islamic calendar. In Medina, Muhammad put in place the Constitution of Medina, which laid out the rights among the people. Through this, he established the first Islamic state.

Muhammad and his followers, took control of Mecca in 630 AD. In later years in Medina, Muhammad unified the tribes of Arabia under Islam. By the time he died in 632 AD, almost all the tribes of the Arabian Peninsula had converted to Islam.

Islamic leaders conquered Iran in 641 AD, and in 642 AD, Egypt was under Islamic control. The Iberian Peninsula (modern-day Spain and Portugal), India, and Indonesia became Islamic lands in the eighth century. The Muslims were stopped in France by their defeat at the Battle of Tours in 732 AD. Nonetheless, Islamic rule continued on the Iberian Peninsula for nearly nine centuries.

In 751 AD, paper-making from China made its way west through the Muslims, allowing the introduction of Islam to the Africans. In the Middle East, the success of Islam changed the culture forever; Islam remains the base institution of the region. Safavid, Seljuk, Ottoman (Ottoman ended the Byzantine Empire), and Mughal Empires, were all "Islamic Empires."

The Islamic Golden Age, the 8th-13th centuries, was marked by the ascension of the Abbasid Caliphate. A Caliphate is the ruler of an Islamic state. The Abbasids were influenced by the Quran's injunction that "the ink of the scholar is more holy than the blood of the martyr." During this time, the Arab world became an intellectual center for science, astronomy, chemistry, physics, mathematics, philosophy, medicine, and education.

The Islamic Empire reached its peak in 750 AD. Then, it covered everything from today's Pakistan and Morocco to the Iberian Peninsula and more. The empire initially began through conquest but grew from trade.

Muhammad was born in 570 AD to a respected clan, but he was orphaned and raised by his uncle Abu Talib, who loved him more than his own children. Muhammad became a trader known for his honesty. At 25, he married a wealthy widow, 15 years older than him, named Khadija. In his late 30s, he started worshipping near Mecca in Hira, a cave in the mountain Jabal al-Nour, meaning Mountain of Light, all by himself. In 610 AD, he claimed that the Angel Gabriel told him about Allah, God, believing he was a prophet. After that, he started preaching to friends, family, and the public. At the time, his people believed in many gods, and he was persecuted for his teachings and beliefs. In 619, his uncle and wife died, making him feel alone in the world. Many people and the government in Mecca wanted him to disappear, and they planned to kill him. To escape, Muhammad traveled to Yathrib, now called Medina.

Muslims in Yathrib wanted revenge on Mecca. They plotted raids on trade caravans from Mecca, which were acts of war. Mecca suffered greatly from the attacks. In 624, the Battle of Badr was fought between 313 Muslim troops and over 1,000 Meccans. The Muslim warriors won and established themselves as a powerful military force. Mecca was under Muslim control, and Muhammad forgave anyone who surrendered and became Muslim.

Muslim's are required to make a pilgrimage to Mecca at least once in a lifetime. Here in Mecca they are gathered. Image by Konevi from Pixabay

Muhammad died in his home in Medina in 632 as the most powerful political and religious man in Arabia. He was buried in Roza-e-Rasool, meaning Tomb of the Prophet, which is next to the Mosque of the Prophet, or Masjid al-Nabwi. After his death, what Gabriel had told Muhammad at Hira would later be written as the Quran or the Muslim holy book. Today, Muslims are taught to learn the Quran as it was written in the original language and not through a translation.

Arabs were tribal people, but Islam brought them together after Muhammad died. Abu Bakr became the first caliph or the Prophet's successor. Abu Bakr united the Arab tribes and expanded the empire to include tribes living under foreign rule. The first three caliphs united many Arab tribes, but the fourth had to deal with civil wars, and there was no expansion. The Umayyad Dynasty lasted from 661-750 AD and continued to expand the Muslim empire. It was a vital empire for trade, knowledge, culture, and more. It extended through military conquest and religious conversion.

Muslim Mosque, where Muslims gather to worship. Image by Shujon Moral from Pixabay

Muslims gathered for worship Nabawi Mosque, Medina, Saudi Arabia - By hikrcn, Adobe

There are two different belief systems in Islam, Sunni, and Shia. Ali was the fourth caliph after Muhammad died, but Shia Muslims believe he should have been the rightful successor. However, most Muslims believe Abu Bakr, the first caliph, was the rightful successor, and these believers are Sunni. In the beginning, Sunni and Shia were political groups, but they morphed into religious beliefs as time went by.

Sunni and Shia Muslims have fought throughout history for religious and political reasons. Still, both sects have made significant contributions to the world and culture. Muslims preserved Roman and Greek scholarly work, which allowed the European Renaissance to happen. Muslim scholars Avicenna and Averroes preserved Aristotle's work. Al-Khwarizmi developed Algebra as an astronomer, mathematician, and geographer. People enjoy coffee worldwide every day, and we can thank the Muslims in Yemen for coffee.

Western Africa

Atlantic Ocean
Senegal River
Niger River
Sahara Desert
Ivory Coast

Where in the World?

Lesson 13

A Closer Look

at what you have learned so far!

Lesson 13

PLUS+ This Lesson's Geography

Western Africa
Atlantic Ocean
Senegal River
Niger River
Sahara Desert
Ivory Coast

Previously Learned Geography a TRUE REVIEW - 6 week review

Lesson 7
Hispania
Gaul
Germania
Alexandria
Carthage

Lesson 8
Indus River
Ganges River
Himalayas
Arabian Sea
Bay of Bengal
Great Indian Desert

Lesson 9
China
Mongolia
Yellow Sea
Yellow River
Yangtze River
Beijing

Lesson 10
Japan
Kyoto
Tokyo
Mt. Fuji
Pacific Ocean
Sea of Japan

Lesson 11
Constantinople
Rome
Athens
Ephesus
Antioch

Lesson 12
Mecca
Medina
Baghdad
Damascus
Tours
Syria

Hint: All geography found on this page, is also the geography that you will be reviewing this week. Refer to these maps as needed when doing your "Memorization Through Repetition" worksheets.

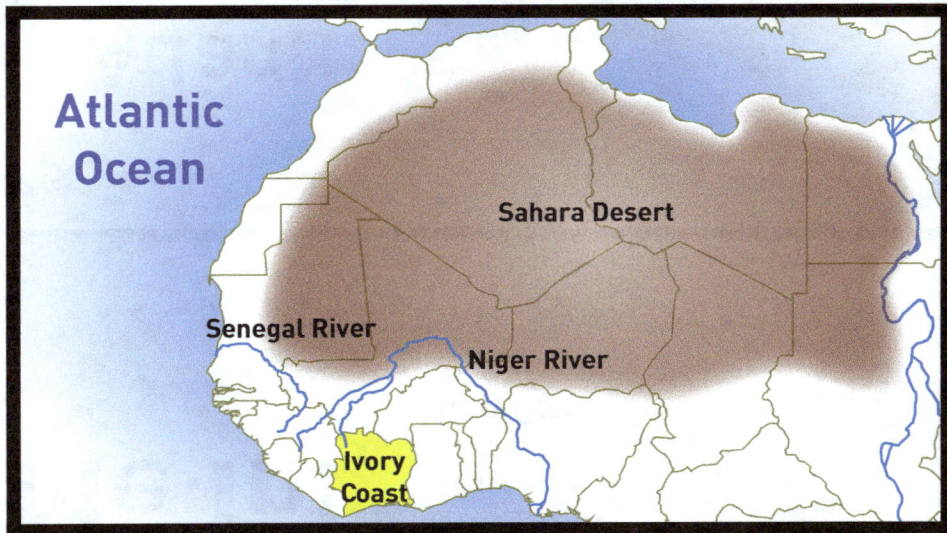

Parent/Teacher: The "A Closer Look" page is intended to show students the accumulated geographic areas taught within their 6-week review period plus new geography. For additional teaching tips on how to utilize this teaching aide for the different learning levels, please refer to page 1.

Zoom Me In!

This Lesson's Geography
Western Africa
Atlantic Ocean
Senegal River
Niger River
Sahara Desert
Ivory Coast

Use this sheet as a reference for this lesson's "Now, let's trace, shade & label" worksheet.

Lesson 13

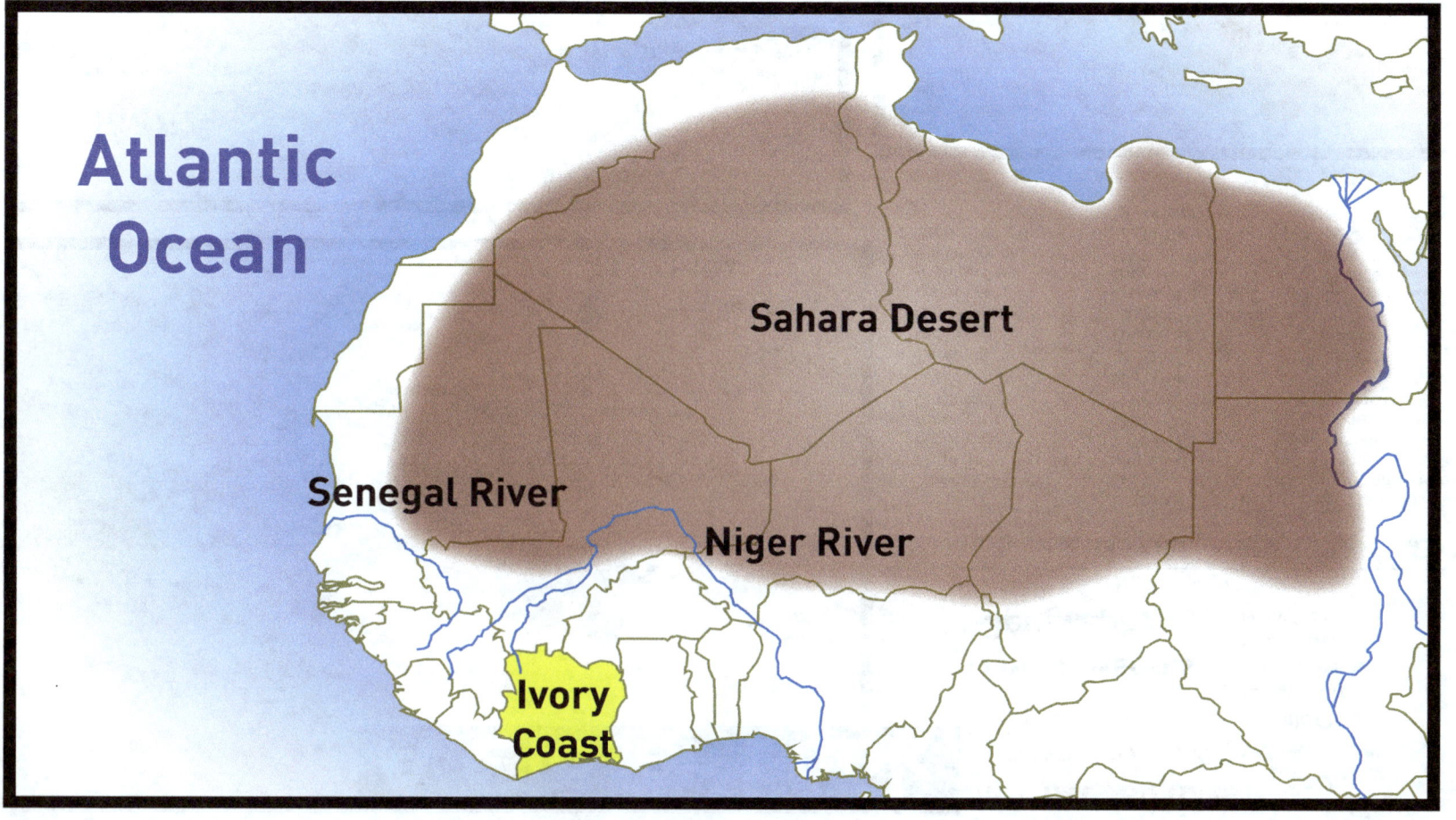

Lesson 13 Geography
Western Africa
Atlantic Ocean
Senegal River
Niger River
Sahara Desert
Ivory Coast

Tid-Bits

Muslim Empire is also Today, you are learning about parts of Western Africa. Let's begin with the Sénégal River. This river is 1,114 miles long and serves as the border between Sénégal, a country to the south of the river, and a nation to the north called Mauritania. The Roman author Pliny the Elder called it Bambotus, which came from a word meaning "hippopotamus." There must have been quite a few from his investigations while writing his Naturalis Historia!

The Senegal River flows through a tropical climate. It serves as the perfect habitat for animals native to this region, including the great white pelican, flamingo, zebra, giraffe, leopard, and banded white mongoose. Along this river is the most dangerous animal in Africa, and some say, the deadliest in the world. Now, you may think that it would be a lion, but you would be wrong. It is the Hippopotamus! Despite them looking rather friendly, these giant Hippos are highly aggressive and unpredictable. They kill more people than lions or crocodiles. Under Senegalese law, it is illegal to kill one except in self-defense. Adult male hippos can weigh about 3,300-pounds, with females reaching 2,800-pounds. Huge males can grow to 4,400-pounds, with some exceptionally enormous hippos reaching 5,800-pounds. Although they are large, they are fast. A hippo can gallop up to 19 miles an hour on land. In water, hippos aren't quite as quick. They do have webbed feet but are not very great swimmers, and they can't float. The hippo moves slowly and purposely in water and is rarely seen in deep water. The ears, eyes, and nose of hippos are high on its head. This allows them to be above the water while the rest of the body is underwater.

Senegal River in north western Africa. Image by Mariusz Prusaczyk from Pixabay

The next most dangerous is the Mosquito. This tiny, deadly insect carries a disease called Malaria, causing 1 out of every 10 deaths!

Now for the Niger River, it has an odd route! The Niger River is Western Africa's 3rd largest behind the Congo and the Nile at 2,600 miles long! It all begins at the Guinea Highlands, the starting point of the river's unusual route. Although its beginning point is only 150 miles from the Atlantic Ocean, it takes a long path in the opposite direction. Instead, it goes into the

Hippopotamus' in the Senegal River - Image by Brigitte from Pixabay

Aerial view to Niger river in Niamey Niger - By homocosmicos, Adobe Stock

Sahara Desert, then turns toward the Gulf of Guinea, then through several countries before entering the ocean.

The Sahara Desert is the world's largest desert that covers 3,630,000 square miles. It is comparable to the size of China and the United States! This desert has quite a few different types of typography. It comprises sand dunes, sand seas, gravel plains, stone plateaus, salt flats, dry valleys, mountains, rivers, streams, and oases. Land formations change regularly and are influenced by rain and wind. Most of the rivers and streams in the Sahara Desert are seasonal or intermittent, meaning they come and go based on the season's weather. The main exception is the Nile River, which crosses the desert from its origins in central Africa to empty into the Mediterranean.

There are about 20 lakes in the Sahara; all are saltwater, with one exception, Lake Chad is the only freshwater lake in the entire desert.

Some of the world's most extensive underground water supplies exist beneath the Sahara Desert, supporting about 90 major oases. Around two million people live in the Sahara Desert, primarily nomads, moving from place to place.

Many animals survive this harsh climate, including the northwest African cheetah, also known as the

Umm al-Ma Lake - Desert Oasis, Sahara, Libya
By Patrick Poendl - Adobe Stock

Caravan of camels making their way through the Sahara Desert - Image by Herbert Bieser from Pixabay

Saharan cheetah. When you think of deserts, you think of Camels. And you would be right, they are the leading animal in the desert. They have a great capacity to resist heat and thirst. Even above 122°F, they can stay without drinking water for many days. The camel is the favorite animal used by nomads. The second favorite animal for nomads is the goat. Animals living in the desert need to be like the Camal; some, like the addax, a large white antelope, can go nearly a year in the desert without drinking. Other animals include the gazelle, monitor lizards, deathstalker scorpions, sand vipers, hyrax, small populations of African wild dogs, red-necked ostrich, secretary birds, Nubian bustards, and various raptors. The dung beetle also resides in the Sahara. It served as a holy symbol to the ancient Egyptians, and it has some impressive adaptability.

Archaeological studies have uncovered dinosaur fossils and Saharan Rock Art, a treasure of carved or painted art on rocks from ancient times. There have been over three thousand sites found!

Daytime temperatures can reach 136°F, but freezing temperatures are not uncommon at night. In the Sahara, the temperature can become as low as 22°F.

This Saharan Cheetah is taking a rest under a tree and out of the sun. By Guntherize - Adobe Stock

African Wild Dog - Image by Pexels from Pixabay

African Hyrax-Image by Andreas Göllner from Pixabay

Herd of gazelles - By: Unknown/- Public Domain

Chad's ancient Ennedi cave paintings, Africa - By Torsten Pursche - Adobe Stock

The Ivory Coast nation was a French Colony until 1960. After its independence from France in 1960, the Ivory Coast was peaceful and prosperous for more than 30 years. But then fell into civil war in 2002. The agreement between the government and the rebels brought back peace to the country.

The Ivory Coast in West Africa is known for its chocolate. The country produces more cocoa than any other place in the world. In addition to chocolate, the Ivory Coast has bananas, pineapples, fish, coffee, lumber, cotton, palm oil, and petroleum. The life expectancy is 57 years, and only 47 percent of adults can read.

Ancient Africa
Ancient Ghana
Ancient Mali
Western Sahara
Fez
Tangier

Where in the World?

Lesson 14

A Closer Look at what you have learned so far!

Lesson 14

PLUS+ This Lesson's Geography

Ancient Africa
- Ancient Ghana
- Ancient Mali
- Western Sahara
- Fez
- Tangier

Previously Learned Geography — a TRUE REVIEW - 6 week review

Lesson 8
- Indus River
- Ganges River
- Himalayas
- Arabian Sea
- Bay of Bengal
- Great Indian Desert

Lesson 9
- China
- Mongolia
- Yellow Sea
- Yellow River
- Yangtze River
- Beijing

Lesson 10
- Japan
- Kyoto
- Tokyo
- Mt. Fuji
- Pacific Ocean
- Sea of Japan

Lesson 11
- Constantinople
- Rome
- Athens
- Ephesus
- Antioch

Lesson 12
- Mecca
- Medina
- Baghdad
- Damascus
- Tours
- Syria

Lesson 13
- Atlantic Ocean
- Senegal River
- Niger River
- Sahara Desert
- Ivory Coast

Hint: All geography found on this page, is also the geography that you will be reviewing this week. Refer to these maps as needed when doing your "Memorization Through Repetition" worksheets.

Parent/Teacher: The "A Closer Look" page is intended to show students the accumulated geographic areas taught within their 6-week review period plus new geography. For additional teaching tips on how to utilize this teaching aide for the different learning levels, please refer to page 1.

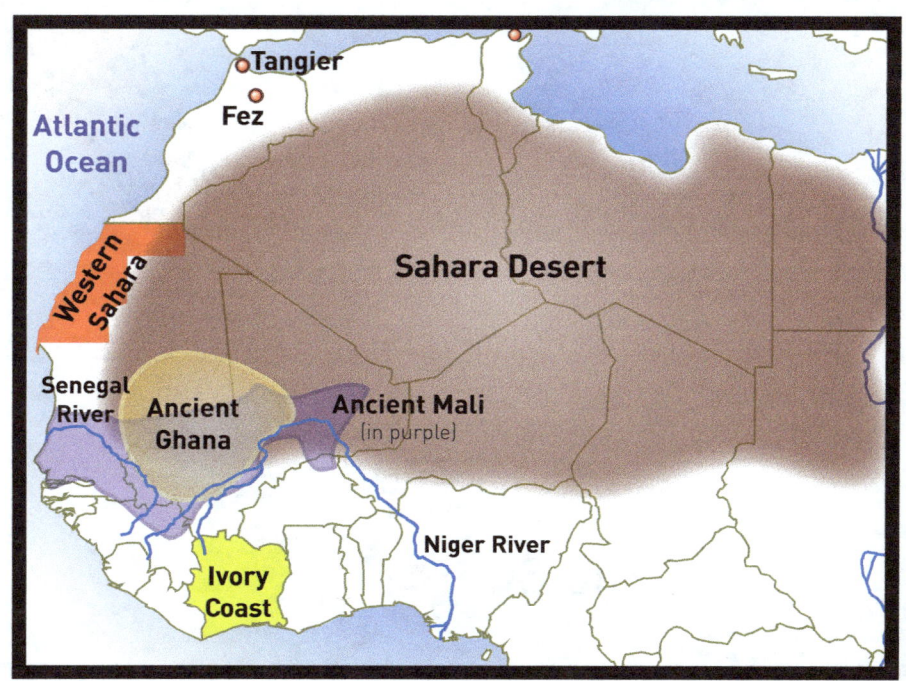

105

Lesson 14

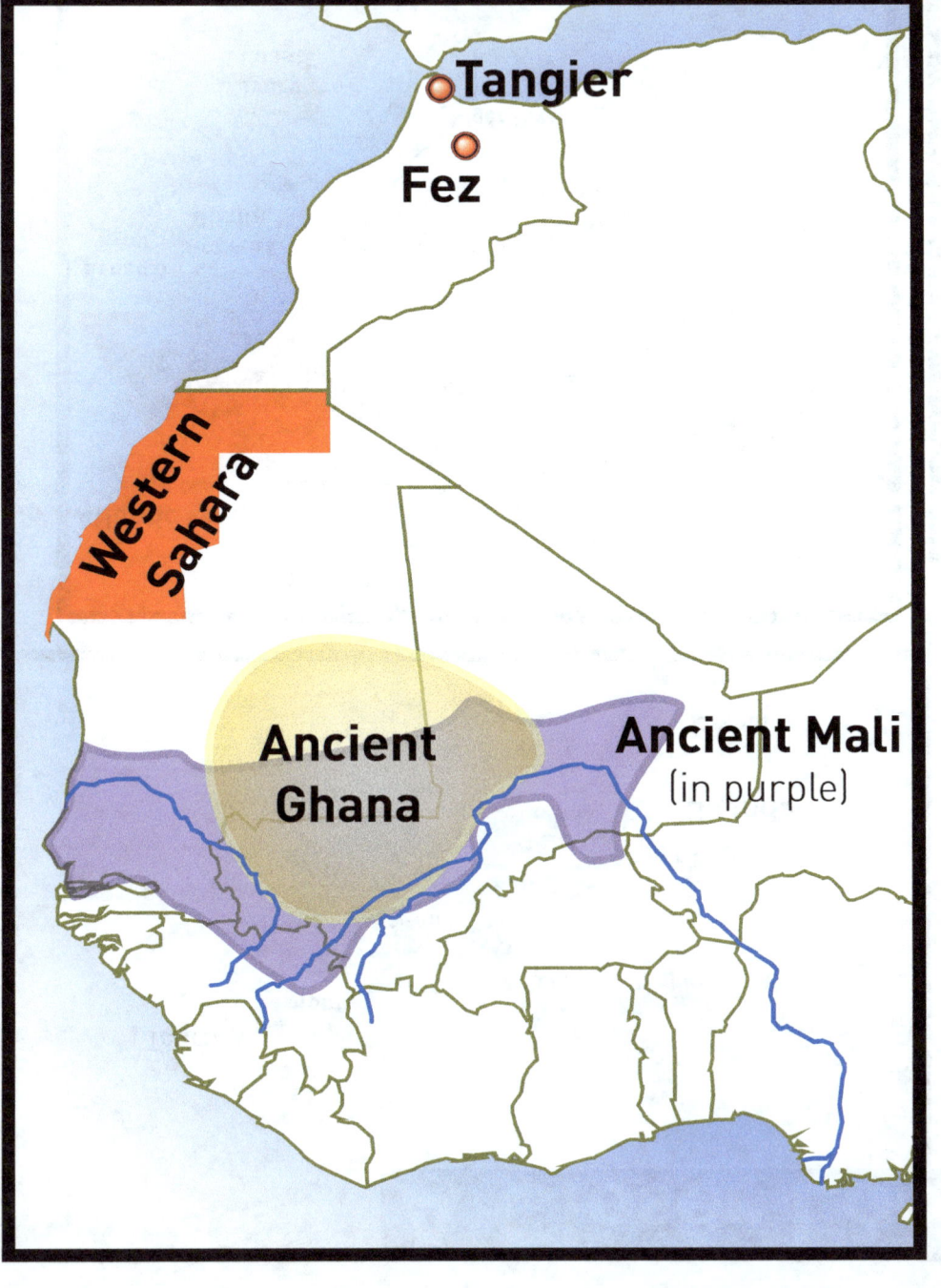

Zoom Me In!

**This Lesson's
Geography:**

Ancient Africa
Ancient Ghana
Ancient Mali
Western Sahara
Fez
Tangier

Use this sheet as
a reference for
this lesson's
"Now, let's trace,
shade & label"
worksheet.

Lesson 14 Geography
Ancient Africa
Ancient Ghana
Ancient Mali
Western Sahara
Fez
Tangier

Tid-Bits

Africa is a massive continent with diverse people, history, and culture. Although we can't cover everything, we will look at the Western African empires of Ghana and Mali and the area around the Sahara Desert.

The Ghana Empire flourished from 600-1200 AD in what is now Mauritania and Mali. However, after civil wars, drought, and significant gold mining and trading decline, the Ghana Empire fell. The Mali Empire then flourished, coming into much of the same territory and more. They reigned for over 400 years, from 1240-1645 AD.

The northern portion of the Ghana Empire was part of the great Sahara Desert, and in the south was rainforest. The Niger and Senegal Rivers were essential to life and trade. When the rivers flooded, it would bring forth necessary minerals from the river beds making the earth fertile for the Ghana people to grow the food they needed. In addition, the Ghana people depended on these rivers for fishing, freshwater for themselves and their animals, such as cattle and goats. The land was rich with natural deposits of gold, iron, copper, ivory, and more. The ancient Ghana people's wealth came primarily from the mining of iron and gold. The iron they used to fashion weapons Iron smiths were considered magicians, for they worked with fire and earth to create iron. Kings of the Ghana empire lived in the capital Koumbi Saleh. This region of Africa was the most significant producer of gold during the Middle Ages. In fact, Ghana became so famous for its gold that it was nicknamed "Land of Gold." And many from all over Europe and Asia would come to trade.

The Mali Empire was in modern-day Burkina Faso and Ghana. However, the empire was wealthier than the Ghana Empire. The most famous ruler was Mansa Musa, who ruled from 1312-1337. He converted to Islam while he was King. He even went on a pilgrimage to Mecca. On his way, he stopped in Cairo, Egypt, where he impressed everyone with his incredible wealth. Mansa Musa and his court spent so much money in Cairo that they impacted the Egyptian economy, taking more than twelve years to normalize.

There were many small tribes and cultural groups within the Mali Empire. People were divided into castes. One of the most revered castes was the farmers. Farmers were highly respected because they provided food. Just below the farmers were the artisans. Other groups included fishermen, scribes, civil servants, soldiers, and slaves.

The Sahara Desert had an incredible amount of salt. As mentioned, the Ghana & Mali Empire's land

Cave dwellings of Ancient Mali - By Unknown, Public Domain

Remnants of Ancient Ghana, By Unknown, Public Domain

Ancient Mali Mosque - By Unknown, Public Domain

Photo: Modern day Fez street where merchants sell their wares. Donkeys and mules are commonly used for transportation in the old city's maze of narrow streets that lead to bustling markets and bazaars. The architecture of the city has been preserved from the ancient days. Around Fez there are large walls, built to defend the medina against attacks, stretch 5 miles around the old city, where no motorized traffic is allowed. The medina is one of the largest urban areas in the world that bans cars.

except one. When these salt lakes dry up, the salt stays behind while the water has vaporized into the atmosphere. Thus, the salt was found in dried lake beds or shallow mines. It was a creamy-grey color and existed in slabs. If traveling by camel, each camel could carry two slabs, weighing 200 pounds each! These salt slabs would often end up at essential trading posts, which would be used to trade for gold, ivory, hides, copper, iron, and more. Thus, if an empire controlled the salt trade, they controlled the gold trade, and both would make the empire wealthy and powerful.

had much gold. These two products depended on one another. The camel transported salt through the hot Sahara Desert or was shipped by boat upon the Niger and Senegal Rivers to these ancient empires. Gold was used to buy salt, and salt was used to buy gold. Gold was a luxury item people used to make things beautiful and show off their wealth. Salt was an essential item because it preserved meat and made food taste better. They were both in high demand and still are today. Now, which would you rather, if you could only have one? Salt or gold?

Aren't the deserts filled with sand, not salt? Yes, that is correct, but as you have learned, all lakes found in the Sahara Desert are salt lakes,

Western Sahara is mainly desert with large flat rocky or sandy surfaces with small mountainous regions to the south and northeast. For this reason, the area was and is sparsely populated. The population consists of Arabs and Berbers. Agriculture consists of fruits and vegetables grown in the various oases and raising camels, sheep, and goats. Western Sahara also boasts rich fishing waters.

Fez - Its full name, Fez-el-Bali, was built towards the end of the eighth century. Built by the Muslim

View of Dakhla, a city of Western Sahara - By Cesare Palma

Dynasty of the Idrissids, the city sits on the banks of the Fez River. In 859 AD, the University of Karueein, as it is now called, was officially founded, giving Fez one of the oldest universities in the world. The city was designed using narrow winding alleyways, a complicated labyrinth to thwart invasions.

Tangier is believed to be founded by the Phoenicians. It was a free city under the Romans. It served as Morocco's largest seaport and commercial center until the founding of Fez in 808 AD. Tangier was captured by the Portuguese in 1471 and then transferred to England as part of the wedding payment called a "dowry" that Catherine of Braganza brought to Charles II. A bit more than 200 years later, the English abandoned the city to the Moroccans in 1684.

Fez has long been famous for its leather trade. Here, workers in one of Fez's tanneries transform animal skins into brightly-coloured leathers by soaking them in vats.

Tangier is a city in northwestern Morocco. It is on the Maghreb coast at the western entrance to the Strait of Gibraltar, where the Mediterranean Sea meets the Atlantic Ocean off Cape Spartel.

Where in the World?

Middle East
Israel
Sinai Peninsula
Suez Canal
Cairo
Gaza Strip

Lesson 15

A Closer Look at what you have learned so far!

Lesson 15

PLUS+ This Lesson's Geography

Middle East *(Modern Day)*
Israel
Sinai Peninsula
Suez Canal
Cairo
Gaza Strip

Previously Learned Geography a TRUE REVIEW - 6 week review

Lesson 9
China
Mongolia
Yellow Sea
Yellow River
Yangtze River
Beijing

Lesson 10
Japan
Kyoto
Tokyo
Mt. Fuji
Pacific Ocean
Sea of Japan

Lesson 11
Constantinople
Rome
Athens
Ephesus
Antioch

Lesson 12
Mecca
Medina
Baghdad
Damascus
Tours
Syria

Lesson 13
Atlantic Ocean
Senegal River
Niger River
Sahara Desert
Ivory Coast

Lesson 14
Ancient Ghana
Ancient Mali
Western Sahara
Fez
Tangier

Hint: All geography found on this page, is also the geography that you will be reviewing this week. Refer to these maps as needed when doing your "Memorization Through Repetition" worksheets.

Parent/Teacher: The "A Closer Look" page is intended to show students the accumulated geographic areas taught within their 6-week review period plus new geography. For additional teaching tips on how to utilize this teaching aide for the different learning levels, please refer to page 1.

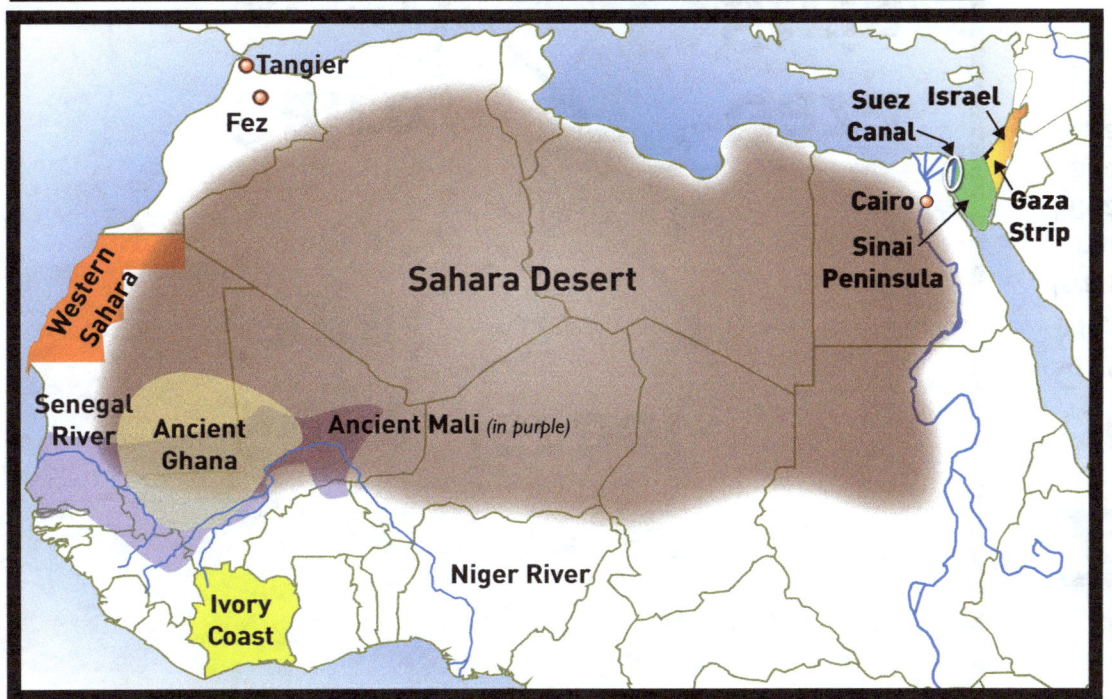

Lesson 15

Zoom Me In!

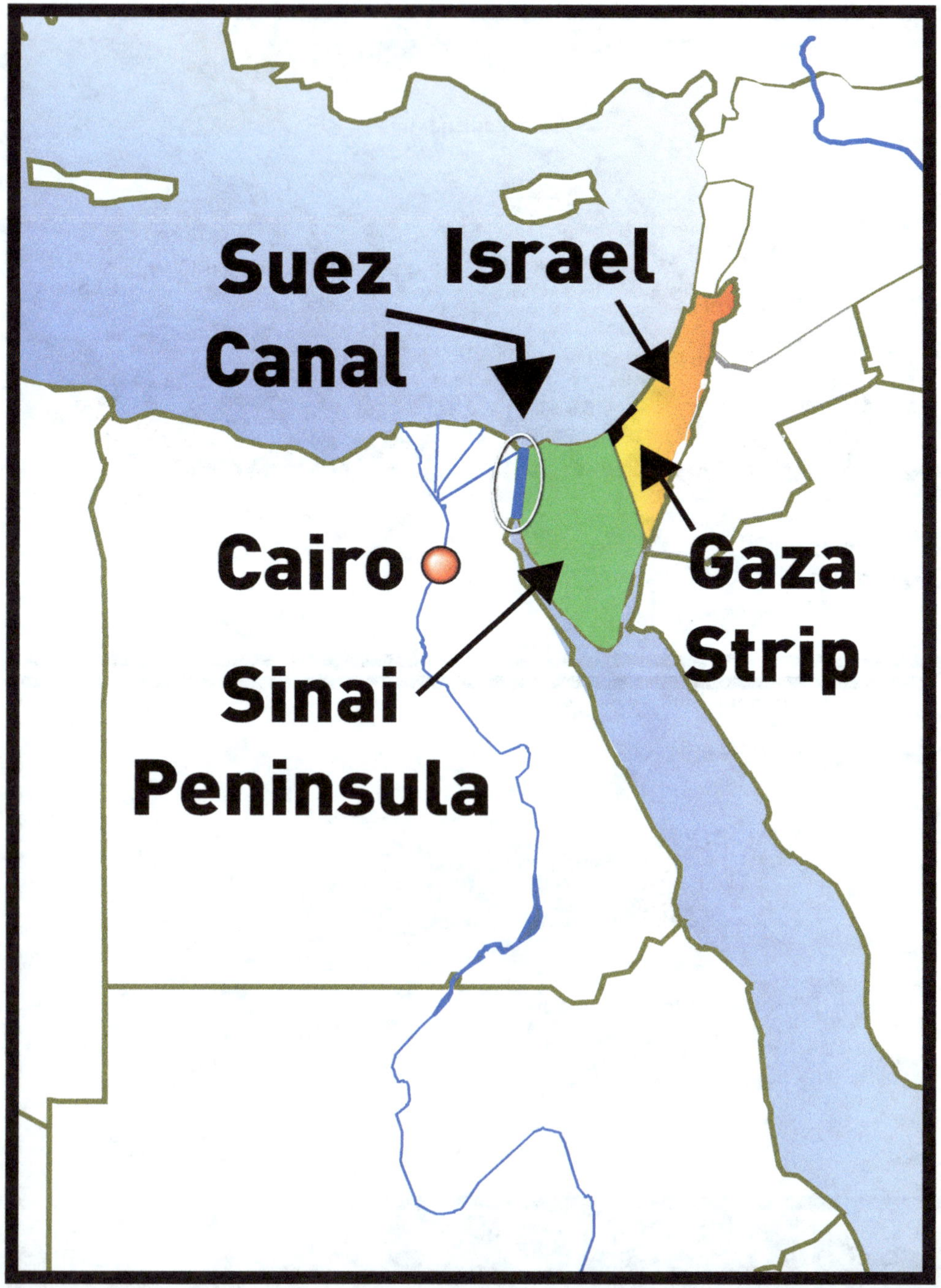

**This Lesson's
Geography**
Middle East *(Modern Day)*
Israel
Sinai Peninsula
Suez Canal
Cairo
Gaza Strip

**Suez
Canal**

Israel

Cairo

**Sinai
Peninsula**

**Gaza
Strip**

Use this sheet as
a reference for
this lesson's
"Now, let's trace,
shade & label"
worksheet.

Lesson 15 Geography
Middle East *(Modern-day)*
Israel
Sinai Peninsula
Suez Canal
Cairo
Gaza Strip

Tid-Bits

Modern-day Israel is home to the most Jewish people in all the world. There are two official languages, which are Hebrew and Arabic. Currently, Israel is relatively tiny. This country's land is 1/6 of 1% of all land in the Middle East, about half the size of Lake Michigan in the U.S., so I think, and tell me if you agree, Israel is a small place for 20 million people!

At the Olympic games, Israel has won five bronze medals, one silver, and one gold. If you ever visit Israel, you will have your pick of museums to explore, for there are more museums per person than any other country in the world. At the Waling Wall, which locally they call "Kotel," an estimated 1 million notes are left each year.

Ever want to go to the lowest point on earth? The Dead Sea in Israel is the lowest you can go at 1,315 feet below sea level. Because the Dead Sea is far below sea level, the water doesn't flow to the ocean, so when the water evaporates, it leaves behind salt. This salt has accumulated for thousands of years, making the Dead Sea about ten times saltier than the ocean. So going swimming in the Dead Sea must be a very different experience; for everyone that enters, floats!

Israel, Old Town & Rock Temple - Image by Walkerssk from Pixabay

The deeper you go down into the Dead Sea, the higher the salt, or salinity, the level becomes. Finally, at about 300 feet down, the salt becomes so thick, it begins to form crystals that fall to the seafloor.

The Dead Sea salt shoreline - By vvvita, Adobe Stock

Relaxation in the Dead Sea - Image by Ri Butov from Pixabay

A close up look at the Dead Sea salt shoreline as it glistens - Image by Gidon Pico from Pixabay

With such a high salt content, it is easy to understand why it is named the Dead Sea, for, upon the shores, there is no evidence of plant life, and within there are no fish or other sea life. Imagine standing at the edge of the Dead Sea. Do you think there would be a difference in the landscape around you than that of other lakes? If you say yes, you would be correct. No plants, no animals, just land covered in salt residues with formations that glitter in the sun.

But despite its barren appearance, this sea offers some surprises. Back in 2011, scientists went deeper into the Dead Sea than ever! There they discovered freshwater springs that were surrounded by colonies of tiny microbes. These tough microbes are called Dunaliella algae. They survive in the most severe environments and are known for their health benefits as they have high concentrations of beta-carotene, essential vitamins, and antioxidants. As mentioned, there is also much "life" on the surface of the Dead Sea, which on most days is dotted by bobbing swimmers. Although, scientists probably wouldn't consider that as "life" native to the Dead Sea!

Moving to the southwest, the Sinai Peninsula is about 23,000 square miles and is a part of NE Egypt, linking Africa and Asia. This peninsula is flat and sandy in the north, and then as you peer to the south, the Sinai rises in prominent ridges. Here the climate is scorching and dry and sparsely vegetated. However, evidence shows that there once was water flowing through the land, long abandoned now. This evidence may indicate that the region was once humid. Limestone quarrying and oil

TOP LEFT: White Canyon Sinai Peninsula, Egypt - By Kotangens, Adobe Stock. BOTTOM LEFT: View from Mount Sinai at sunrise. Beautiful mountain landscape in Egypt. By Anton Petrus - Adobe Stock. Sinai Peninsula as seen from outer space. Photo compliments of NASA

Suez Canal as seen from outter space. Photo compliments of NASA

Stranded Ships on the Suez Canal. By Unknown, Public Domain

Stranded Sailors playing football upon a ship marooned on the Suez Canal

drilling are the main economic activities; nomadic herding is practiced. "Jabal Musa" in Arabic means "Mount of Moses" or "Mt. Sinai." This peninsula is said to be the place where Moses received the Ten Commandments. It is also the site where, in 1844, one of the oldest manuscripts of the New Testament was found. Sinai was the scene of fighting during the Arab-Israeli Wars of 1956, 1967, and 1973. Israel occupied, then withdrew from the peninsula in 1956. In 1967, Israel again drove the Egyptians from Sinai, establishing a defense line along the Suez Canal. In the 1973 war, the Egyptian army crossed the Suez Canal and recaptured territory in the Sinai. Under the Camp David accords (1978) and Egyptian-Israeli peace treaty (1979), Israel returned Sinai to Egypt.

Along the west side of the Sinai Peninsula is the modern-day Suez Canal planning began in 1854 when a Frenchman negotiated an agreement with Egypt to form the Suez Canal Company (SCC). Building the Suez Canal required massive manpower. The Egyptian government initially supplied most labor by forcing the poor to work for nominal pay and under threat of violence. In 1861, tens of thousands of workers used picks and shovels to dig the canal by hand. The project slowed to a stop after Egypt banned the use of forced labor in 1863. In response, the SCC began using custom-made steam and coal-powered shovels and dredgers to dig the canal. This outstanding canal was the first of its kind, and it changed trade routes coming to and from Asia and Europe forever.

Many years later, a fleet of ships was stranded in the canal for more than eight years! During 1967's Six-Day War between Egypt and Israel, the Suez Canal was shut down by Egypt and blockaded on both sides. At the time of the closure, 15 international shipping vessels were moored at the canal's midpoint. They would remain stranded in the waterway for eight years, eventually earning the nickname the "Yellow Fleet" for the desert sands that caked their decks. The crews made the most of it by passing the time, forming a floating community, and hosting sporting and social events. As the years passed, the fleet even developed stamps and an internal system of trade. The 15 stranded

Inauguration celebration of the Suez Canal completion as depicted in this artist rendering. By Unknown, Public Domain

The caption on the artist rendering reads: "The Ishmus of Suez Maritime Canal: The cutting near Chalouf" By Unknown, Public Domain

ships were finally allowed to leave the canal in 1975. Unfortunately, only two vessels were still seaworthy enough to make the voyage under their power.

The city of Cairo in Egypt covers about 193 square miles with 22 million people. It is the largest city in all of Africa and the Middle East.

The Arabic name for Cairo is al-Qahirah, which means "the conqueror," "the vanquisher," or "the victorious." Today, Cairo is home to the only remaining ancient wonder of the world. The pyramids!

In Cairo, their week is a bit different than ours. Sunday is the first day of the workweek, and their weekend is Friday and Saturday. Lastly, the Nile runs through Cairo, and there are two large islands in the middle of the city.

Gaza Strip is a small piece of land made up of towns, villages, and farmland and sits on the Mediterranean. It is 25 miles long, 6 miles wide, and sits between Israel to the north and east with Egypt's Sinai Peninsula to the south. Gaza has been continuously inhabited for more than 3,000 years and was a crossroads of ancient civilizations. Unfortunately, this tiny strip of land is a hotbed of conflict. For four centuries, the Ottoman Empire ruled until it was briefly interrupted by France and Egypt. Then, during World War I, Britain took control of Gaza and the rest of Palestine. Then Egypt took control of the Strip during the 1948 Arab-Israeli war.

Gaza Strip, war and poverty ravaged country. Image by hosny salah from Pixabay

Gaza Strip flag – Image by hosny salah from Pixabay

The Strip's population tripled in 1948-49 when it absorbed about a quarter of the hundreds of thousands of Palestinian refugees displaced from areas that are now part of Israel.

Then in the 1967 war, Israel captured the Gaza Strip from Egypt.

In 2007 the Hamas Islamists took control of the Gaza Strip. In response to the Hamas control, Israel tightened the closure of its

borders with Gaza, curbing fuel supplies and limiting the movement of people because the Hamas Islamists fire rockets toward Israel. Although the Hamas Islamists have control, it is considered a Palestinian territory. About 1.5 million Palestinians live in Gaza; more than half are refugees from past wars with Israel. Gaza has one of the highest population densities and demographic growth rates in the world. Most Gazans live on less than $2 a day, and up to 80 percent are dependent on food aid.

**Cairo, Egypt on the Nile at sunset.
By Givaga, Adobe Stock**

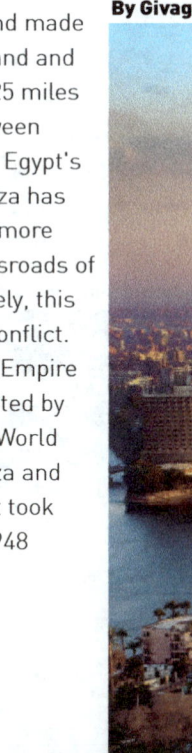

Where in the World?

Lesson 16

African Waters
- Congo River
- Lake Victoria
- Zambezi River
- Orange River

117

A Closer Look at what you have learned so far!

Lesson 16

PLUS+
This Lesson's Geography

African Waters
Congo River
Lake Victoria
Zambezi River
Orange River

Previously Learned Geography a TRUE REVIEW of the last 6 weeks.

Lesson 10
Japan
Kyoto
Tokyo
Mt. Fuji
Pacific Ocean
Sea of Japan

Lesson 11
Constantinople
Rome
Athens
Ephesus
Antioch

Lesson 12
Mecca
Medina
Baghdad
Damascus
Tours
Syria

Lesson 13
Atlantic Ocean
Senegal River
Niger River
Sahara Desert
Ivory Coast

Lesson 14
Ancient Ghana
Ancient Mali
Western Sahara
Fez
Tangier

Lesson 15
Israel
Sinai Peninsula
Suez Canal
Cairo
Gaza Strip

Hint: All geography found on this page, is also the geography that you will be reviewing this week. Refer to these maps as needed when doing your "Memorization Through Repetition" worksheets.

Parent/Teacher: The "A Closer Look" page is intended to show students the accumulated geographic areas taught within their 6-week review period plus new geography. For additional teaching tips on how to utilize this teaching aide for the different learning levels, please refer to page 1.

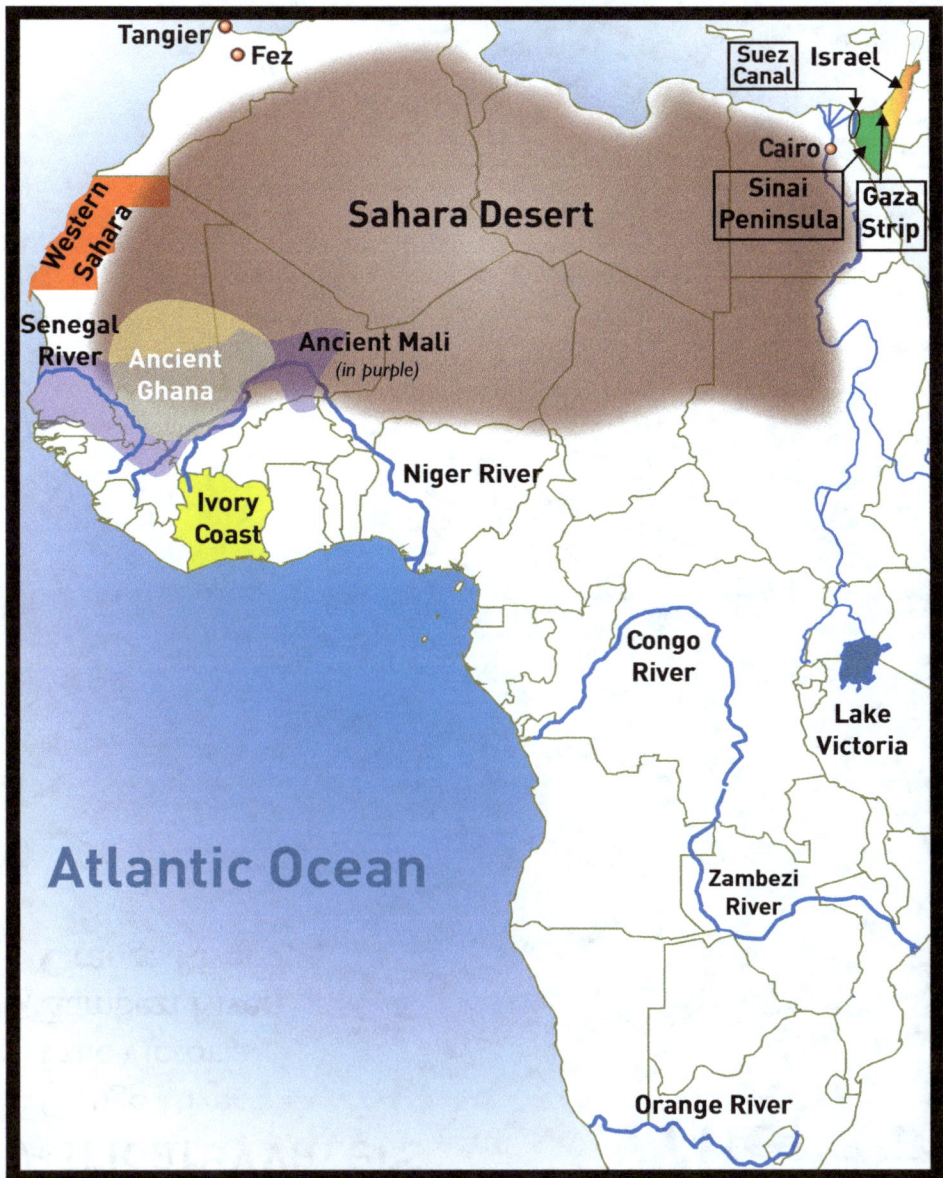

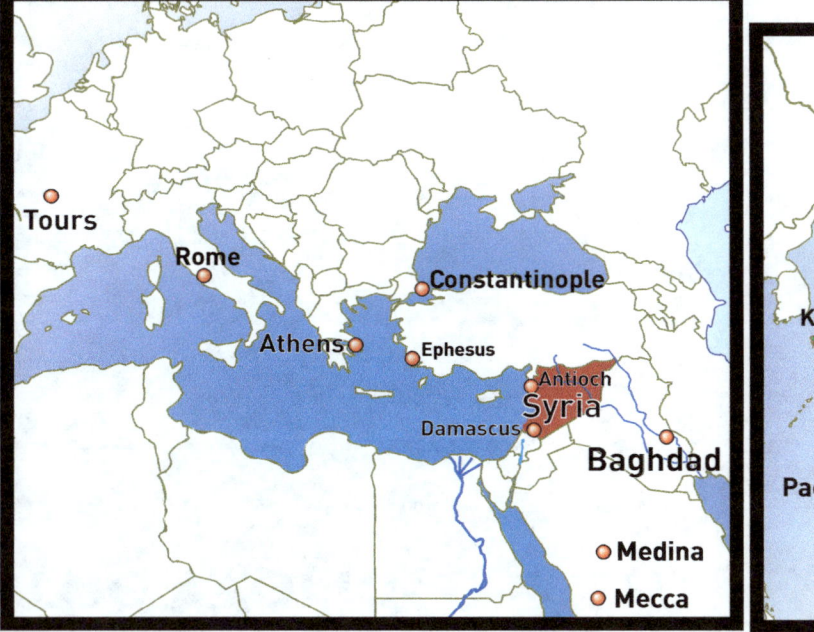

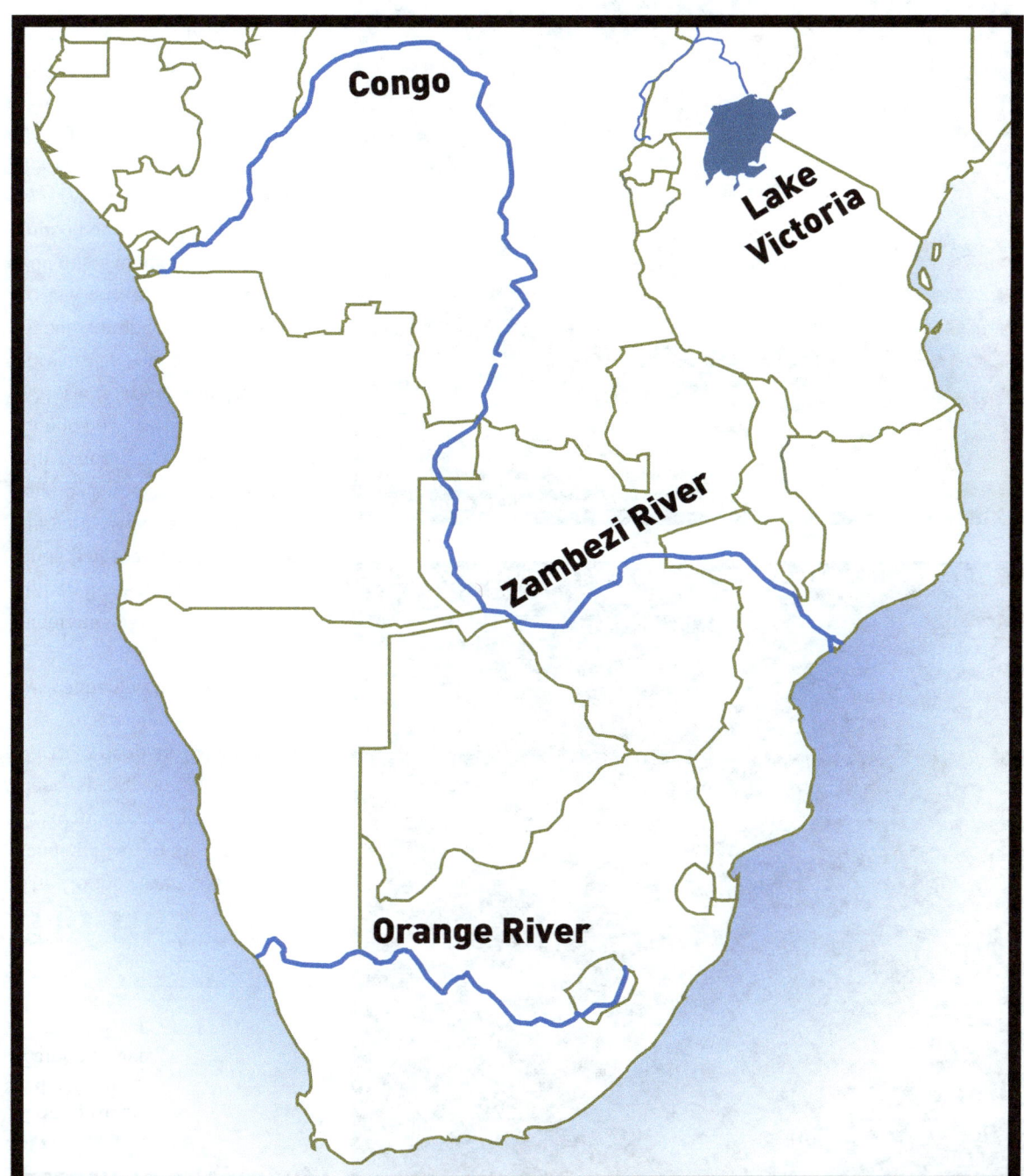

Lesson 16

Zoom Me In!

This Lesson's Geography
African Waters
Congo River
Lake Victoria
Zambezi River
Orange River

Use this sheet as a reference for this lesson's "Now, let's trace, shade & label" worksheet.

Lesson 16 Geography
African Waters
Congo River
Lake Victoria
Zambezi River
Orange River

Tid-Bits

The Congo River is the 9th longest river on the planet at 2,920 miles. It is also the deepest river on Earth, with parts as deep as 700 feet. It is the second-longest river in Africa, behind the Nile River. Beginning its journey in the highlands of northeast Zambia, it then flows north, then west, ending at the Atlantic Ocean at Banane. There are over 4,000 islands within the river, with over fifty that are ten miles long. The Congo has several breathtaking waterfalls, rough rapids, and three main tributaries: the Kasai, Sangha, and Ubangi Rivers. The rapids stretch over 200 miles long and have as much power as all waterfalls and rivers in the United States combined. The Congo River, once in each direction, crosses the equator twice.

The Congo is the financial artery that makes trade possible;

The Bonobo, also called the Pygmy Chimpanzee - Image by Sasin Tipchai from Pixabay

Elephants along the river. Image by Stephen Lawrence from Pixabay

there's no way into the heart of the Congo except by the river. Much of the Congo is impassible except by pirogues -- dugout canoes. And only the truly adventurous ever traverse certain parts of the river.

The river's environment, including the vast 1.3 million square mile river basin, serves as home to a wide variety of animals, including hippos, manatees, crocodiles, elephants, and at least 700 species of sea creatures. In addition, the Congo River basin contains about 1,000 species of birds. And some animals are only found here, which means that they are endemic. Some endemic animals include the Congo peafowl, dryas monkey, and bonobo. Additionally, it's home to more mammals, birds, and fish than any other part of Africa.

A woman from the Democratic Republic of Congo makes her way along the Congo River in her pirogue to trade her wares. Image by Tracy Angus-Hammond from Pixabay

East of the Congo river lies the source of the great Nile River, Lake Victoria. This is a vast lake located in east-central Africa along the equator and borders Uganda, Kenya, and Tanzania. It is Africa's largest lake, with a surface area of 26,600 square miles. It is considered a tropical freshwater lake. It is the largest of its kind globally and the second-largest freshwater lake measured by surface area. The only more enormous freshwater lake is Lake Superior in North America. This body of water is named after Queen Victoria of the United Kingdom. The average depth is 130 feet, with the deepest point being 276 feet. Approximately 80 percent of the lake's water comes from rain. The other 20 percent comes from small streams or tributaries that flow into the lake.

Lake Victoria - Image by valerossi from Pixabay

Zambezi River flows for 2,200 miles and is the fourth-longest river in Africa. Only the Nile, Congo, and Niger are longer. It begins in the wetlands of the Mwinilunga District of north-western Zambia, near the border where Zambia, Angola, and the Congo meet. As you can see on the map, the Zambezi comes very near the Congo!

There are several waterfalls on the Zambezi, including the breathtakingly impressive Victoria Falls, one of Africa's most popular sightseeing spots. Unfortunately, the river is frequently interrupted by rapids and has never been a means of long-distance travel.

Along the river, numerous animals can be found. At the water's edge, crocodiles and hippos are abundant. Large animals such as elephants, lions, zebras, giraffes, and buffalo can be found near the river in many areas. In addition, numerous birds can be spotted along the river, including pelicans, egrets, and African fish eagles.

Many fish species can be found in the river, including yellowfish, catfish, tigerfish, and cichlids. Additionally, bull sharks, which some call the Zambezi Sharks, typically live in coastal waters.

Aerial of Victoria Falls of the Zambezi River - By Michael, Adobe Stock

Lion cub near the Zambezi River. By Ignatius Tan - Adobe Stock

deposits on the Namibian coast. The first diamond discovered was in 1867, which lay beneath layers of silt and sand along the river's shore. There still exist diamond deposits along the final course and mouth of the Orange. The diamond zone is restricted since it is possible to find deposits of diamonds in the rich alluvial beds along this stretch. The rights of diamond mining lie with the government, which earns income from the sale of these precious stones.

Its waters are quiet and peaceful, which presents opportunities for water sports and leisurely canoe trips. Thankfully, it lacks dangerous water animals like crocodiles and hippos that inhabit other African rivers like the Nile. During months of sweltering temperatures, its water does not reach the sea. The Orange River's contribution to agriculture lies with the farmers for the use of its waters for irrigation and growth of citrus fruits, which do exceptionally well in the climate of the southern African region. They also cultivate grapes for export in various forms, including raw, dried, and processed for winemaking.

A beautiful landscape of a sunrise over the mountains and calm waters of the Orange River, in the Richtersveld National Park, South Africa. By Udo Kieslich, Adobe Stock

However, they have been known to swim very far up the Zambezi River. Watch out!

A tremendous source of hydroelectric power on the Zambezi is the Kariba Dam. At 420 feet high and 1,900 feet long, it is one of the largest dams in the world.

Moving southward, the Orange River is the longest in South Africa, at about 1,299 miles long. Its source comes from the Drakensburg Mountains in Lesotho, flowing westward through South Africa until it reaches the Atlantic Ocean. And the name... is the Orange River orange? Nope! The person who discovered the river, a Dutch navigator, named it in honor of the Dutch prince, William of Orange.

Just like ocean waves bring shells to the shore, guess what the Orange River deposits on its banks? Diamonds! For thousands of years, the river has made

A Closer Look

at what you have learned so far!

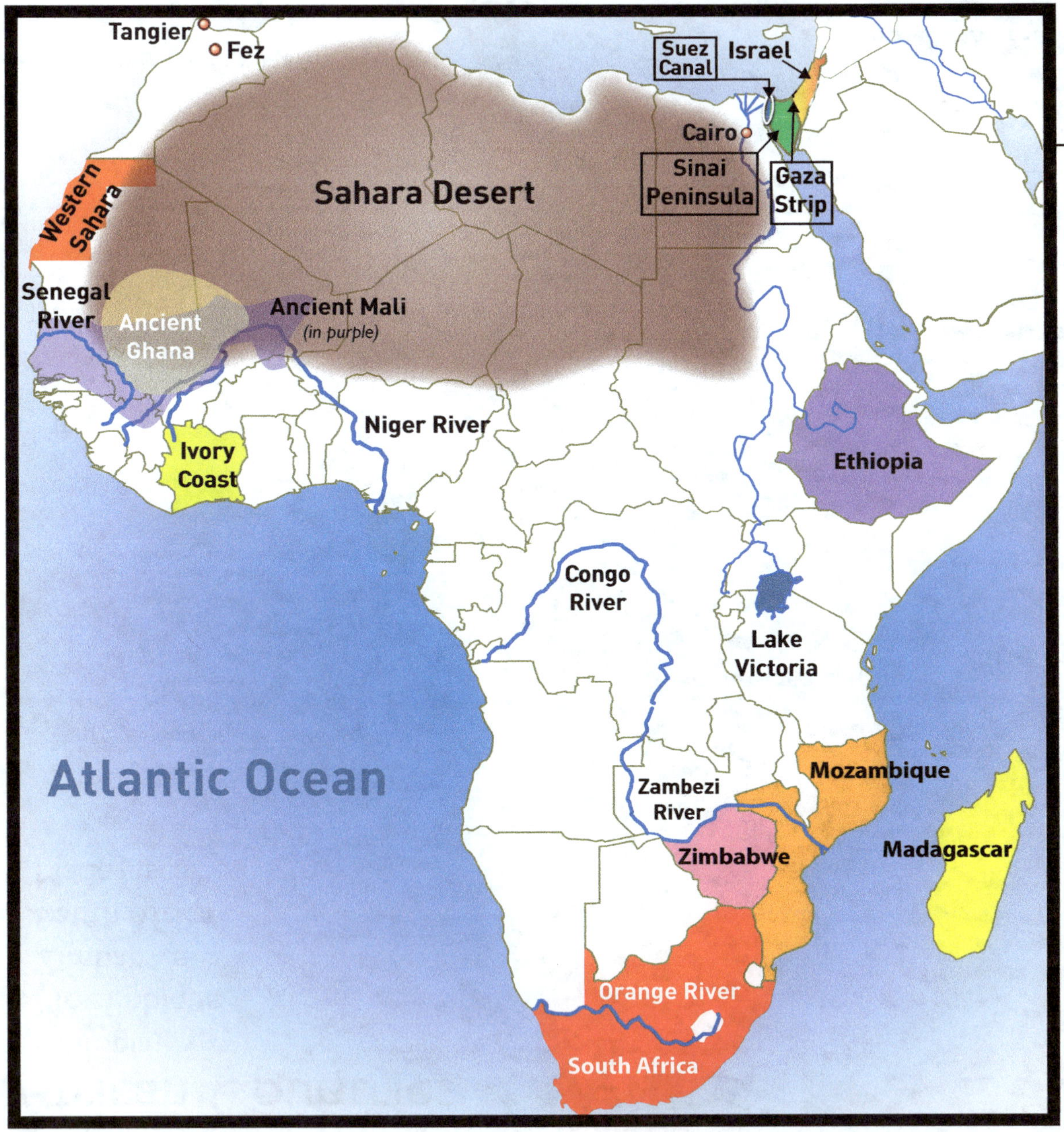

PLUS+

This Lesson's Geography

Lesson 17

African Countries

Ethiopia
Mozambique
Zimbabwe
South Africa
Madagascar

Hint: All geography found on this page, is also the geography that you will be reviewing this week. Refer to these maps as needed when doing your "Memorization Through Repetition" worksheets.

Previously Learned Geography
TRUE REVIEW of the last 6 weeks.

Lesson 11
Constantinople
Rome
Athens
Ephesus
Antioch

Lesson 13
Atlantic Ocean
Senegal River
Niger River
Sahara Desert
Ivory Coast

Lesson 15
Israel
Sinai Peninsula
Suez Canal
Cairo
Gaza Strip

Lesson 12
Mecca
Medina
Baghdad
Damascus
Tours
Syria

Lesson 14
Ancient Ghana
Ancient Mali
Western Sahara
Fez
Tangier

Lesson 16
Congo River
Lake Victoria
Zambezi River
Orange River

Parent/Teacher: The "A Closer Look" page is intended to show students the accumulated geographic areas taught within their 6-week review period plus new geography. For additional teaching tips on how to utilize this teaching aide for the different learning levels, please refer to page 1.

Tangier
Fez
Suez Canal
Israel
Cairo
Sinai Peninsula
Gaza Strip
Sahara Desert
Western Sahara
Senegal River
Ancient Ghana
Ancient Mali *(in purple)*
Ivory Coast
Niger River
Ethiopia
Congo River
Lake Victoria
Atlantic Ocean
Zambezi River
Mozambique
Zimbabwe
Madagascar
Orange River
South Africa

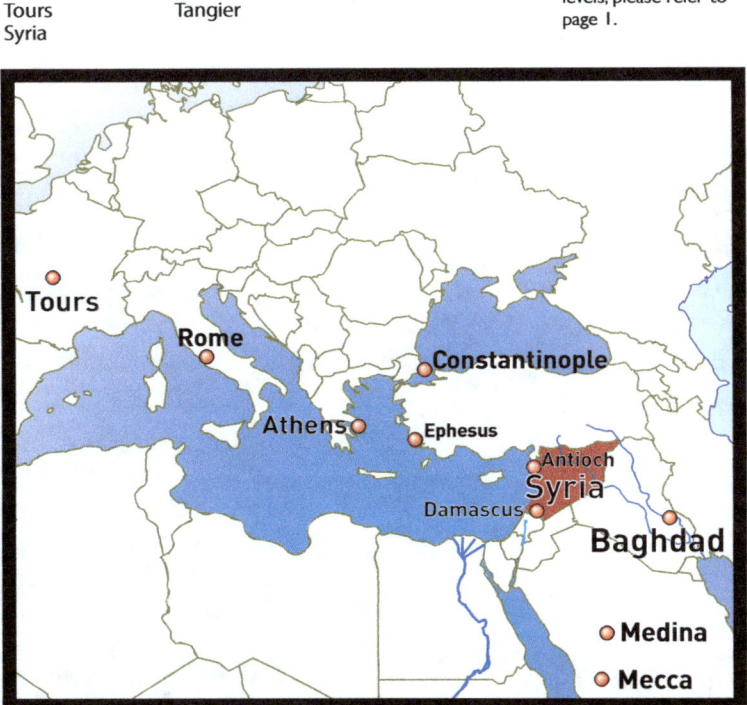

Tours
Rome
Constantinople
Athens
Ephesus
Antioch
Syria
Damascus
Baghdad
Medina
Mecca

Lesson 17

Zoom Me In!

This Lesson's Geography:

African Countries
Ethiopia
Mozambique
Zimbabwe
South Africa
Madagascar

Use this sheet as a reference for this lesson's "Now, let's trace, shade & label" worksheet.

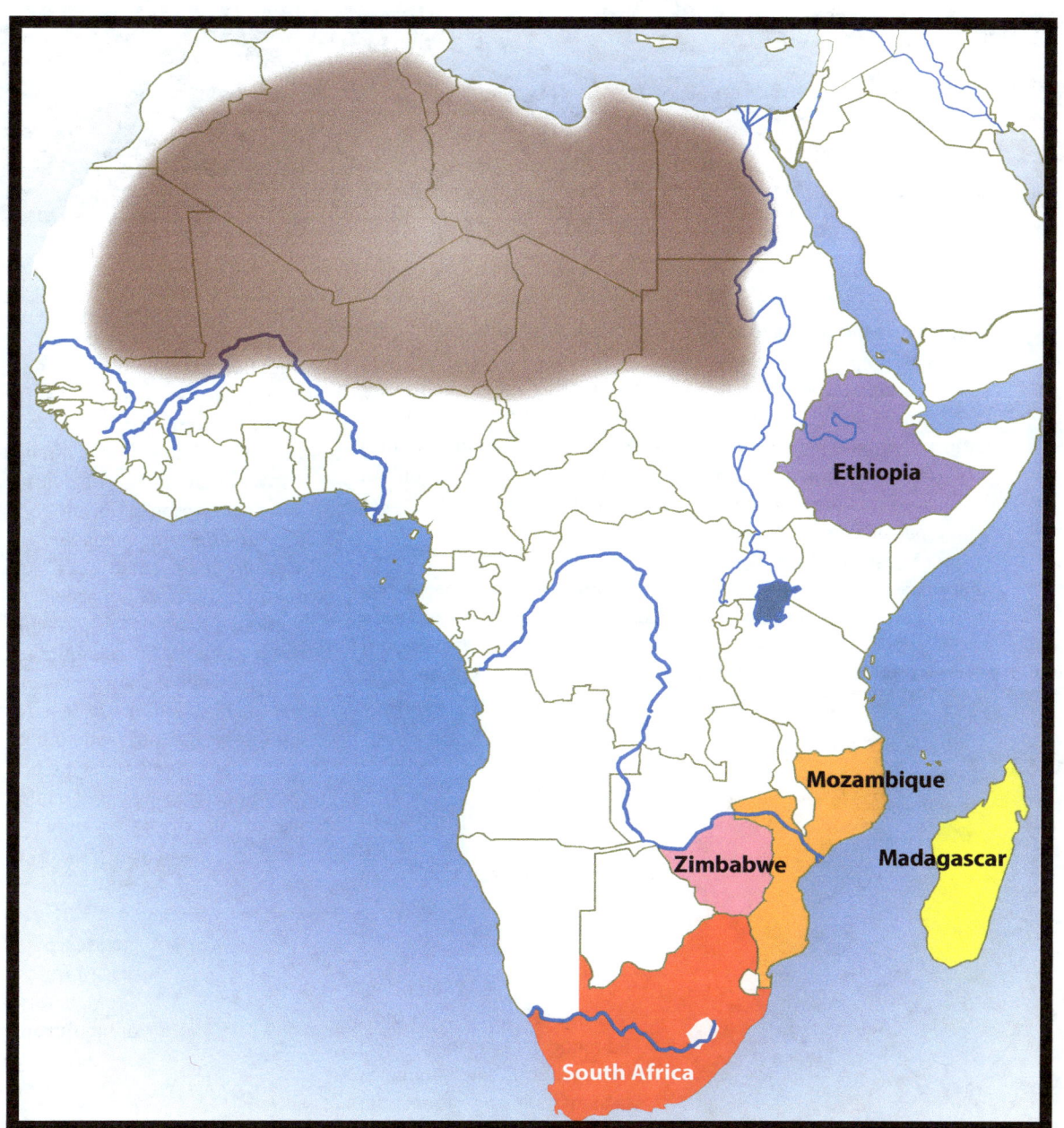

Lesson 17 Geography
African Countries
Ethiopia
Mozambique
Zimbabwe
South Africa
Madagascar

Tid-Bits

Ethiopia is 426,373 square miles, which makes it approximately as big as Spain and France, combined! The capital is Addis Ababa, which means "new flower." Ethiopia has a lot of mountains. In fact, more than 70% of the continent's mountains are found here. In Ethiopia, there is a place called Danakil Depression. The Danakil Depression is bordered by the Ethiopian Plateau on the west. To the east lies the Danakil Alps, beyond which is the Red Sea. This place is the lowest point on the African continent and the hottest place on Earth. While this area is not the friendliest, it attracts many visitors looking to experience an out-of-this-world landscape. Salt flats, active volcanoes, hot springs, and crater lakes of lava bubbling from the Earth's mantle are found here!

Here in Ethiopia lies the Great Rift Valley, which can be seen from outer space! This most distinct physical detail cuts through Ethiopia from the northeast to the south of the country.

In Ethiopia, there are more than 80 different ethnic groups. Among these groups, there are even more languages with over 200 dialects spoken in the country.

The Church of St. Mary of Zion in the holy northern city of Axum in Ethiopia claims to hold possession of the Ark of the Covenant. According to the Old Testament, The Ark of the Covenant is a large, gold-covered wooden chest that keeps Moses' Ten Commandments. It also served

Dallol, Danakil Depression, Ethiopia – By Cristina, Adobe Stock

as the place of the presence of God. It was held at the Temple of Solomon in Jerusalem for centuries, then vanished after Jerusalem was sacked. Since then, the Ark's location has remained unknown. Rumors of its whereabouts include being stolen by the Knights Templar, hidden in a rebuilt French cathedral, and buried alongside Alexander the Great in Greece.

The Ethiopia Meskel celebration is an annual religious holiday in the Ethiopian Orthodox church. It commemorates the discovery of the True Cross upon which Jesus was crucified by the Romans. In the 4th century BC, the legend goes that the Roman Empress Helena received a vision in a dream telling her where to find the cross. So she ordered the people of Jerusalem to collect wood, and the smoke from a colossal bonfire apparently indicated the location where the cross was buried. It is believed that a piece of the cross that Saint Helena discovered was brought to Ethiopia and is located somewhere in the mountains of Amba Geshen.

Ethiopia follows the Julian calendar of 12 months of 30 days each plus a 13th month of 5 or 6 days. Thus, it is roughly 7 and a half years

Erta Ale volcano crater, lava lake, Danakil Depression, Ethiopia, By homocosmicos, Adobe Stock

The Ethiopia Meskel Celebration, Ethiopia

behind the Gregorian calendar, which we follow.

The Ethiopian new year begins on September 11th and on September 12th in leap years. As with many countries that fall along the Earth's equator, the sun dictates time in Ethiopia. The sunrise marks the beginning of the day, and the sunset marks the end of the day. Interestingly, what most of the world would call 7:00, Ethiopians call 1:00. Both noon and midnight are 6:00 in Ethiopia.

Coffee, one of the world's most popular beverages, was discovered in Ethiopia, in the region of Kaffa. But, I wonder, could that be pronounced, café?

Ethiopia is the home of the Black Jews, known as the Falashas, or Beta Israel. Ethiopia adopted Christianity in the 4th century, making it one of the oldest Christian nations in the world.

Moving southward, the Republic of Mozambique was a Portuguese colony for nearly 500 years, known for crops such as cashew nuts, which are really seeds of the cashew fruit! Additionally, they grow cassava, and all sorts of spices, from chili to garlic.

Mozambique was torn by a civil war that lasted for 16 years after achieving its independence from Portugal in 1975. Finally, in 1992 the fighting ceased. Mozambique is a poor country, with half of the people living on less than $1 a day.

Maputo, the capital, is a vibrant city with a population of 1.5 million. It has white sandy beaches that run for 1,500 miles and features islands and coral reefs where over 1,200 species of fish can be found.

Maputo Elephant Reserve is home to a herd of more than 400 elephants! Here they live protected and enjoy a home with lakes, wetlands, swamp forests, grasslands, and mangrove forests.

Zimbabwe is rich in fantastic nature views with its picturesque African landscape. Victoria Falls in Zimbabwe is considered one of the world's wonders (pictured in Lesson 16). There are also breathtaking views of the highland mountains, tropical evergreen, hardwood forests, and rivers. Trees include teak and mahogany, knobthorn, msasa, and baobab.

The Great Zimbabwe Ruins are an impressive set of stone complexes built between the 13th and 15th centuries when the ancient Kingdom of Munumatapa existed.

Education is essential to the Zimbabweans with the highest literacy rate in Africa at 90% of the population. Sadly, many Zimbabweans survive on just one meal a day. Relief agencies say 25% of Zimbabweans require food aid.

Interestingly, it is believed that Zimbabwe was once home to a place called Ophir. An ancient country full of wealth from which King Solomon gain his ivory, gold, and other precious items.

Each culture defines what "beautiful" is from a social

Mozambique grown spices being sold at market - Image by teresa cotrim from Pixabay

Maputo Elephant Reserve is home to a hard of more than 400 elephants - Image by anujohanna from Pixabay

standpoint. For the Zimbabweans, a big stomach among men is a sign of wealth. It implies that they can afford meat daily. This is an attractive feature!

The primary grain for consumption is maize, although millet and sorghum are the principal grains in parts of the Zambezi Valley. After grinding, the flour is cooked into a thick porridge eaten with green vegetables or meat. A wide range of green vegetables are grown in kitchen gardens and collected wild. They generally are prepared with onion and tomato and sometimes with groundnut (peanut) sauce. Bread can be a staple in their diet if you live in an urban area. But for those that live in rural areas, it isn't as important.

Foods that are eaten seasonally include milk, boiled or roasted groundnuts, boiled or roasted maize, fruits, termites, and caterpillars.

Moving to the tip of the African continent, South Africa! The South Africans love their sports. Namely, soccer, cricket, and rugby. In fact, South Africa is the only country in the world to have hosted the Soccer, Cricket, and Rugby World Cup!

South Africa carries the dubious title of being home to the Cape Floral Region. Situated at the tip of Africa, this majestic, floral kingdom is the only one to be fully contained within a single country. Incredibly, it has the highest known concentration of plant species in the world. Its nearest rival, the South American rain forest, has only one-third the number of species. Even more remarkable is that 70 percent of the Cape's impressive 9,600 plant species grow

Cape Town Stadium in South Africa where the world cup is played. Image by falco from Pixabay

nowhere else on Earth.

South Africa has an incredibly varied terrain. It has deserts, wetlands, grasslands, bush, subtropical forests, mountains, and escarpments. Very diverse!

South Africa is extremely rich in mining and minerals. It is considered the world's leader with nearly 90% of all the platinum metals on Earth and around 41% of all the world's Gold!

Rounding the southern tip of South Africa was a noteworthy feat during the Age of Discovery. So many were searching for the East Indies, and back then, there was no Suez Canal that they could cut through! So many ships in search of trade would make the brave and treacherous trips down the west side of Africa to then head east in their adventure, that is, if they made it. More than 2,000 shipwrecks off the South African coast, most dating back at least 500 years.

The Karoo region in the Western Cape is home to some of the best fossils of early dinosaurs. In fact, it is estimated that some 80% of the mammalian fossils found to date were found in the Karoo.

Madagascar is the fourth largest island in the world, approximately 226,642 square miles. The only larger islands are Borneo, Greenland, and New Guinea.

Almost all of the plant and animal species found on Madagascar are unique to the island. There are two seasons: a dry, cooler season that starts in May and ends in October - then a hot, rainy season begins in November and lasts until April.

Zimbabwe's savanna grasslands, Image by Mike Wall from Pixabay

The population of Madagascar is 21,290,000 and is one of the poorest countries in Africa. The people in this territory face many problems, including poor health care, a flawed educational system, economic issues, and malnutrition.

Of the people, 52% maintain their indigenous religious beliefs, with 41% Christian and 7% Islam. Madagascar has two official languages, the first is French, and the second is Malagasy. Madagascar was under French rule from 1895-1957.

The ecological diversity of Madagascar has led some ecologists to refer to Madagascar as the "eighth continent." In 2010 this island was classified by Conservation International as a biodiversity hotspot. More than 85% of Madagascar's 13,900 plant species are found nowhere else in the world. For example, there are around 170 palm species. A lot of those native plant species are used as herbal remedies for a variety of afflictions.

Madagascar is well known for its unique style of wood carving! The art has a distinct regional style evident in the architectural elements. Sculptors create balcony railings, different household goods, furniture, and wooden sculptures in this art style.

ABOVE: Baobob trees in Madagascar.
By Unknown, Public Domain

LEFT: Madagascar style wood carving.
By Unknown, Public Domain

Women walking along the coast in Madagascar - Image by aga2rk from Pixabay

Ancient Mesoamerica Regions   Where in the World?   Lesson 18

Gulf of Mexico
Yucatan Peninsula
Olmec Civilization
Maya Civilization
Aztec Civilization

A Closer Look
at what you have learned so far!
PLUS+ This Lesson's Geography:

Lesson 18

Ancient Mesoamerica Regions
Gulf of Mexico
Yucatan Peninsula
Olmec Civilization
Maya Civilization
Aztec Civilization

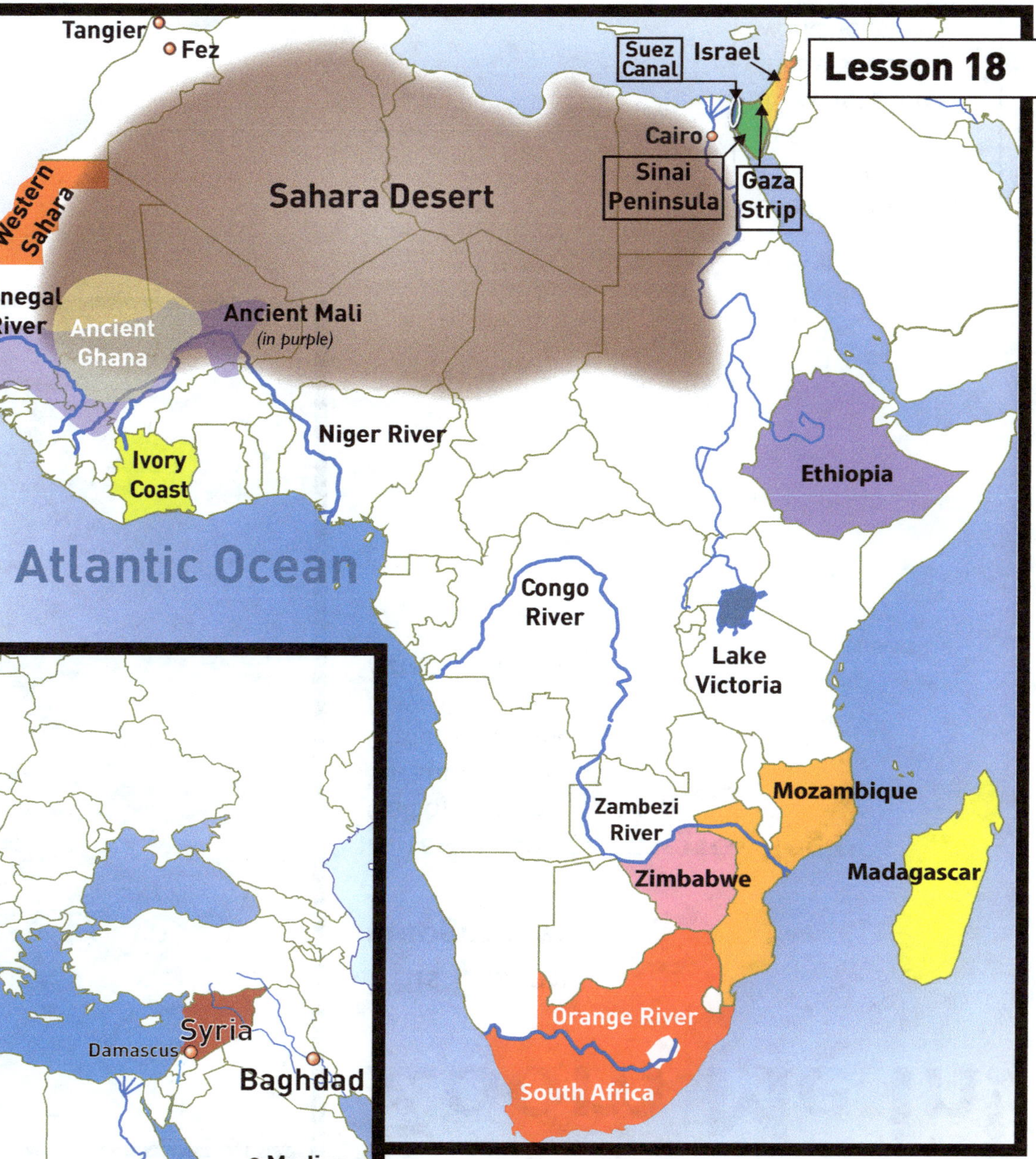

Previously Learned Geography
TRUE REVIEW
of the last 6 weeks.

Lesson 12
Mecca
Medina
Baghdad
Damascus
Tours
Syria

Lesson 13
Atlantic Ocean
Senegal River
Niger River
Sahara Desert
Ivory Coast

Lesson 14
Ancient Ghana
Ancient Mali
Western Sahara
Fez
Tangier

Lesson 15
Israel
Sinai Peninsula
Suez Canal
Cairo
Gaza Strip

Lesson 16
Congo River
Lake Victoria
Zambezi River
Orange River

Lesson 17
Ethiopia
Mozambique
Zimbabwe
South Africa
Madagascar

131

Lesson 18

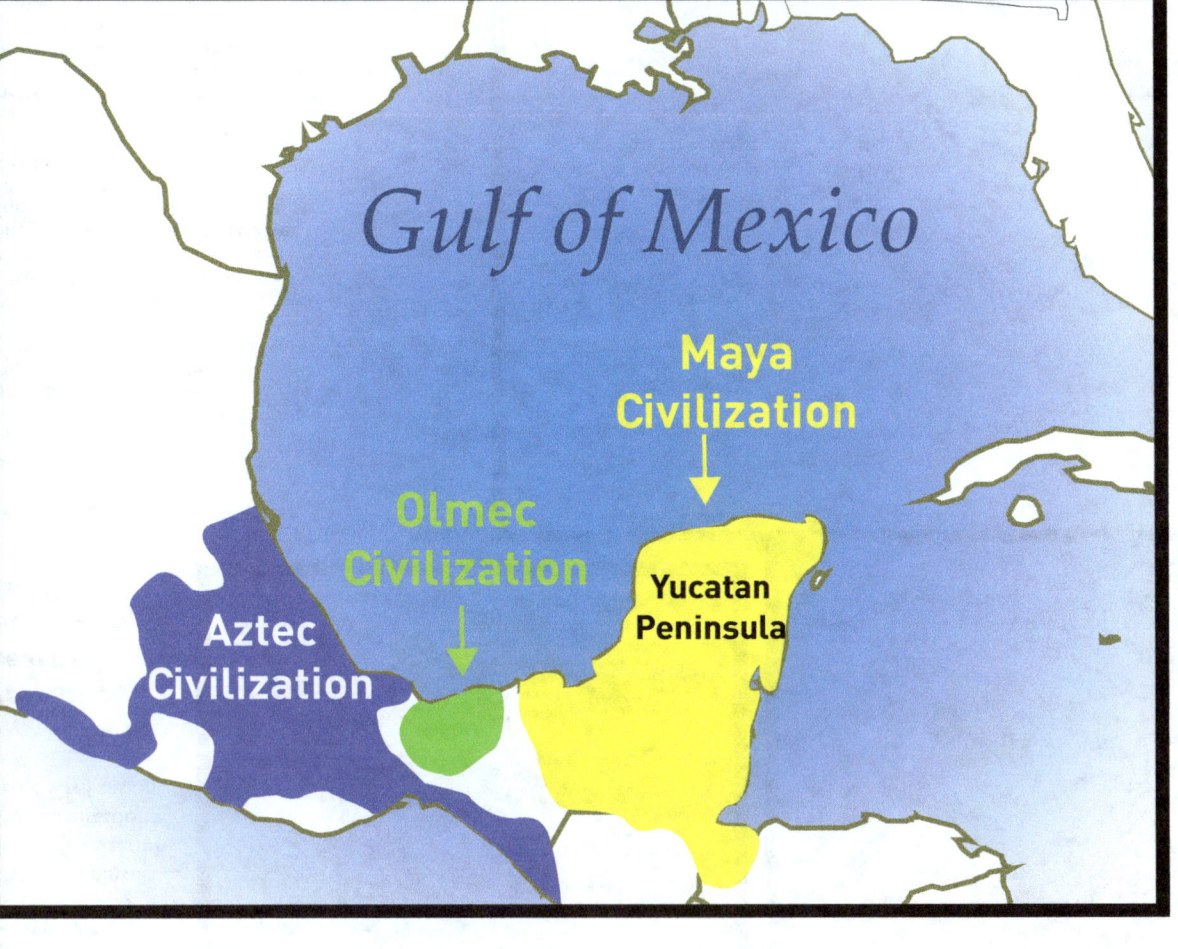

Zoom Me In!

This Lesson's Geography:

Ancient Mesoamerica Regions
Gulf of Mexico
Yucatan Peninsula
Olmec Civilization
Maya Civilization
Aztec Civilization

Use this sheet as a reference for this lesson's "Now, let's trace, shade & label" worksheet.

Lesson 18 Geography
Ancient Mesoamerica Regions
Gulf of Mexico
Yucatan Peninsula
Olmec Civilization
Maya Civilization
Aztec Civilization

Tid-Bits

Today, you are learning about ancient Mesoamerica! Let's begin with a large body of water north of Mesoamerica and south of North America, the Gulf of Mexico, the ninth-largest body of water on the planet at 600,000 square miles. The coastline measures approximately 3,540 miles from the tip of Florida to the tip of the Yucatan Peninsula. And let's not forget about Cuba with its 236 miles of additional coastline. This area supports some of the largest fisheries in the world.

These waters and the bordering coastline of North America and Cuba have an astonishing diversity of animals. There are 29 marine mammal species in the Gulf of Mexico, including the bottlenose dolphins, humpback whales, sperm whales, minke whales, and the West Indian manatee.

The coasts off the Gulf offer a range of habitats, including submerged vegetation and over 5 million acres of wetlands.

Bottle nose Dolphin - By Bernard Beaussier, Adobe Stock

The waters within the Gulf of Mexico are surprisingly shallow along the continental shelf. However, it contains a trough called 'Sigsbee Deep' that measures down 14,383 feet, which is almost 3 miles deep! The Gulf Stream, originating in the warm waters of the Gulf of Mexico, is one of the strongest ocean currents in the world.

The first European exploration of the Gulf of Mexico was by Amerigo Vespucci in 1497. In fact, the North and South American continents were named for him.

The Yucatán Peninsula is about 70,000 square miles and separates the Caribbean Sea from the Gulf of Mexico. The people that live here on the peninsula are primarily descendants of the great ancient Mayan Civilization.

This land is mainly flat, heavy in limestone, rising to about 500 feet in the south. The plain continues north and west, stretching under the shallow Gulf of Mexico water for about 150 miles from the low, sandy shoreline. In the north, rainfall is light and is absorbed by the porous limestone. Water for people and their livestock comes from underground rivers and wells. It is often pumped by windmills, surface pools (aguadas), or natural water-filled sinkholes (cenotes). The land has tropical, dry, and rainy seasons, but generally, the climate is hot and dry in the north and in the south hot and humid.

RIGHT: A Cenote on the Yucatan Peninsula - Image by Emilian Danaila from Pixabay

Gulf of Mexico - Image by Jan Haerer from Pixabay

Additionally, each year the Yucatan becomes a target for hurricanes. It is hurricane season, from June to November. However, the most significant risk of encountering a hurricane is between August and October.

Magnificent forests of tropical hardwoods provide the basis for a lumber industry here on the Yucatan, and among the woods and beyond, the land teems with tropical life, including the jaguar, the armadillo, the iguana, and the Yucatán turkey. In addition, fishing is an important industry along the Yucatán coast.

The Olmec civilization was sophisticated and reigned in Mesoamerica for 1,000 years before the Aztecs. There were pre-Olmec cultures in the region; however, the Olmecs have been referred to as the "cultura madre," meaning the 'mother culture,' of Central America.

The Olmec civilization thrived roughly between 1200 BC and 400 BC. The Olmecs left behind much of their artwork. The most famous of these are the 'colossal heads,' which were carved from basalt boulders. Seventeen 'colossal heads' have been found measuring between 3.28 feet and 9.8 feet tall.

By 400 BC, the Olmecs vanished, the cause of which remains a mystery.

Olmec Civilization "colossal head," By Zbiq, Adobe Stock

The ancient Mayan civilization is well known for developing its own written language, style of architecture, mathematical and astronomical systems, and the Mayan calendar.

As mentioned, the descendants of the Mayan Civilization still exist in the region. While most have adopted modern culture, some celebrate their traditional heritage by speaking the Mayan language.

The Mayan architecture is a marvel! It is considered to be one of the most sophisticated of ancient architecture. They built massive temples, sculptures, and stone pyramids.

Ancient Mayan children were named based on the calendar.

Each day in the Mayan calendar had a different name for both boys and girls.

Beauty, as with all cultures, was important to the Mayans.

Ancient Mayan Calendar, By Unknown, Public Domain

Although their standard of beauty is different than ours. Their idea of beauty included a long head. To accomplish this, they would press a board on a baby's head to create a flat forehead and bind the rest of the head in a basket to shape it properly. In addition, they preferred women that were cross-eyed. Lastly, the Mayans loved a long nose. Some would even attach clay extensions to make their noses seem larger.

Mayans had a bright smile, quite literally! They would insert precious gemstones into their teeth as it was considered fashionable for people of all classes. This was done by hand drilling a hole in a tooth, inserting the gem, and setting it with natural glue.

The Aztecs were an ethnic group who lived in a successful and thriving society from the 14th to the 16th century. They reside in the area we now call central Mexico. Their culture dominated the area. Their practices and traditions were steeped in mythology and religion. They are most well known for their practice of human sacrifice. However, before they settled down and began building their civilization, they lived a nomadic existence, continually moving and never settling in one place. It is believed that they were always on the move because they were constantly battling with other tribes. These fights were often caused because the Aztecs believed in gods who needed human sacrifice; they would take prisoners from other tribes to kill them in religious rituals.

The Aztecs valued education, and as soon as their city was built, they organized an education system for everyone. The Aztec leaders wanted their people to be a success. To achieve this, they knew they needed to develop the minds of their society. So girls, boys, adults, and even slaves went to school.

The Aztec clothing was a symbol of social status. The poorer the people, the less they wore. The male slaves and common people would wear only a loincloth, a simple material covering the crotch area. If a man was higher on the social ladder, he would have a pattern or fringe on the loincloth as an indication of this. The poor women wore skirts and blouses. Like the men, the higher the woman's social class, the more decoration she could add to the material, along with wearing jewelry. Royalty would be allowed to wear feathers and the color turquoise.

The Aztecs loved sports and games and were very competitive. Ullamaliztli is a well-known Aztec ball game. It was such an essential game to their culture that they built a court to play on as soon as they settled in their capital city. The game gets its name from the word ulli, which means rubber, and describes the type of ball used. The goal of the game was to get the ball through a hoop. To do this, players could use their hips, knees, and arms, and because the ball was large and heavy, the players wore protective clothing, including pads and helmets. This clothing guarded them from the stone wall of the court into which they would often be thrown against.

The Aztecs had a very strict and organized legal system. It was common for people to be sentenced to death for their crimes. To face the death penalty, a person would have to commit robbery, destroy crops, sell stolen property, or murder.

For other crimes deemed less severe, people would be sentenced to slavery or have their homes destroyed. Sometimes the criminal's family also faced punishment. The Aztec prison had different sections for holding people, depending on the seriousness of their crimes. The conditions in prison were horrible, and many prisoners died.

The Aztecs were destroyed by the Spanish in the Conquest of Jalisco in 1521. The Aztecs were a dominant society, yet in 1519, their domination began to falter as the Spanish conquistadors arrived in Mexico, led by Cortes, intending to take gold, land, and power from the natives. The Aztecs wouldn't stand for this. The result was a war that the Spanish won in 1521.

Reproduction interpretation of an Aztec pyramid. Disneyland Tokyo. By Unknown, Public Domain

Mesoamerica

Mexico City
Chichen Itza
Lake Texcoco
Mayapan
Oaxaca

Where in the World?

Lesson 19

A Closer Look
at what you have learned so far!
PLUS+ This Lesson's Geography:

Mesoamerica
Mexico City
Chichen Itza
Lake Texcoco
Mayapan
Oaxaca

Previously Learned Geography
TRUE REVIEW of the last 6 weeks.

Lesson 13
Atlantic Ocean
Senegal River
Niger River
Sahara Desert
Ivory Coast

Lesson 14
Ancient Ghana
Ancient Mali
Western Sahara
Fez
Tangier

Lesson 15
Israel
Sinai Peninsula
Suez Canal
Cairo
Gaza Strip

Lesson 16
Congo River
Lake Victoria
Zambezi River
Orange River

Lesson 17
Ethiopia
Mozambique
Zimbabwe
South Africa
Madagascar

Lesson 18
Gulf of Mexico
Yucatan Peninsula
Olmec Civilization
Maya Civilization
Aztec Civilization

Hint: All geography found on this page, is also the geography that you will be reviewing this week. Refer to these maps as needed when doing your "Memorization Through Repetition" worksheets.

Parent/Teacher: The "A Closer Look" page is intended to show students the accumulated geographic areas taught within their 6-week review period plus new geography. For additional teaching tips on how to utilize this teaching aide for the different learning levels, please refer to page 1.

Lesson 19

137

Lesson 19

Zoom Me In!

This Lesson's Geography:

Mesoamerica
Mexico City
Chichen Itza
Lake Texcoco
Mayapan
Oaxaca

Use this sheet as a reference for this lesson's "Now, let's trace, shade & label" worksheet.

Lesson 19 Geography
Mesoamerica
Mexico City
Chichen Itza
Lake Texcoco
Mayapan
Oaxaca

Tid-Bits

Mexico City is built right on a lake called Texcoco. The ancient Aztecs built their civilization on the island in the middle of the lake - the city was called Tenochtitlan. In 1519, Cortes, the conquistador, arrived on the scene, then shortly after that came Spain with him. They conquered the Aztecs, taking their city. After some time of occupying the island, they figured out that flooding was challenging to control. To fix this problem, they drained the lake. Now, the entire lake basin is almost entirely occupied by Mexico City. This wasn't the best for a growing city of 22 million people because the city is sinking. Over the last century, it has sunk 33 feet!

Mexico City has had many nicknames in the past. Including "City of the Palaces," "City of Hope," and "Capital in Movement." The last of which is understandable!

The population of Mexico City has grown by more than 20 million people in just over 110 years, from 500,000 in 1900 to 21.2 million people in 2012. As a result, Mexico

Chichen Itza, By jgpatino, Adobe Stock

City is the largest metropolitan area in the western hemisphere and the largest Spanish-speaking city globally.

Mexico City's Metro is the largest in Latin America and the cheapest in the world at only 3 pesos per journey which is about $0.15 U.S. (2018). Every day 4-5 million people use the bus system.

The city is so big and the traffic so bad that the wealthy use helicopters to get from one place to another. You can often see them landing on the tops of buildings.

Basilica of Our Lady of Guadalupe. The old basilica and cityscape of Mexico City on the far, By WitR, Adobe Stock

Mexico City takes its arts and entertainment seriously! With over 160 museums, 100 art galleries, and 30 concert halls. Mexico City has the fourth-highest number of theaters globally after New York, London, and Toronto. The 10,000-seat National Auditorium in Mexico City was named the Best Venue in the world. Other forms of entertainment include the largest amusement park in Latin America and the city's famous Zócalo, which turns into one of the world's biggest ice skating rinks each winter. Mexico City was the first city in Latin America to host the Olympic Games, with the Summer Olympics in 1968.

Before the turn of the 21st century, thousands of children and adults were dying. Suffering diseases because of the extreme air pollution of the city. In 1991, the air quality was announced as a public risk for 355 days out of the year. Since then, the government has taken several steps to reduce air pollution, which has resulted in a massive improvement to the situation. Early this century, an average of 478 crimes were reported each day in the city. Now, Mexico City has one of the highest police to resident ratios anywhere as it is reported that there is one police officer for every 100 residents. Mexico City has seen a vast decrease in crime rates in recent years.

Chichen Itza is classified as one of the New Seven Wonders of the World. The term Chichen Itza means 'the mouth at the well of Itza.' And it is thought

Ruins of Mayapan, Yucatán, Mexico, By Suzanne Plumette, Adobe Stock

that Itza means 'water magicians.' El Castillo temple is the famous pyramid that makes the site of Chichen Itza so unique. It actually sits upon another much older temple. It is believed that the city fell at approximately 1000 AD after 400 years. The construction of Chichen Itza was well planned as its erected temples and pyramids are in clusters. Of these clusters, the Great North Platform is home to the most visited sites of Chichen Itza, including the Kukulkan Pyramid, the Great Ball Court, and the Temple of the Jaguars. During the Spring and Autumn each year, the sun's rays create a shadow across the Kukulkan Pyramid that looks like a serpent slithering down the staircase.

Do you like to make echoes with your voice? Well, if you visited Chichen Itza, you could make some very unusual echoes. For example, if you clap once from one end of the Ball Court, it produces nine echoes, and a clap in front of the Kukulkan Pyramid creates an echo resembling a chirp.

Lake Texcoco is the famed drained lake now sitting under Mexico City and was once the home of the Aztec Civilization that resided on an island in the

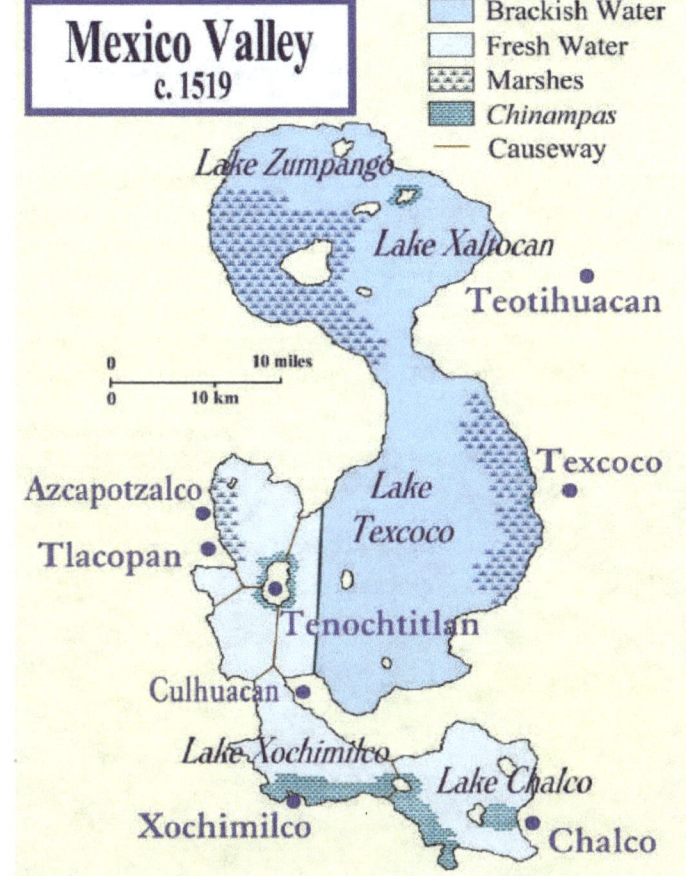

middle of the lake. Before its draining, Lake Texcoco is thought to be the size of 2,189 square miles with a depth of 500 feet. In the hotter months of the year, the lake's depth fell, creating several interconnected lakes.

Mayapan is considered the last significant Mayan capital and is the most studied Mayan settlement in the region. Mayapan's city center within the Yucatan Peninsula is only 4 square miles and housed 12,000 people within its walls and about 5,000 citizens living out their lives in the rural areas. Around the city, there are defense walls that together are 5.6 miles long and had 12 entrances.

The ruins of Mayapan number 4,000 structures in all but not all have been excavated. Within Mayapan, there are twenty-six breathtaking cenotes. One might be tempted to take a swim in one! A cenote is a freshwater sinkhole.

This is a map of the Valley of Mexico on the eve of the Spanish conquest of Mexico. It shows the major towns within the Valley, in particular, the island capital of the Aztecs, Tenochtitlan. The map also shows the five lakes that once existed within the Valley, highlighted to differentiate the brackish from the fresh waters. - By Madman2001

Cultural Festival in Oaxaca, Mexico, By Unknown, Public Domain

Architecture in Oaxaca, Mexico, By Unknown, Public Domain

The city of Oaxaca de Juárez is the capital of the state of Oaxaca. You'll find many colonial-era structures. Here people celebrate the Zapotec and Mixtec cultural festivals. The Zapotec and Mixtec are two indigenous people groups who have lived in Oaxaca for thousands of years and still thrive there today. An estimated 800,000-1 million people keep to their traditional language and customs.

Oaxaca is located 280 miles Southeast of Mexico City, where the Sierra Madre mountain range is. This mountainous terrain encloses a temperate central valley that reaches the Pacific coast. The lay of the land within the valley provides for a mild, spring-like climate year-round. The rainy season lasts from May through September, with rain generally in the afternoons. The coastal area remains hotter and drier, while temperatures in the mountains remain cooler year-round.

Oaxaca is known for its variety of moles and chocolates. In addition, the blend of Zapotec, Mixtec, and Spanish traditions provides a unique style of music, dance, and art.

BOTTOM LEFT & RIGHT: Cenotes found on the Yucatan Peninsula in Chichen Itza, by Arthur (left), by By Subbotina Anna, Adobe Stock

Where in the World?

Lesson 20

Dominion of Canada
Ontario
Quebec
New Brunswick
Nova Scotia

A Closer Look
at what you have learned so far!
PLUS+ This Lesson's Geography:

Dominion of Canada
Ontario
Quebec
New Brunswick
Nova Scotia

Lesson 20

Previously Learned Geography
TRUE REVIEW of the last 6 weeks.

Lesson 14
Ancient Ghana
Ancient Mali
Western Sahara
Fez
Tangier

Lesson 15
Israel
Sinai Peninsula
Suez Canal
Cairo
Gaza Strip

Lesson 16
Congo River
Lake Victoria
Zambezi River
Orange River

Lesson 17
Ethiopia
Mozambique
Zimbabwe
South Africa
Madagascar

Lesson 18
Gulf of Mexico
Yucatan Peninsula
Olmec Civilization
Maya Civilization
Aztec Civilization

Lesson 19
Mexico City
Chichen Itza
Lake Texcoco
Mayapan
Oaxaca

Hint: All geography found on this page, is also the geography that you will be reviewing this week. Refer to these maps as needed when doing your "Memorization Through Repetition" worksheets.

Parent/Teacher: The "A Closer Look" page is intended to show students the accumulated geographic areas taught within their 6-week review period plus new geography. For additional teaching tips on how to utilize this teaching aide for the different learning levels, please refer to page 1.

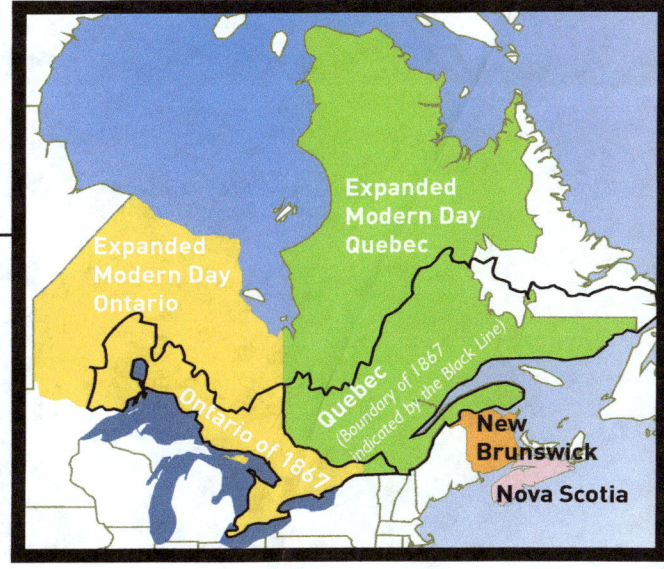

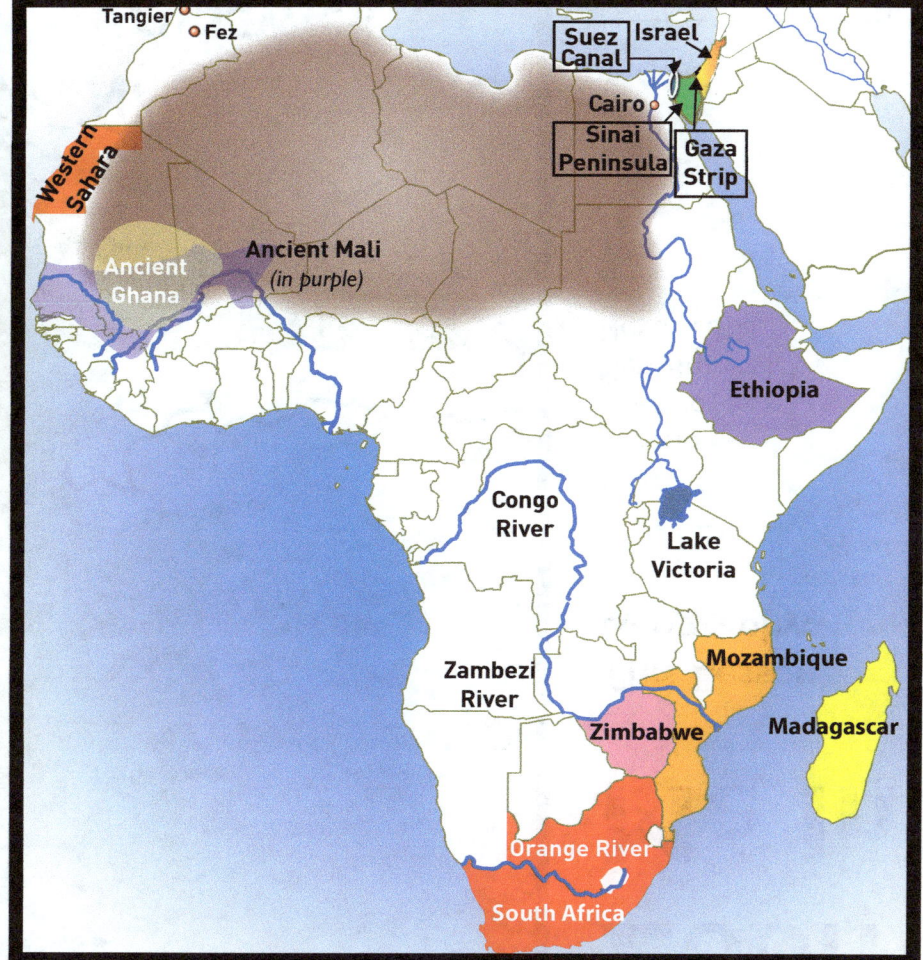

143

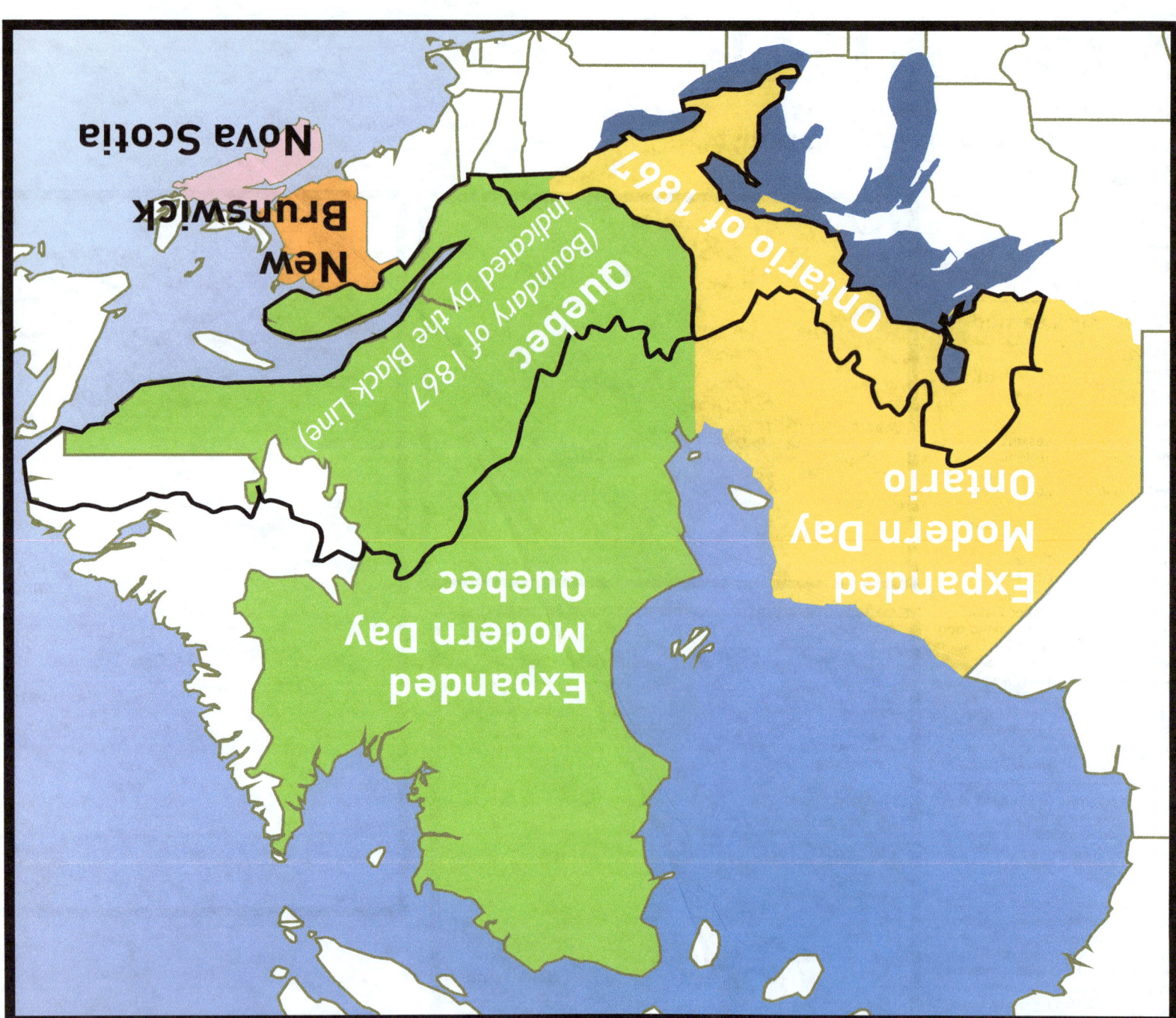

Lesson 20 Geography
Dominion of Canada
Ontario
Quebec
New Brunswick
Nova Scotia

Tid-Bits

The British North America Act of 1867 merged the Province of Canada, New Brunswick, and Nova Scotia to form the Dominion of Canada. The provinces of Ontario and Quebec replaced the former Province of Canada.

The map above shows light orange for present-day Ontario and bright green for present-day Quebec. The black line over each indicates the boundary lines created with the British North America Act of 1867.

Canada's Province Ontario is the most populous province and is home to the capital city, Ottawa. Additionally, Ontario is one of the original four provinces that joined the Confederation on July 1st, 1867;

Toronto Skyline, Ontario, Pixabay

Ontario's pre-Confederation name was Upper Canada. The name Ontario is believed to come from a Huron word meaning "great lake." Which makes sense since this province borders all but one of the Great Lakes.

Part of Ontario's waterfront is a beach called Wasaga. It is the longest freshwater beach on earth, situated on three of the five Great Lakes, including Lake Huron, Lake Erie, and Lake Ontario. In addition, the beach is home to the world's largest freshwater island called Manitoulin. Ontario has a unique underground pedestrian system that connects over 1,200 stores and restaurants. It is called "Path" and is over 17 miles long.

Wasaga Beach, Ontario, Canada - By Unknown, Public Domain

The arrival of Samuel de Champlain, the father of New France.
Painting by Unknown, Public Domain

The longest covered bridge, New Brunswick, Pixabay

The Province of Quebec was first discovered by Jacques Cartier, a French explorer that landed here in 1535. Then in 1608, Samuel de Champlain arrived and set up a fur-trading post.

The Quebec city has a beautiful 400-year history set against the backdrop of a walled city filled with narrow, winding cobbled streets. It is charming and reminiscent of old European cities.

The word "Kebec" is an Algonquin word meaning "where the river narrows."

Quebec City's 400th anniversary was celebrated in 2008, and it is the oldest French-speaking community in North America. In fact, only about 1.5% of the people speak only English.

Quebec City is the only walled city north of Mexico. Its walls are over 15,000 feet. On average, there are 149 days per year when the snow is at least one inch deep. In July, the average temperature is 77°F, and in January, it dips on average to 18°F.

Old Town, Quebec, Pixabay

New Brunswick boasts some wonderful inventions and fantastic scenery! We'll start with a yummy creation! The inventor of the ice cream cone was born in Sussex corner, the Dairy Capital of Canada. There was a baker there named Walter Donelly who made a bad batch of dough. He was at a loss with what to do with his hard, crispy pastry until he tried rolling it up to hold something.... Eureka! An ice cream cone!

The world's longest covered bridge was completed in Hartland in 1899. It is 1,282 feet long and spans the Saint John River. The area boasts an impressive 62 covered bridges, and when you pass through you are supposed to make a wish!

The Eel River Sand Bar, near Dalhousie, is one of the longest natural sandbars in North America. The meaningful part of this sandbar is that freshwater laps its shores on one side and saltwater on the other.

Aerial view of Nova Scotia, By Unknown, Public Domain Hopewell Rocks at the Bay of Fundy, Pixabay

New Brunswick has the largest tidal whirlpool in the Western Hemisphere. It is called the "Old Sow" off of Deer Island. It can be seen 3 hours before high tide.

Watch the Saint John River crash through a narrow gorge and tumble into the harbor at low tide. Then, come back at high tide and watch the same river go the other way. The Bay of Fundy's incredible tides are too strong for the mighty Saint John River, forcing the waters to flow upstream twice a day, every day. It is a fantastic phenomenon where the water feels like it's flowing backward.

The Bay of Fundy has the highest tides globally and is home to many types of sharks, including threshers, makos, porbeagles, and the great white shark. In addition, up to 15 species of whales can be seen in the waters.

Campobello Island is the location of the Roosevelt Campobello International Park – and the former summer home of President Franklin D. Roosevelt. It has 34 rooms, including 18 bedrooms.

The Head Harbor Lightstation on Campobello Island is the second oldest lighthouse in New Brunswick. It's accessible on foot when the waters are low tide, which means you can walk out to the lighthouse. But don't get stuck out there at high tide!

In Nova Scotia's capital, Halifax, there was the most enormous man-made explosion before Hiroshima in World War II. In 1917 about 2,000 people were killed and 9,000 injured when the SS Mont Blanc, a French cargo ship loaded with wartime explosives, collided with an empty Norwegian ship. It caught fire and 25 minutes later exploded. Later this incredible explosion caused a tsunami pressure wave that caused considerable damage.

Nova Scotia enjoys four distinct seasons. Winters are cold and snowy. The summer temperatures are usually in the 68-74°F range. But look out for Atlantic Hurricane Season when Nova Scotia suffers the brunt of tropical storms and hurricanes.

East Quoddy Lighthouse on Campobello Island New Brunswick Canada at Low Tide - By warren_price, Adobe Stock

Canadian Waters

Great Bear Lake
Great Slave Lake
Hudson Bay
Baffin Bay
Labrador Sea

Where in the World?

Lesson 21

A Closer Look
at what you have learned so far!
PLUS+ This Lesson's Geography:

Lesson 21

Canadian Waters
Great Bear Lake
Great Slave Lake
Hudson Bay
Baffin Bay
Labrador Sea

Previously Learned Geography
TRUE REVIEW of the last 6 weeks.

Lesson 15
Israel
Sinai Peninsula
Suez Canal
Cairo
Gaza Strip

Lesson 17
Ethiopia
Mozambique
Zimbabwe
South Africa
Madagascar

Lesson 19
Mexico City
Chichen Itza
Lake Texcoco
Mayapan
Oaxaca

Lesson 16
Congo River
Lake Victoria
Zambezi River
Orange River

Lesson 18
Gulf of Mexico
Yucatan Peninsula
Olmec Civilization
Maya Civilization
Aztec Civilization

Lesson 20
Ontario
Quebec
New Brunswick
Nova Scotia

Hint: All geography found on this page, is also the geography that you will be reviewing this week. Refer to these maps as needed when doing your "Memorization Through Repetition" worksheets.

Parent/Teacher: The "A Closer Look" page is intended to show students the accumulated geographic areas taught within their 6-week review period plus new geography. For additional teaching tips on how to utilize this teaching aide for the different learning levels, please refer to page 1.

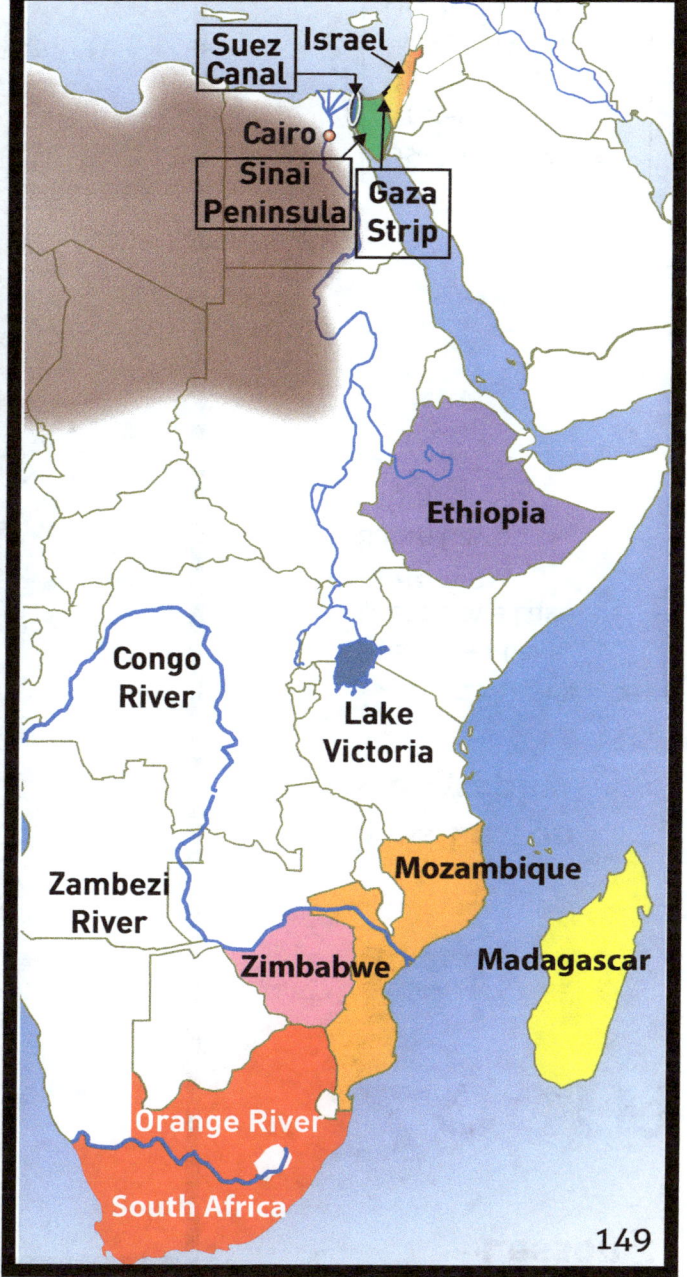

149

Lesson 21

Zoom Me In!

This Lesson's Geography:

Canadian Waters
Great Bear Lake
Great Slave Lake
Hudson Bay
Baffin Bay
Labrador Sea

Use this sheet as a reference for this lesson's "Now, let's trace, shade & label" worksheet.

Lesson 21 Geography
Canadian Waters
Great Bear Lake
Great Slave Lake
Hudson Bay
Baffin Bay
Labrador Sea

Tid-Bits

First on our list of Canadian waters is the Great Bear Lake. With a surface area of 12,028 square miles and a maximum depth of 1,463 feet, the Great Bear Lake is the largest lake that is entirely on Canadian soil. The shoreline of this magnificent lake is 1,690 miles. Being so far north, this lake is covered with ice from late November until July each year. The lake's name comes from the words "Satudene" from the Denesuline language meaning "grizzly bear water people."

The Great Slave Lake, although not the biggest, is the deepest lake in North America and is the 10th largest lake in the world. It is 2,014 feet deep and covers 10,502 square miles.

It is believed that the North American aboriginal people were the first settlers around the lake. With the fur trade routes being established, maps were needed, and the Great Slave Lake was put on European maps when fur traders were moving northwest from Hudson Bay in the mid 18th century. The name 'Great Slave' came from the Slavey Indians, one of the tribes living on its southern shores at that time. The large lake was referred to as "Grand lac des Esclaves" which was eventually translated into English as "Great Slave Lake."

Aerial view of Great Slave Lake in Canada, By Unknown, Public Domain

**BELOW: Northern lights over a houseboat on Great Slave Lake, in the town of Yelloknife, Canada
Image by: Vincent Demers**

ABOVE: The Great Bear Lake, Canada, By Unknown, Public Domain

In the 1930s, gold was discovered in the northern portion of the lake. This lead to the establishment of Yellowknife, which became the capital of the Northwest Territory.

Hudson Bay is a large body of saltwater. It is 470,000 square miles and is the second-largest bay after the Bay of Bengal. This bay is relatively shallow, with an average depth of only 330 feet. It is about 850 miles long and 650 miles wide.

The bay was named for Sir Henry Hudson, an English explorer who sailed for the Dutch East India Company. Hudson explored the bay beginning August 2, 1610, on his ship aptly named "Discovery," which made several trips to North America. The bay was discovered on Hudson's fourth voyage as he down the west side of Greenland into the bay. There the ship got stuck! The ship and crew were trapped in the ice over the harsh winter. The crew survived onshore at the southern tip of James Bay. Take a look at a larger map and try to find James Bay. James Bay jets down from Hudson Bay at the southern tip, sitting between Ontario and Quebec. You can also look on the picture provided by NASA (right).

NASA satelite photo of Hudson Bay. Public Domain

When the ice cleared in the spring, the adventure-filled Hudson wanted to explore the rest of the area. Still, the crew wasn't up for the challenge and declared mutiny against Hudson on June 22, 1611. They abandoned him and a few other of his crew on a small boat. Historians believed he didn't survive long after.

Baffin Bay is located between Baffin Island and the southwest coast of Greenland, and it is connected on the south end to the Atlantic by the Davis Strait and the Labrador Sea. On the northern side, the Nares Strait connects Baffin Bay with the Arctic Ocean.

This bay is freezing! Because of this, the bay is not able to be navigated most of the year. In addition, the ice cover and high density of floating ice and icebergs would stop any would-be sea-goers.

SATELLITE IMAGE OF THE NORTH WATER POLYNYA, MAY 27, 2015

This region of Baffin Bay is where most of the aquatic life lives. The nature of the Polynya creates a warm microclimate providing refuge for narwhal, beluga, walrus, and bowhead whales to feed themselves, mate, and rest. Thin ice forms in some areas, but the Polynya is kept warm by wind, tides, and an ice bridge on

However, in the spring and summer months, there is an area of 31,000 square miles called the "North Water Polynya" that warms up and allows for travel.

its northern edge. This area of Baffin Bay was named the "North Water" by the 19th-century whale hunters who relied on it for spring passage. This Polynya is one of the most biologically productive marine areas in the Arctic Ocean.

Polar bear walking upon the pack ice in Hudson Bay, Adobe Stock

Sir Henry Hudson, By Unknown, Public Domain

Baffin Bay pictured from the shores of Greenland. Adobe Stock

The Labrador Sea is an extension of the North Atlantic Ocean between the Labrador Peninsula and Greenland. The Labrador Sea is about 11,155 feet deep and 621 miles wide, joining the Atlantic Ocean. It becomes shallower the closer it gets to Baffin Bay as it passes through the Davis Strait.

The water temperature varies depending on the time of year. It dips just below freezing in the winter, with the northern and western parts covered in ice between December and June. Then in the summer months, it soars up to 41–43 °F. That is still cold! During the winter, two-thirds of the sea is covered in ice.

The Labrador Sea has drifting ice that serves as a breeding ground for seals in early spring. The sea is also home to Atlantic salmon and several marine mammal species. While abundant to the north, Beluga whales in Baffin Bay, whose population reaches 20,000, are rare in the Labrador Sea, especially since the 1950s. However, the sea contains one of the two significant types of Sei whales. Also common are Minke and Bottlenose whales.

Along the coastal banks, the Labrador duck was a common bird until the 19th century, but it is unfortunately extinct. Other coastal animals include the Labrador wolf, caribou, moose, black bear, red fox, Arctic fox, wolverine, Snowshoe hare, grouse, osprey, raven, ducks, geese, partridge, and American wild pheasant.

Humpback whales feeding among giant icebergs in the Labrador Sea, Ilulissat, Greenland, Adobe Stock

Ice floe and icebergs floating in the Davis Strait in the Labrador Sea off of Greenland. Adobe Stock

South America West

Venezuela
Colombia
Ecuador
Peru
Bolivia
Chile

Where in the World?

Lesson 22

Arctic Ocean

Greenland

Baffin Bay

Iceland

Faroe Islands

Great Bear Lake

Great Slave Lake

Hudson Bay

Labrador Sea

North Pacific Ocean

North Atlantic Ocean

Gulf of Mexico

Hawaii

Germania

Gaul

Hispania

Black Sea

Mongolia

China

Korea

Sea of Japan

Yellow Sea

Mt. Fuji

Mediterranean Sea

Himalayas

Arabian Desert

Sahara Desert

Ivory Coast

Ethiopia

Sao Tome & Principe

Arabian Sea

Bay of Bengal

North Pacific Ocean

Venezuela

Colombia

Ecuador

Peru

Bolivia

Argentina

South Pacific Ocean

South Atlantic Ocean

Mozambique

Zimbabwe

Madagascar

South Africa

Indian Ocean

A Closer Look
at what you have learned so far!

PLUS+ This Lesson's Geography:

South America (West)
Venezuela
Colombia
Ecuador
Peru
Bolivia
Chile

Previously Learned Geography
TRUE REVIEW of the last 6 weeks.

Lesson 16
Congo River
Lake Victoria
Zambezi River
Orange River

Lesson 17
Ethiopia
Mozambique
Zimbabwe
South Africa
Madagascar

Lesson 18
Gulf of Mexico
Yucatan Peninsula
Olmec Civilization
Maya Civilization
Aztec Civilization

Lesson 19
Mexico City
Chichen Itza
Lake Texcoco
Mayapan
Oaxaca

Lesson 20
Ontario
Quebec
New Brunswick
Nova Scotia

Lesson 21
Great Bear Lake
Great Slave Lake
Hudson Bay
Baffin Bay
Labrador Sea

Lesson 22

Hint: All geography found on this page, is also the geography that you will be reviewing this week. Refer to these maps as needed when doing your "Memorization Through Repetition" worksheets.

Parent/Teacher: The "A Closer Look" page is intended to show students the accumulated geographic areas taught within their 6-week review period plus new geography. For additional teaching tips on how to utilize this teaching aide for the different learning levels, please refer to page 1.

Lesson 22

Zoom Me In!

This Lesson's Geography:

South America (West)
Venezuela
Colombia
Ecuador
Peru
Bolivia
Chile

Use this sheet as a reference for this lesson's "Now, let's trace, shade & label" worksheet.

Lesson 22 Geography
South America (West)
Venezuela
Colombia
Ecuador
Peru
Bolivia
Chile

Tid-Bits

Venezuela is a northern coastal country in South America. It is the 33rd largest country in the world, with a total area of 353,841 square miles. The population of Venezuela is 28.9 million, while its capital city of Caracas is home to 1.9 million people. The people of Venezuela speak Spanish, and it is their official language. Although the country doesn't have an official religion, most people follow the Roman Catholic Church.

Like all countries, Venezuela has imports that provide needed goods for their people. In addition, there are exports that bring money into the country. Their exports include steel, cement, aluminum, and agricultural products. Their imports include electronics, chemicals, and food.

Venezuela has only two seasons. No matter what, though, it's hot! Part of the year is considered hot and dry; the other part of the year is deemed to be hot and wet.

Here in Venezuela, schoolchildren can choose when they want to go to school between two times per day. In the morning or afternoon... which would you choose? Older children can even choose to take classes at night!

There is a fun tradition of roller skating to church with the family in Venezuela on Christmas day!

Do you like to dance? Well, in Venezuela, they have an official national dance called Joropo. And their music is a mix of Spanish and African, full of percussion instruments. It is a common sight to see the Venezuelan people dancing in the streets. Jaropo is performed during national holidays and festivals. Their most celebrated festival during the year is called "The Red Devils of Yare." The participants are beautifully costumed and play red devils that battle on Corpus Christi Day. The battle always ends with virtue winning over the devils, which signifies Christianity's win over Satan.

Like many of us, the Venezuelan people have Christmas trees in their homes and set up nativity scenes in their front yards to celebrate Christmas.

An interesting difference in their country is that they do not have water heaters or bathtubs. As a result, they often take cold showers at night. Remember, Venezuela is hot no matter what time of year!

In Venezuela exists the highest waterfall in the world! It is called Angel Falls and has a height of 3,212 feet and a plunge of 2,648 feet. In the hot Venezuelan land, there is a good deal of water that evaporates before arriving below.

Venezuela's name comes from the word Veneziola, which means "Little Venice." It was named by Amerigo Vespucci, who saw houses that reminded him of Venice. Although it was Christopher Columbus who was the first to discover the coastline.

Street performers in Venezuela performing the Joropo dance! By Unknown, Public Domain

Moving east to the country of Columbia. The name "Colombia" is the last name of the explorer that discovered this area. Who was this famous explorer? If you said Christopher Columbus, you were right!

Here in Columbia, 99% of the population speak

Multicoloured Tanager, endemic bird species can only be found in Colombia. By Unknown, Public Domain

Colombia is the only country in South America with a coastline on both the Pacific Ocean and the Caribbean Sea. Bogota is the capital and is the second-largest capital city in South America. At 8,661 feet above sea level, it is one of the highest capital cities in the world. Colombia is classed as a "megadiverse" country, ranking as the 2nd most biodiverse country in the world. This means that it has many different types of species within the same class. This includes butterflies, orchids, the most amphibian species, and more species of birds than all of Europe and North America combined.

Colombia is the world's leading source of the precious gem emerald. And the other precious commodity, coffee. While Tejo is the national team sport in Columbia, the most popular is football. We call their type of "football" by a different name in the U.S.; we call it soccer. Other popular and successful sports of Colombia include roller-skating, weightlifting, baseball, boxing, motorsport, and cycling.

To the south we go! Ecuador sits at the northwestern edge of South America and is the smallest country on the continent. The equator runs right through Ecuador. What is the equator? Well, if you said something like, "it's an imaginary line running around the world that acts as a boundary between the Northern and Southern hemi-spheres, well, you would be right! And this is how Ecuador got its name. They sound similar, don't they?

By Alejo Fernández (1475-1545) - Photo by historian Manuel Rosa., Public Domain, Painting of Christopher Columbus. Painted sometime between 1531 and 1536. It is the only state sponsored portrait of the First Admiral of the Indias called Don Cristoval Colon known today as Christopher Columbus in English.

Spanish, which is the official language of Colombia. However, in addition to Spanish, there are also many indigenous languages spoken throughout the country. Colombia has a population of over 45 million people.

The area covered by modern-day Colombia was originally inhabited by the indigenous tribes Muisca, Quimbaya, and Tairona. In 1499 the Spanish arrived, making the area a Spanish colony called New Granada.

Angel Falls, the tallest continuous waterfall in the world. Located in Venezuela. By Unknown, Public Domain

LEFT: Introducing the "Magnificent Frigatebird" This unique avian creature uses its impressive wingspan of 8 feet to soar into skies, reaching up more than 8,000 feet in altitude according to BBC Nature. Their elegant, effortless flight is only upstaged by the bright red sac on the front of the males' chests, which balloon up to try and make them more appealing to the female in mating season.

Part of the frigate family, this species is also known as the man-o'-war bird, due to its tendency to attack other birds in the air and steal their food.

RIGHT: The Galápagos giant tortoise They are the largest living species of tortoise, with some weighing up to 920 pounds. This tortoise can live in the wild for over 100 years, making them one of the longest-living vertebrates. Captive Galapagos tortoises can live up to 177 years. For example, a captive individual, Harriet, lived for at least 175 years. Spanish explorers, who discovered the islands in the 16th century, named them after the Spanish galápago, meaning "tortoise".

This country is about the size of Colorado in the United States. The Andes Mountains run through the country's middle, and within the mountain range are many volcanoes. The Andes mountains serve as the Andean Volcanic Belt. They are the most extensive mountain range in the world, running through a few South American countries.

Even though Ecuador is small, it has an incredibly diverse landscape, including the well-known Galapagos Islands off the coast. The Galapagos Islands are admired for having some of the most exciting and unique animals in the world.

Like bananas? Well, Ecuador's fertile farmlands grow more bananas than any other country in the world.

Incas ruled Ecuador until the Spaniards arrived in the 1500s. Then, the Spanish ruled Ecuador until 1822.

Next is Peru, which is famous for its incredible and biodiverse geography. Peru is divided into three different habitats: the Pacific coastal region, the mountainous region of the Andes, and the tropical Amazon Jungle.

The coastal region has moderate temperatures, low precipitations, and high humidity, except for its warmer, wetter northern reaches. In the mountain region, rain is frequent in summer. The temperature and humidity diminish as you go higher, all the way up to the frozen peaks of the Andes. The Peruvian Amazon is characterized by heavy rainfall and high temperatures. Except for its southernmost part, it has cold winters and seasonal rainfall.

Because of Peru's biodiverse nature, the wildlife teems with over 21,462 species of plants and animals. Peru has over 1,800 species of birds, of which 120 are endemic. If you were wondering what endemic means, it means that they are only in this place and nowhere else in the whole world! There are 500 species of mammals and over 300 species of reptiles. Some of the rare species of mammals include the puma, jaguar, and spectacled bear.

Peruvian Jaguar, endemic to Peru's Amazon Jungle

Machu Picchu, found high in the Andes Mountains in Peru, Pixabay

Salar de Uyuni salt flats in Bolivia, Pixabay

The birds of Peru produce large amounts of guano (bird excrement), an economically vital export for fertilizer. Off the coast of Peru, the Pacific holds large quantities of sea bass, flounder, anchovies, tuna, crustaceans, and shellfish. Of course, that are many sharks and various types of whales too!

In addition to this diverse geography, Machu Picchu, the 15th century Inca citadel, sits 7,970 feet above sea level in the Andes Mountains. It is included in the New Seven Wonders of the World. Created as a "royal" estate, Machu Picchu was built around 1450–1460. The amount of time used by the Incan people was brief, approximately 80 years before being abandoned, seemingly due to destruction from the Spanish conquests in other parts of the Inca Empire.

Bolivia is a landlocked country found in the heart of South America. 60% of the Bolivian people are indigenous; therefore, the country is rich in culture. In fact, their rich indigenous heritage has 37 official languages! The main languages are Spanish, Quechua, Aymara and Guaraní.

The name of the country stems from Bolivia's first president Simon Bolivar. He played a leading role in establishing Venezuela, Bolivia, Colombia, Ecuador, Peru, and Panama as sovereign states, independent of Spanish rule.

One of the Bolivian treasures is Isla del Sol. This mythical birthplace of the Sun God lies on the Bolivian side of Lake Titicaca. It is home to a collection of 80 ruins.

Lake Titicaca, which straddles the border

Isla del Sol, a mythical birthplace of the Sun God, over 80 ruins reside on the shores of Lake Titicaca, Pixabay

between Peru and Bolivia, is the world's highest lake. Its altitude is 12,507 feet above sea level and is also South America's largest lake by volume.

Another treasure in Bolivia is the surreal and overwhelming beauty of Salar de Uyuni salt flats. This vast salt flat land is 4,085 square miles, making Bolivia home to the most extensive salt flats globally.

At Salar de Uyuni, a hotel called Palacio de Sal translates to "Palace of Salt." It was constructed in 1993-1995 with one million 14-inch blocks of salt used for the floor, walls, ceiling, and furniture, including beds, tables, chairs, and sculptures.

Many natural resources can be found in Bolivia, including Lithium which is used to make batteries. To be sure, there are such batteries in a clock at the National Congress building in La Paz that runs backward! This is to remind citizens to think differently.

Like other surrounding countries in South America, the guinea pig is raised and eaten as traditional meat, playing a significant role in the Bolivian diet. Guinea pigs require much less room than traditional livestock and reproduce quickly.

Now for the long and narrow country running along the Pacific coastline, Chile. On the east side of the country lies the Andes Mountain Range. The climate varies tremendously from north to south because of the sheer vertical length of the country. Chile has a dry desert climate in the north; centrally, it is beautifully warm and moderate; to the south, it is rainy.

Chile has some energetic and fun festivals! Fiesta de la Virgen del Carmen de La Tirana is a religious festival that lasts a week in July. People celebrate for 24 hours a day, singing and dancing, wearing brightly colored costumes and clothing. The Festival International de la Cancion (International Song Festival) is an extremely popular music festival for South America. Lastly, the Fiesta de San Pedro is a festival that prays for good weather at sea and good catches for the year. Fishermen decorate their boats, and at night everyone lights candles.

Reaching back in time, Spain conquered and colonized the region in the mid-16th century, replacing Inca rule in the north and center, but failing to conquer the independent Mapuche who inhabited south-central Chile. After declaring its independence from Spain in 1818, Chile emerged in the 1830s as a relatively stable authoritarian republic. In the 19th century, Chile saw significant economic and territorial growth, ending Mapuche resistance in the 1880s and gaining its current northern territory in the War of the Pacific (1879–83) after defeating Peru and Bolivia. As a result, Chile is today one of South America's most economically, socially stable, and prosperous nations, with a high-income economy and high living standards.

Fiesta de la Virgen del Carmen de La Tirana is a religious festival, Pixelbay

Picturesque scene in Chile with the backdrop of the Andes Mountains, Pixelbay

South America East

Argentina
Uruguah
Paraguay
Brazil
French Guiana
Suriname
Guyana

Where in the World?

Lesson 23

A Closer Look

at what you have learned so far!

PLUS+ This Lesson's Geography:

South America (East)
Argentina
Uruguay
Paraguay
Brazil
French Guiana
Suriname
Guyana

Previously Learned Geography
TRUE REVIEW of the last 6 weeks.

Lesson 17
Ethiopia
Mozambique
Zimbabwe
South Africa
Madagascar

Lesson 18
Gulf of Mexico
Yucatan Peninsula
Olmec Civilization
Maya Civilization
Aztec Civilization

Lesson 19
Mexico City
Chichen Itza
Lake Texcoco
Mayapan
Oaxaca

Lesson 20
Ontario
Quebec
New Brunswick
Nova Scotia

Lesson 21
Great Bear Lake
Great Slave Lake
Hudson Bay
Baffin Bay
Labrador Sea

Lesson 22
Venezuela
Colombia
Ecuador
Peru
Bolivia
Chile

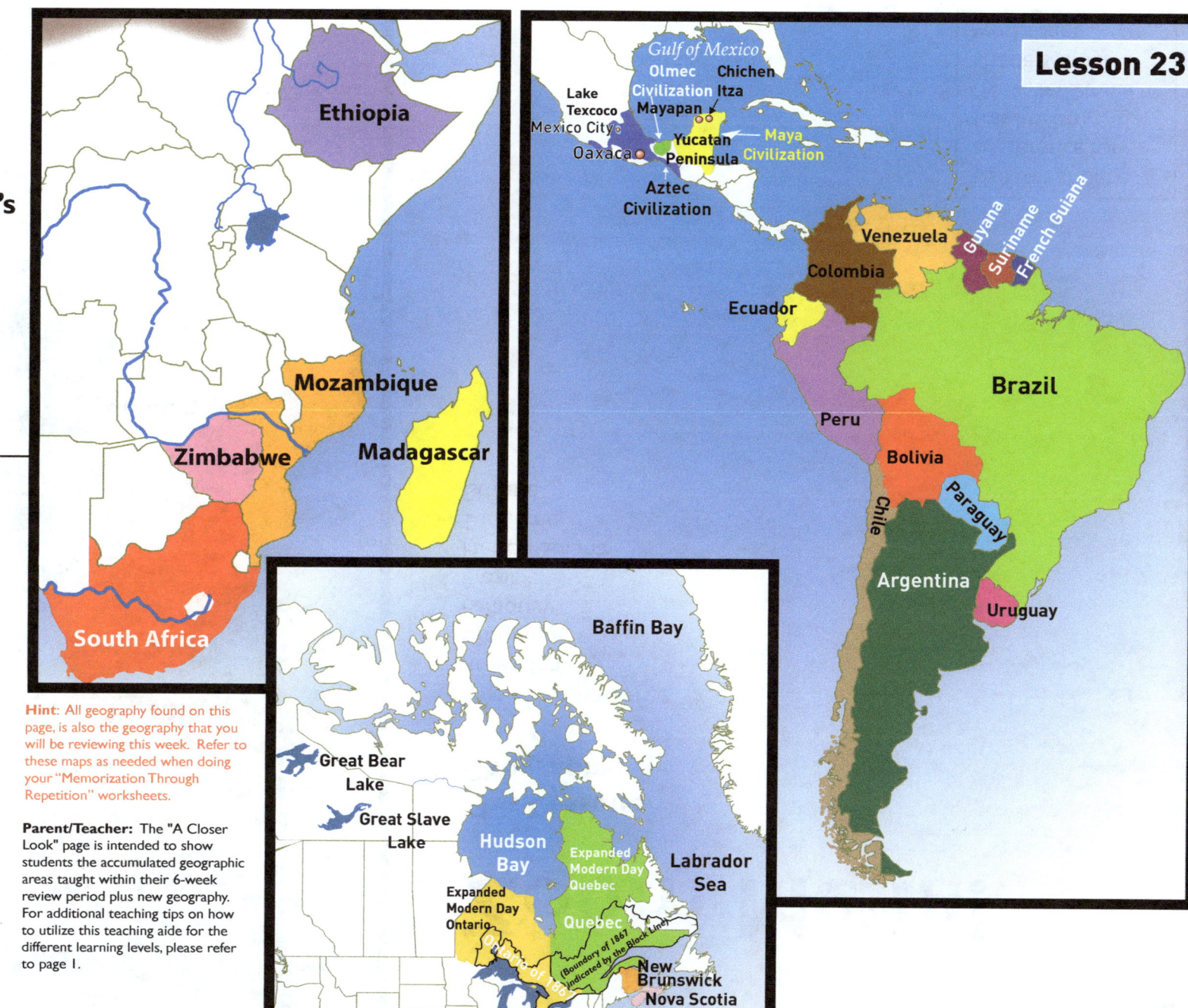

Hint: All geography found on this page, is also the geography that you will be reviewing this week. Refer to these maps as needed when doing your "Memorization Through Repetition" worksheets.

Parent/Teacher: The "A Closer Look" page is intended to show students the accumulated geographic areas taught within their 6-week review period plus new geography. For additional teaching tips on how to utilize this teaching aide for the different learning levels, please refer to page 1.

Lesson 23

163

Lesson 23

Zoom Me In!

This Lesson's Geography:

South America (East)
Argentina
Uruguay
Paraguay
Brazil
French Guiana
Suriname
Guyana

Use this sheet as a reference for this lesson's "Now, let's trace, shade & label" worksheet.

Lesson 23 Geography
South America (East)
Argentina
Uruguay
Paraguay
Brazil
French Guiana
Suriname
Guyana

Tid-Bits

The description of the country by the word "Argentina" was found on a Venetian map as early as 1536. The Italian naming "Argentina" means "land of silver" or "Costa Argentina," meaning "coast of silver."

The mainland of Argentina has a surface area of 1,073,518 square miles. Its coastal border over the Río de la Plata and South Atlantic Ocean is 3,180 miles long.

Argentina's highest point is Mount Aconcagua at 22,831 feet above sea level and also serves as the highest point in the Southern and Western Hemispheres. The lowest point is Laguna del Carbón in the San Julián Great Depression, at 344 feet below sea level.

Although the most populated areas are generally temperate, which means not too hot nor too cold. Argentina has an exceptional climate diversity, ranging from subtropical in the north to polar in the far south. The average annual precipitation ranges from 6 inches in the driest parts to over 79 inches in the westernmost parts of the country. Average annual temperatures range from 41 °F in the far south to 77 °F in the north.

With Argentina, most of the world that knows the Tango knows that it comes from Argentina! Tango has been around since the beginning of the 20th century and has spread throughout the world as a sensual dance of love. Ushuaia is the capital city of the Tierra del Fuego province, located in the most southern part of Argentina. Sometimes referred to as 'the end of the world.' Here you can see

"The end of the World" the tip of Argentina. By Unknown, Public Domain

The Argentina dance, the Tango. By Unknown, Public Domain

One of many of the diverse landscapes in Argentina. By Unknown, Public Domain

An Uruguay cattle rancher. By Unknown, Public Domain

Iguazu Falls – junction of the waterfalls marks the border between Brazil, Argentina, and Paraguay. Adobe Stock

penguins, seals, and whales. The temperatures here range from a maximum of 60° F to -32°F.

Uruguay is home to an estimated 3.44 million people, of whom 1.8 million live in the metropolitan area of its capital and largest city, Montevideo. With an area of approximately 68,000 square miles. Uruguay is geographically the second-smallest nation in South America, after

Suriname. The name "Uruguay" comes from the Uruguay River, which means "river of the painted birds" in the Guarani language. The river starts in Brazil and ends in the Rio de la Plata Basin, forming the water border between Uruguay and Argentina.

It is ranked first in the region for democracy, peace, lack of corruption, quality of living, freedom of press, prosperity, and security. This is all the more impressive, considering the country was ruled by a military dictatorship until 1985.

In Uruguay, cows outnumber people four to one. It is a nation of 12

million cattle but just three million people.

Uruguay is the only country in Latin America that is entirely outside of the tropics. The land is located within the temperate zone, so extreme temperatures are rare.

Paraguay is the smallest landlocked country in South America that lies on both banks of the Paraguay River, which runs through the center of the country from north to south. Due to its central location in the continent, it is sometimes referred to as Corazón de

Sudamérica, which translates to "Heart of South America."

The name of the country comes from the river of the same name. Which may mean "river of crowns" or "the river where men live and are ornate with crowns of various feathers."

In Paraguay, the overall climate varies from tropical to subtropical, having only wet and dry periods. Between October and March, warm winds blow from the Amazon Jungle in the north, while the period between May and August brings cold winds from the Andes.

Having no mountains to protect this region, Paraguay experiences winds up to 100 mph. These winds influence the temperature significantly and suddenly; between April and September, temperatures will sometimes drop below freezing. Conversely, January is the hottest summer month, with an average daily temperature of 84 degrees F°.

The Paraguay people are made up of 80% Mestizos, who are of mixed Spanish and Native-American ancestry. Paraguay is a bilingual nation with Guaraní as its first

Paraguay River, from which the name of the country was derived. Pixabay

language and Spanish, its second. It is also one of few South-American countries to retain its native tongue as an official language. Interestingly, Guaraní is an onomatopoeic language, which means that many of its words imitate the natural sounds of animals and the natural environment. In Paraguay, pistol dueling is still legal as long as both parties are registered, blood donors. Eek!

In 1811, Paraguay gained independence from Spain. However, three dictators governed it during the first 60 years of independence. The country's third dictator, Francisco López, waged war against Uruguay, Brazil, and Argentina in 1865-1870. Half the male population was killed during the conflict. This war became known as the "War of the Triple Alliance."

Although Paraguay lacks a coastline, they have the largest navy of any landlocked country in South America with naval aviation, river defense corps, and a coastguard.

Brazil is the largest country in South America and has some fantastic features! The name Brazil comes from a tree that is named Brazilwood. Portuguese is the official language of the people. Portugal had claimed the land in 1500, but after 322 years, they broke free and became an independent country under their own rule in 1822.

Important cities include Rio de Janeiro, Salvador, and Fortaleza. Brazil's Atlantic coastline runs for 4,655 miles. And because of how large the country is, Brazil covers 3 time zones. Brazil is one of 77 founding members of the United Nations. The Amazon River flows through Brazil and is the second-longest – do you remember what river is the longest? If you said the Nile in Africa, you would be right! 60% of the Amazon Rainforest is in Brazil, and the climate is primarily tropical. This tropical climate is home to various animals, including armadillos, tapirs, jaguars, and pumas.

Football, which we call soccer, is by far the most popular sport in all of Brazil. The Brazil team has won the World Cup many times.

2002 World Cup Champions, Brazil, By Unknown, Public Domain

Christ the Redeember statue, Rio de Janeiro, Brazil, Pixabay

Brazilian Flamingos, Pixabay

Suriname is home to both 2 and 3-toed sloths which are known for being slow moving mammals with a tendency to hang upside down from branches. Pixabay

with half of its 281,612 people (2018) living in the metropolitan area of Cayenne, it's capital. Fun fact: Cayenne Pepper is named after the capital Cayenne!

The territory was initially inhabited by Native Americans. The first French establishment was recorded in 1503, but the French presence did not take until the foundation of Cayenne in 1643. Guiana then became a slave colony and saw its population increase until the official abolition of slavery during the French Revolution.

Dutch colonial inspired architecture in Suriname. By Unknown, Public Domain

French Guiana is an overseas department and region of France. Since 1981, when Belize became independent, French Guiana has been the only territory of the mainland Americas that is still part of a European country.

It has a very low population density of only 3.4 inhabitants per 9 square miles,

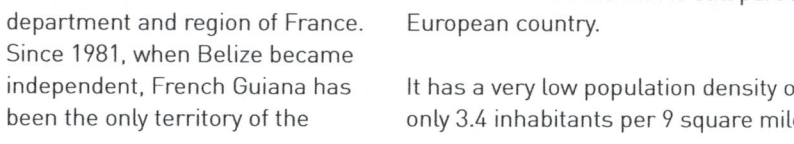

The Atlantic coastline in French Guiana, Pixabay

Guiana temporarily became a French department in 1797. Still, it was gradually transformed into a penal colony by establishing a network of camps and penitentiaries spread over the coast where prisoners were sentenced to forced labor.

Guiana is derived from an Amerindian language and means "land of many waters." This "land of many waters" consists of two main geographical regions. First, there is a coastal strip where the majority of the people live. Then there is the dense, near-inaccessible rainforest that gradually rises to the modest peaks of the Tumuc-Humac mountains along

the Brazilian frontier. Suriname is a unique blend of culture within the boundaries of a small country on the northeastern coast of South America.

Suriname's earliest inhabitants were the Surinen Indians,

after whom the country is named. Spain explored Suriname in 1593, but by 1602 the Dutch began to settle the land, followed by the English. In exchange for New Amsterdam (New York), the English transferred sovereignty to the Dutch in 1667. With the Dutch influence, the official language is Dutch, with the area's

colonial-era architecture being Dutch-inspired.

Suriname is a small country compared to most South America, with 64,000 square miles and only 545,672 people.

The rolling hills are tropical rainforests and makeup 80% of the total landscape.

Picturesque Suriname landscape, by Unknown, Public Domain

Guyana's Giant Otter, Pixabay

Guyana's Harpy Eagle, Pixabay

Guyana's Kaieteur Falls, Pixabay

An example of Guyana's diverse landscape, Pixabay

The highest hill has an elevation of 4,199 feet above sea level. Beyond the rain forests are lakes that makeup 16% of the total landmass. Suriname, formerly known as Dutch Guiana, gained independence in 1975 The main export of Suriname is bauxite, which is an aluminum ore that is exported to several major countries across the world. Other significant exports include bananas, shrimp, and rice.

Suriname and neighboring Guyana are the only two countries that drive on the left in South America.

Guyana is a sovereign state on the northern mainland of South America. It is, however, often considered part of the Caribbean region because of its strong cultural, historical, and political ties with other Anglo Caribbean countries and the Caribbean community.

Initially inhabited by many indigenous groups, Guyana was settled by the Dutch before coming under British control in the late 18th century. It was governed as British Guiana, with mostly a plantation-style economy until the 1950s. It gained independence in 1966 and officially became a republic within the Commonwealth of Nations in 1970. The legacy of British rule is reflected in the country's political administration and diverse population, which includes Indian, African, Amerindian, and multiracial groups.

Guyana is the only South American nation in which English is the official language. The majority of the population, however, speak Guyanese Creole, an English-based creole language.

Like most countries, Guyana can be divided into five natural regions. A narrow and fertile marshy plain along the Atlantic coast, where most of the population lives. More inland, there is a white sand belt that contains much of Guyana's mineral deposits. Third, there are dense rain forests in the southern part of the country, and a dryer savannah is found in areas in the southwest. Lastly, the smallest interior lowlands consist mostly of mountains that gradually rise to the Brazilian border.

The local climate is tropical and generally hot and humid, though moderate northeast trade winds are experienced along the coast. There are two rainy seasons, the first from May to mid-August, the second from mid-November to mid-January.

There is a vast diversity of wildlife, including rare species such as the giant otter and the harpy eagle.

North Atlantic

Greenland
Iceland
Denmark Strait
Davis Strait

Where in the World?

Lesson 24

A Closer Look
at what you have learned so far!

PLUS+ This Lesson's Geography:

North Atlantic
Greenland   Denmark Strait
Iceland   Davis Strait

Lesson 24

Previously Learned Geography TRUE REVIEW of the last 6 weeks.

Lesson 18
Gulf of Mexico
Yucatan Peninsula
Olmec Civilization
Maya Civilization
Aztec Civilization

Lesson 19
Mexico City
Chichen Itza
Lake Texcoco
Mayapan
Oaxaca

Lesson 20
Ontario
Quebec
New Brunswick
Nova Scotia

Lesson 21
Great Bear Lake
Great Slave Lake
Hudson Bay
Baffin Bay
Labrador Sea

Lesson 22
Venezuela
Colombia
Ecuador
Peru
Bolivia
Chile

Lesson 23
Argentina
Uruguay
Paraguay
Brazil
French Guiana
Suriname
Guyana

Hint: All geography found on this page, is also the geography that you will be reviewing this week. Refer to these maps as needed when doing your "Memorization Through Repetition" worksheets.

Parent/Teacher: The "A Closer Look" page is intended to show students the accumulated geographic areas taught within their 6-week review period plus new geography. For additional teaching tips on how to utilize this teaching aide for the different learning levels, please refer to page 1.

171

Lesson 24

Zoom Me In!

This Lesson's Geography:

North Atlantic
Greenland
Iceland
Denmark Strait
Davis Strait

Use this sheet as a reference for this lesson's "Now, let's trace, shade & label" worksheet.

Lesson 24 Geography
North Atlantic
Greenland
Iceland
Denmark Strait
Davis Strait

Tid-Bits

The description of the country by Greenland is an autonomous constituent country within the Kingdom of Denmark between the Arctic and Atlantic Oceans, east of the Canadian Arctic archipelago. Though geographically a part of the continent of North America, Greenland has been politically and culturally associated with Europe for more than a millennium - specifically Norway, Denmark, and Iceland. Most of its residents are Inuit, whose ancestors began migrating from the Canadian mainland in the 13th century, gradually settling across the island.

Eric the Red. Drawing used in a 1688 Icelandic publication. Part of the Fiske Icelandic Collection. Created by Argrimur Jonsson. Public Domain

Greenland is the world's largest island. However, much of the land is quite unfriendly to live on, for three-quarters of it is covered by the only permanent ice sheet outside Antarctica. With a population of about 56,480, it is the least densely populated territory globally; again, outside of Antarctica who has no permanent residents. About a third of the population lives in Nuuk, the capital. The Arctic Umiaq Line ferry acts as a lifeline for western Greenland, connecting the various cities and settlements.

The early Viking settlers named the island Greenland. Back in the Icelandic sagas, the Norwegian-born Icelander Erik the Red was exiled from Iceland for manslaughter. So he set out on ships to explore an icy land known to lie to the northwest. After finding a habitable area and settling there, he named it Greenland, hoping that the pleasant name would attract settlers.

From 986 AD, Greenland's west coast was settled by Icelanders and Norwegians with 14 boats led by Erik the Red. They formed three settlements—the 'Eastern Settlement,' the 'Western Settlement,' and the 'Middle Settlement.' Norse Greenlanders submitted to Norwegian rule in the 13th century under the Norwegian Empire.

Iceland is a Nordic island country in the North Atlantic, with a population of 348,580 and 40,000 square miles. The capital, which is the largest city, is Reykjavík. Reykjavík and the surrounding areas in the country's southwest are home to over two-thirds of the population.

Iceland is volcanically and geologically active. The interior consists of a plateau characterized by sand and lava fields, mountains, and glaciers. Many glacial rivers flow to the sea through the lowlands. That is, the meltwater from the

A look over the Icelandic landscape streaked with aurora borealis. Adobe Stock

One of the last written mentions of the Norse Greenlanders records a marriage which took place in 1408 in the church of Hvalseky, pictured above. The Hvalsey church is the best-preserved Nordic ruins in Greenland. Adobe Stock

173

glaciers creates these rivers. Iceland is warmed by the strong Gulf Stream. As a result, it has a temperate climate, despite a high latitude just outside the Arctic Circle. Its high latitude keeps summers chilly, with most of the archipelago having a tundra climate.

Since 1981 a prominent feature of Iceland has been the Blue Lagoon, which is a geothermal spa. This spa is located in a lava field and receives special water from a nearby geothermal power station.

Why is this spa so unique? The warm waters are rich in minerals like silica and sulfur. Bathing in the Blue Lagoon is said to help some people suffering from skin diseases such as psoriasis or eczema. The water temperature in the bathing and swimming area of the lagoon averages between 99–102 °F. This man-made lagoon's water is renewed every two days and is the largest in the world.

The spa gets its superheated water vented from the ground near a lava flow used to run turbines that generate electricity. After going through the turbines, the steam and hot water pass through a heat exchanger to provide heat for a municipal water heating system. Then the water is fed into the

One of many ice caves to be found in Iceland. Adobe Stock

A look over the Icelandic landscape. Adobe Stock

TOP LEFT & RIGHT: Iceland's famed blue lagoon. Adobe Stock

lagoon for everyone to enjoy.

The water gets its rich mineral content from underground geological layers that are pushed up at high pressure to the surface by scorching 464°F water. This is the water that the power plant uses. Because of its mineral concentration, water cannot be recycled and must be deposited in the nearby lava field.

The "Blue" in the lagoon comes from one of the minerals called silicate. The silicate makes the water a milky blue shade.

The Denmark Strait, or the Greenland Strait, is an oceanic strait between Greenland and Iceland. The strait connects the Greenland Sea, an extension of the Arctic Ocean, to the Irminger Sea, a part of the Atlantic Ocean. It stretches 300 miles long and 180 miles wide at its narrowest.
One of the most remarkable features of The Denmark Strait is the cataract found on the western side of the Denmark Strait. It is the world's highest underwater waterfall, with water falling almost 11,500 feet.

This spectacular phenomenon is formed by temperature differences between water masses from the opposite sides of the Denmark Strait. The eastern side is much colder than the western. This temperature difference causes these two sides to be different densities. When the two meet up at the top ridge of the strait, the colder, denser water flows downwards and underneath the warmer, lighter water, thus creating a downward flow of water or waterfall.

Denmark Strait's underwater waterfall. Public Domain

A Polar Bear jumps across the pack ice along the Davis Strait. By Tony, Adobe Stock

The Davis Strait is a northern arm of the Labrador Sea. It lies between mid-western Greenland and Nunavut on Canada's Baffin Island. To the north is Baffin Bay. The strait was named for the English explorer John Davis (1550–1605), who explored the area while seeking a northwest passage. By the 1650s, it was used for whale hunting. With a water depth of between 3 feet and 6,562 feet, the strait is substantially shallower than the Labrador Sea and Baffin Bay.

A Closer Look
at what you have in the last 6 lessons!

You are nearing the finish line! There is no new geography from this point forward, just review! **Congratulations!**

TrueReview 1

Previously Learned Geography TRUE REVIEW of the last 6 weeks.

Lesson 19	**Lesson 20**	**Lesson 21**	**Lesson 22**	**Lesson 23**	**Lesson 24**
Mexico City	Ontario	Great Bear Lake	Venezuela	Argentina	Greenland
Chichen Itza	Quebec	Great Slave Lake	Colombia	Uruguay	Iceland
Lake Texcoco	New Brunswick	Hudson Bay	Ecuador	Paraguay	Denmark Strait
Mayapan	Nova Scotia	Baffin Bay	Peru	Brazil	Davis Strait
Oaxaca		Labrador Sea	Bolivia	French Guiana	
			Chile	Suriname	
				Guyana	

Hint: All geography found on this page, is also the geography that you will be reviewing this week. Refer to these maps as needed when doing your "Memorization Through Repetition" worksheets.

Parent/Teacher: The "A Closer Look" page is intended to show students the accumulated geographic areas taught within their 6-week review period plus new geography. For additional teaching tips on how to utilize this teaching aide for the different learning levels, please refer to page 1.

A Closer Look
at what you have in the last 5 lessons!

Previously Learned Geography TRUE REVIEW of the last 5 weeks.

Lesson 20	Lesson 21	Lesson 22	Lesson 23	Lesson 24
Ontario	Great Bear Lake	Venezuela	Argentina	Greenland
Quebec	Great Slave Lake	Colombia	Uruguay	Iceland
New Brunswick	Hudson Bay	Ecuador	Paraguay	Denmark Strait
Nova Scotia	Baffin Bay	Peru	Brazil	Davis Strait
	Labrador Sea	Bolivia	French Guiana	
		Chile	Suriname	
			Guyana	

TrueReview 2

You are nearing the finish line! There is no new geography from this point forward, just review! **Congratulations!**

Hint: All geography found on this page, is also the geography that you will be reviewing this week. Refer to these maps as needed when doing your "Memorization Through Repetition" worksheets.

Parent/Teacher: The "A Closer Look" page is intended to show students the accumulated geographic areas taught within their review period. For additional teaching tips on how to utilize this teaching aide for the different learning levels, please refer to page 1.

A Closer Look
at what you have in the last 4 lessons!

You are nearing the finish line! There is no new geography from this point forward, just review! **Congratulations!**

TrueReview 3

Previously Learned Geography TRUE REVIEW of the last 4 weeks.

Lesson 21
Great Bear Lake
Great Slave Lake
Hudson Bay
Baffin Bay
Labrador Sea

Lesson 22
Venezuela
Colombia
Ecuador
Peru
Bolivia
Chile

Lesson 23
Argentina
Uruguay
Paraguay
Brazil
French Guiana
Suriname
Guyana

Lesson 24
Greenland
Iceland
Denmark Strait
Davis Strait

Hint: All geography found on this page, is also the geography that you will be reviewing this week. Refer to these maps as needed when doing your "Memorization Through Repetition" worksheets.

Parent/Teacher: The "A Closer Look" page is intended to show students the accumulated geographic areas taught within their review period. For additional teaching tips on how to utilize this teaching aide for the different learning levels, please refer to page 1.

A Closer Look

at what you have in the last 3 lessons!

Previously Learned Geography TRUE REVIEW of the last 3 weeks.

Lesson 22
Venezuela
Colombia
Ecuador
Peru
Bolivia
Chile

Lesson 23
Argentina
Uruguay
Paraguay
Brazil
French Guiana
Suriname
Guyana

Lesson 24
Greenland
Iceland
Denmark Strait
Davis Strait

TrueReview 4

You are nearing the finish line! There is no new geography from this point forward, just review! **Congratulations!**

Hint: All geography found on this page, is also the geography that you will be reviewing this week. Refer to these maps as needed when doing your "Memorization Through Repetition" worksheets.

Parent/Teacher: The "A Closer Look" page is intended to show students the accumulated geographic areas taught within their review period. For additional teaching tips on how to utilize this teaching aide for the different learning levels, please refer to page 1.

A Closer Look
at what you have in the last 2 lessons!

You are nearing the finish line! There is no new geography from this point forward, just review! **Congratulations!**

TrueReview 5

Previously Learned Geography TRUE REVIEW of the last 2 weeks.

Lesson 23
Argentina
Uruguay
Paraguay
Brazil
French Guiana
Suriname
Guyana

Lesson 24
Greenland
Iceland
Denmark Strait
Davis Strait

Hint: All geography found on this page, is also the geography that you will be reviewing this week. Refer to these maps as needed when doing your "Memorization Through Repetition" worksheets.

Parent/Teacher: The "A Closer Look" page is intended to show students the accumulated geographic areas taught within their review period. For additional teaching tips on how to utilize this teaching aide for the different learning levels, please refer to page 1.

A Closer Look
at what you have in the last lesson!

You have crossed the finish line! **Congratulations!**   **TrueReview 6**

Previously Learned Geography
TRUE REVIEW of last week's lesson.

Lesson 24
Greenland
Iceland
Denmark Strait
Davis Strait

Hint: All geography found on this page, is also the geography that you will be reviewing this week. Refer to these maps as needed when doing your "Memorization Through Repetition" worksheets.

Parent/Teacher: The "A Closer Look" page is intended to show students the accumulated geographic areas taught within their review period. For additional teaching tips on how to utilize this teaching aide for the different learning levels, please refer to page 1.

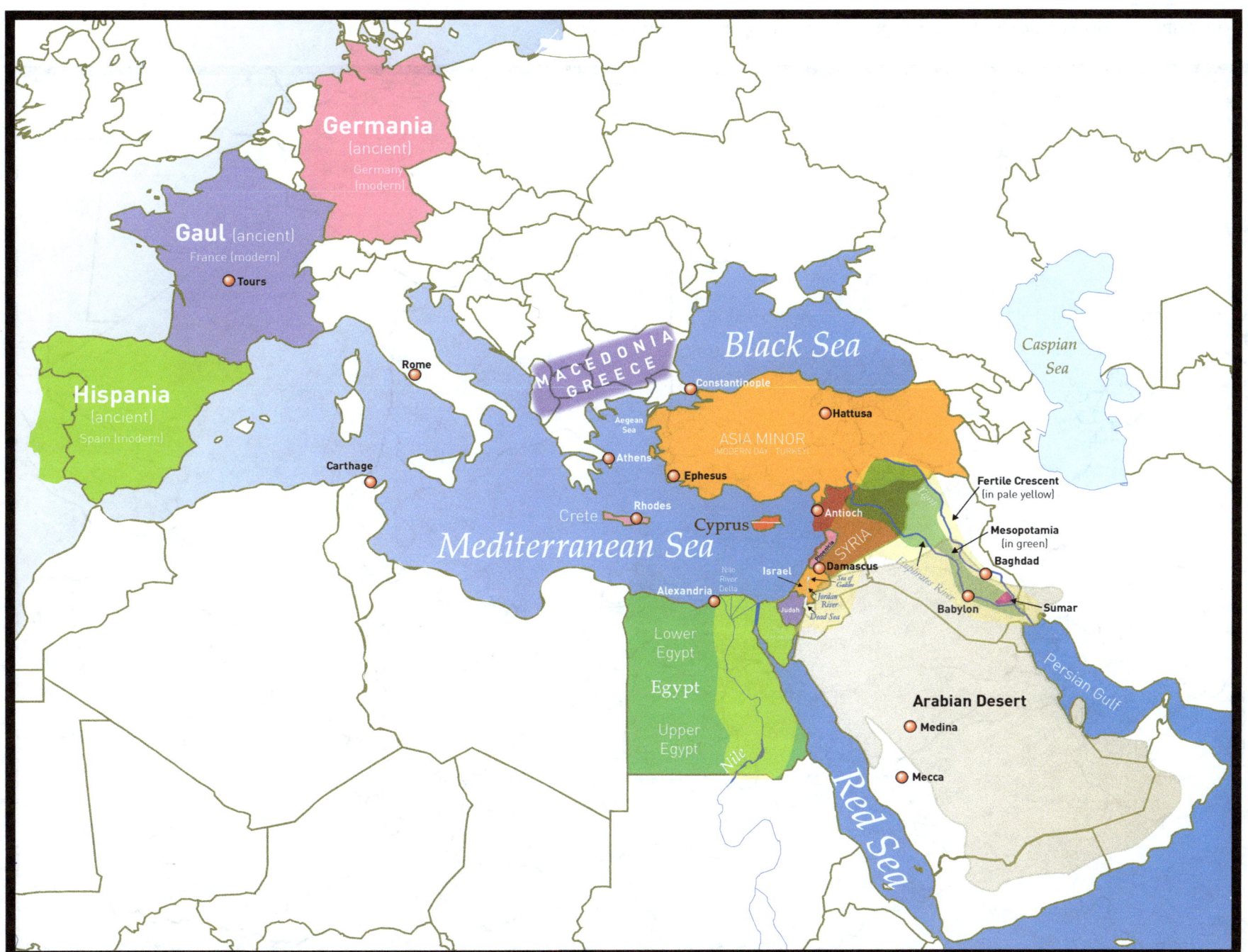

Blank Summary Black Line Map of all Geography for Lessons 1-7, and 11-12

Full Color Summary Map of all Geography for Lessons 8-10

Blank Summary Black Line Map on the Reverse, page 186.

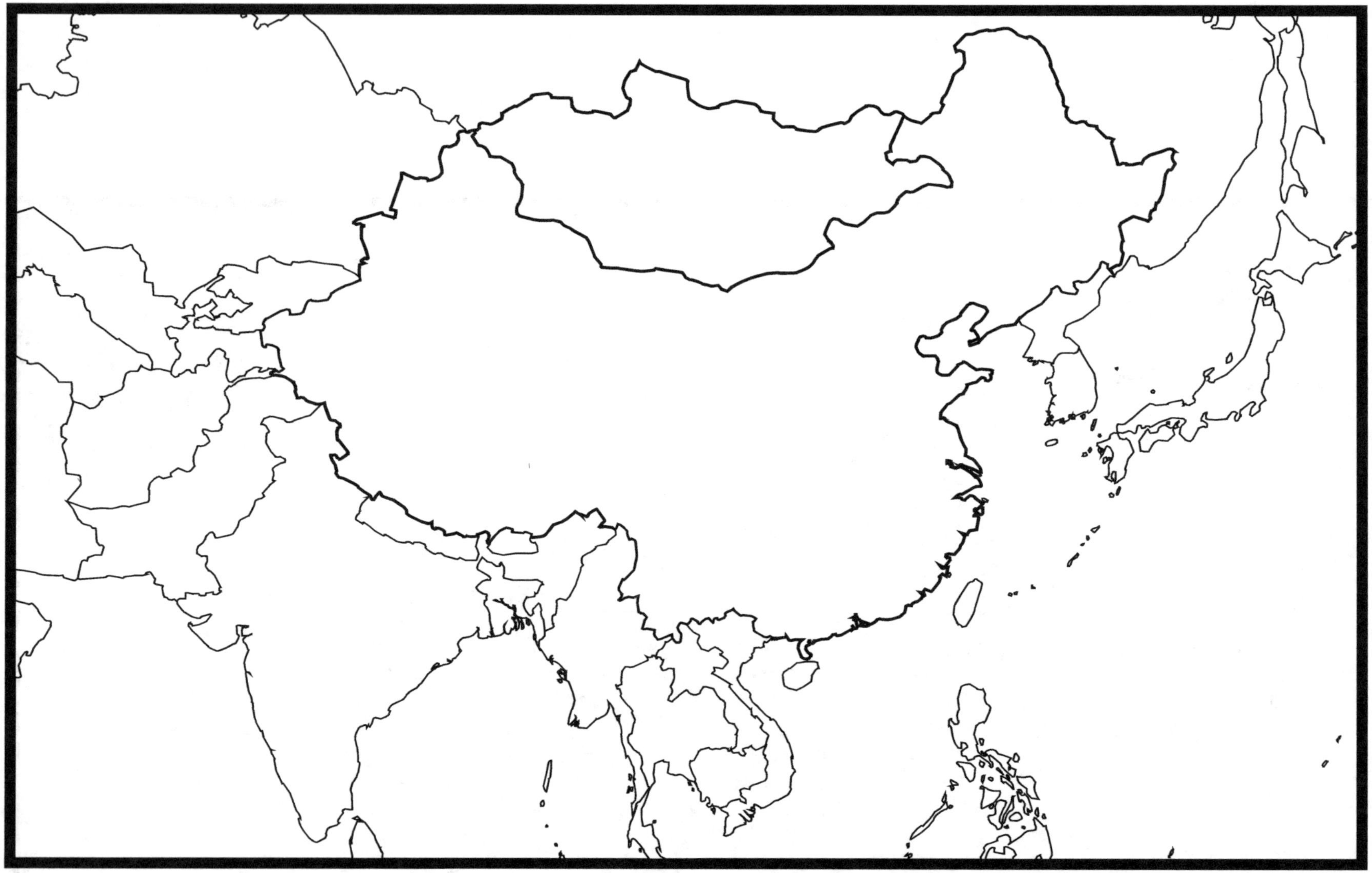

Blank Summary Black Line Map of all Geography for Lessons 8-10

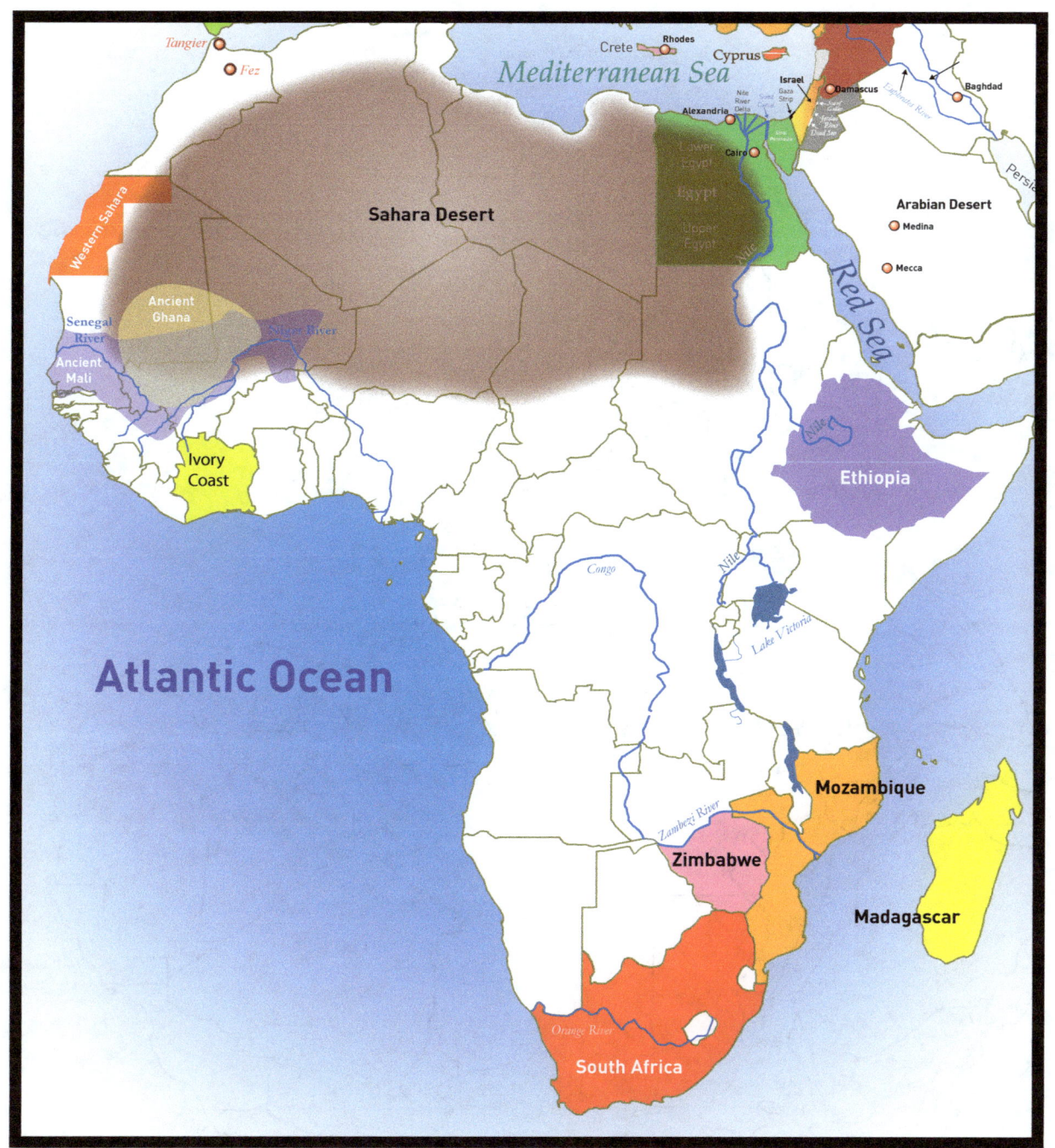

Full Color Summary Map of all Geography for Lessons 13-17

Blank Summary Black Line Map on the Reverse, page 188.

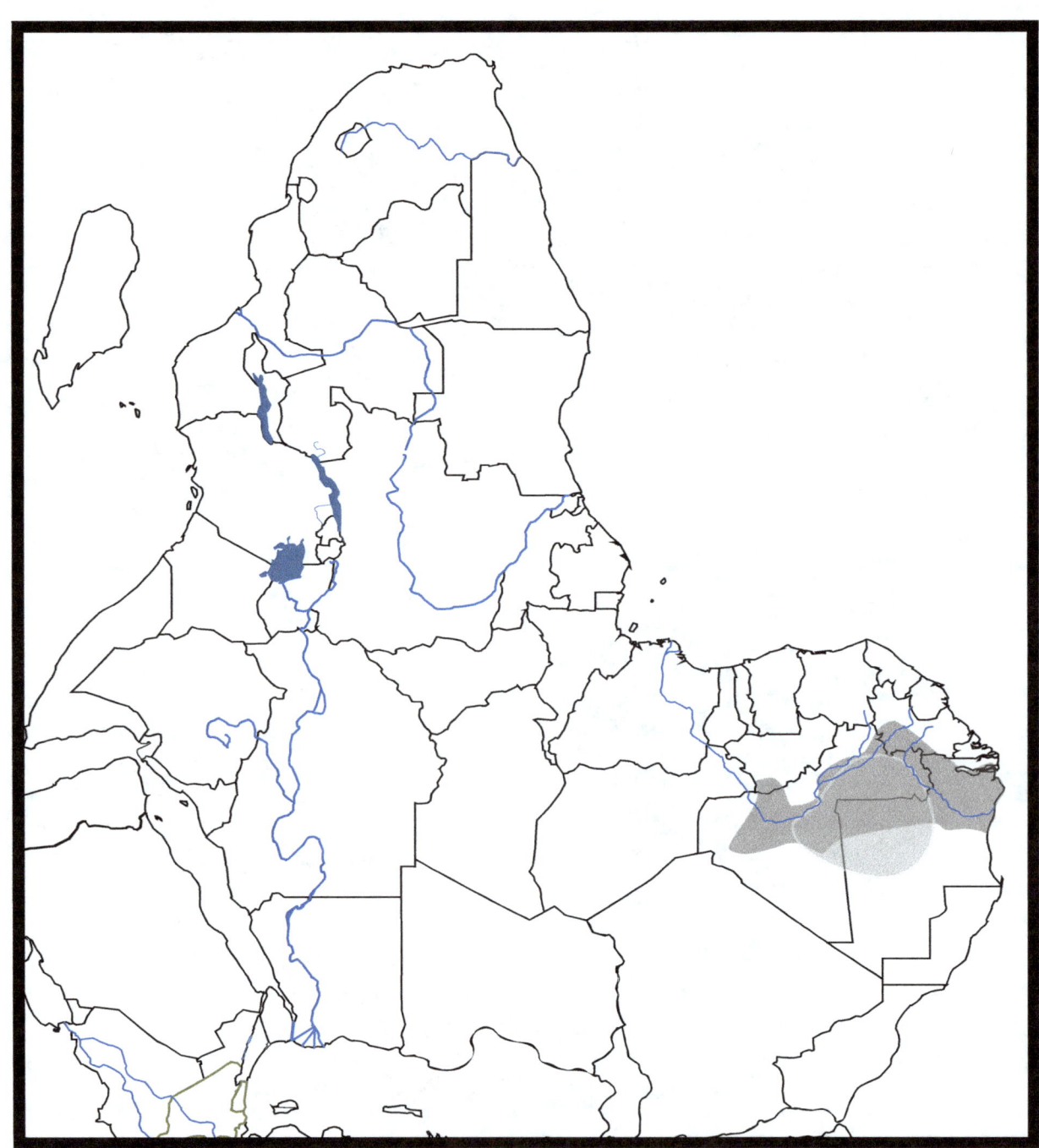

Blank Summary Black Line Map of all Geography for Lessons 13-17

Full Color Summary Map of all Geography for Lessons 18 & 19, 22 & 23

Blank Summary Black Line Map on the Reverse, page 190.

Blank Summary Black
Line Map of all
Geography for Lessons
18 & 19, 22 & 23

Full Color Summary Map of all Geography for Lessons 20, 21, & 24

Blank Summary Black Line Map on the Reverse, page 192

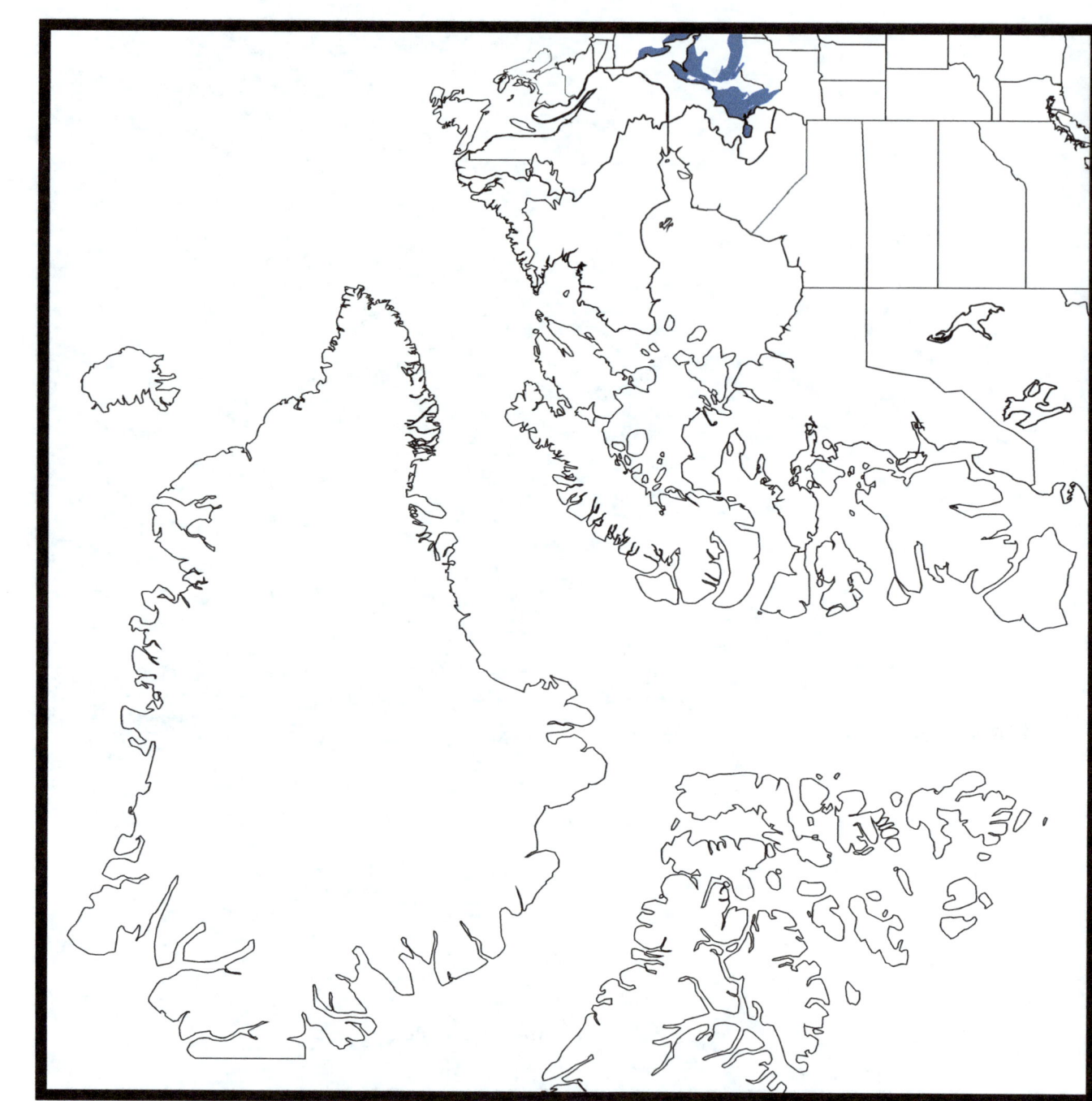

Blank Summary Black Line Map of all Geography for Lessons 20, 21, & 24

Additional Geography Books

"Europe and Asia, Continents, Oceans & More!"
(Digitial Download & Paperback)

"United States & Capitals PLUS Physical Features" 2 BOOKS (that work together)**:**
Student & Teacher Resource Guide*
Includes the Tid-Bits and Master Maps"
(Digitial Download & Paperback)
Student Map Worksheet Book that includes TrueReview*
(Digitial Download & Paperback)
*Digital and Paperback can be bundled or sold separately.

Review Games & More

Musical Hop Scotch Mat

Enlarged Map Sets,
Black Line Maps, along with 2 Review Games for these books:

"Ancient Empires & More!"

"Europe and Asia, Continents, Oceans & More!"

Be sure to check out all resources that compliment the "Where in the World?" Geography Series

http://bit.ly/WhereInTheWorldGeo